IF YOU'VE
SEEN ONE,
YOU'VE
SEEN THE
MALL

IF YOU'VE SEEN ONE, YOU'VE SEEN THE MALL

Europeans and American Mass Culture

ROB KROES

UNIVERSITY OF ILLINOIS PRESS   URBANA AND CHICAGO

This book is printed on acid-free paper.

Library of Congress Cataloging-in-Publication Data

Kroes, Rob.

If you've seen one, you've seen the mall :

Europeans and American mass culture / Rob Kroes.

p.   cm.

Includes bibliographical references and index.

ISBN 0-252-02200-9 (cloth : alk. paper). —

ISBN 0-252-06532-8 (pbk. : alk. paper)

1. Popular culture—United States. 2. Europe—Civilization—American influences. 3. Americanization. I. Title.

E169.04.K755   1996

940—dc20   95-32455

CIP

Contents

Acknowledgments

In 1991–92, at the Netherlands Institute for Advanced Study, a research group studied the reception of forms of American mass culture in Europe. Robert W. Rydell and I, as cochairs of the research project, brought together for longer or shorter visits a number of colleagues from Europe and the United States. If I thank them here, it is because their intellectual company and friendship gave this book its final shape. In particular I thank those who constituted the core group: Doeko Bosscher, Hans Bertens, David Ellwood, Mel van Elteren, Mick Gidley, and David Nye. Finally I mention Kate Delaney; out of sheer interest she worked her way through an earlier Dutch version of this book before I had the benefit of her language expertise for this English version.

Introduction

"They all laughed at Christopher Columbus . . ." We know the line and can probably hum the tune. Radio and phonograph records have brought it to our attention, subliminally perhaps, as one of the many snippets of American popular culture that have become part and parcel of our everyday acoustic environment. The line is oddly reminiscent of the advertising one-liners that Americans have developed into a form of commercial art: "They all laughed when I sat down at the piano." It is an art of salesmanship that aims at shaming Americans into the conformity of the consumer culture. Consumers can hope to buy their way out of social embarrassment—by using the right detergent, the right mouthwash, or the right suntan lotion. Commercial slogans, hammering their message home, serve as instruments of social control. Americans have become equipped with a keen sense of others watching them. They have a third eye with which to watch themselves, the prying eye of the others who are their constant judges and censors. If they have internalized anything, it is not the Oedipal father figure but the jingle of the mass media.

Columbus was different. People may have laughed at him, yet he was not to be shamed out of setting sail into the unknown. He returned to Europe as the discoverer of the "New World," and since then America has never left Europe. Europeans have never stopped laughing at America, yet their collective imagination has filled with a repertoire of Americana. They may have reacted vehemently to it, producing a litany of anti-Americanism that has been one long attempt at exorcism, driving out the devil of a pernicious American culture. Nevertheless, the devil was not simply to be wished away. If cultural guardians were watching the front door, American culture slipped in through the rear entrance. It found a loving welcome among those, mostly of the younger generations, who aimed to wrest cultural control out of parental hands. What to older generations may have seemed to be the mindless conformity of American culture became the stuff of cultural revolt for younger generations. American culture has always met both rejection and acceptance in Europe. Insofar as it has come to constitute an element of European cultural history, it has always shown a dual face.

During the academic year of 1991–92 this complex cultural history was the focus for research by an international group of scholars at the Netherlands Institute for Advanced Study (NIAS). These scholars' common focus was the dual nature, the Januslike face, of American culture as it has been perceived and received in Europe. Forms of American mass culture and the media of their transmission to Europe, from traveling Wild West shows to Vietnam movies, all have shaped our collective awareness of America as a powerful counterpoint to established European cultures. Many of our images of what makes America tick have been mediated through such potent cultural forms. They have shaped a discourse of rejection and acceptance, in addition to giving shape to our everyday cultural setting.

Two words have served as the key concepts in this discourse: *Americanism* and *Americanization*. Americanism in particular has served as the central diagnostic concept, irrespective of whether the thrust of an argument was toward the rejection or advocacy of America. In its positive sense the term served as the shorthand reference to America's hallowed repertoire of guiding ideals, explaining the nation's course and destiny to the American people while at the same time providing an inspiration to non-Americans abroad. When, at the time of the autocratic Second Empire, French Republican sentiment sought a provocative mode of expression, it came up with what became a central icon of Americanism: the Statue of Liberty. In this gift to the American nation France paid tribute to the American republic as the safe haven of a "Liberté éclairant le monde" (Liberty enlightening the world). When in the dark days of Italian fascism author Cesare Pavese led the life of an internal émigré, the chosen locus for his imaginary migration was America as the safe haven of liberty and democracy. More often than not, however, *Americanism* has been a term of rejection in Europe. In its negative sense the term symbolizes America as the antithesis to Europeanism, to everything that European intellectuals conceive of as their common cultural heritage. To the extent that there has been anti-Americanism in Europe, it has been directed against Americanism in this latter, pernicious sense.

The word *Americanization* does not really have such a dual face. It normally serves in a discourse of rejection to point to the variety of processes through which America exerts its dismal influence on European cultures. In its polemical, denunciatory thrust the term tends to beg the question as to whether baneful cultural and social trends in Europe truly are due to an American influence rather than to parallel and relatively autonomous forces that are at work on both sides of the Atlantic. Even in the case of a clear and undeniable impact of American culture, however, the word *Americanization* is unduly alarmist. It reduces the complex processes of cultural influence, of borrowing, imitation, and reception, to the stark binary form of a zero-sum game. In a field of two opposite alternatives, of Europeanism versus Americanism, any degree of Americanization will in this view imply an equal degree of de-Europeanization.

To the extent that the word *Americanization* can serve any useful analytical purpose at all, it should be taken as a shorthand reference to what is essentially a black box in the simple diagram of cultural transmission and reception. If in this process there are obviously senders and receivers as well as modes and means of transmission, the black box is the semiotic dark room where messages undergo a process of translation, where they are decoded and reencrypted, decontextualized and recontextualized, and made to fit the receivers' frames of reference. The black box in this sense is not unlike the children's toys that we know as Transformers, whose changing configurations of constituent elements produce widely divergent meanings from essentially empty signifiers. Of course, the elements of an American mass culture transmitted to Europe are never so purely devoid of meaning (although a long tradition of European anti-American rhetoric has tended to make that claim), yet when they pass through the black box of the semantic transformer, they do come out in different configurations.

In this study I propose to focus on this black box and to analyze the process of Americanization in terms of its mediation and transformation. Because I will concentrate on these processes as they occur in Europe, however, I must provide a sense of the prevailing attitudes and traditions, in their different European national settings, toward America and American culture. To the extent that American culture has penetrated ever more powerfully into the realm of European cultures, it always has had to pass through the highly charged field of tension between the poles of Europeanism versus Americanism. The first chapter therefore offers an exploration of the repertoires of discourse and metaphors that Europeans have used to make sense of American culture as distinct from European culture(s). The outcome often was one of rejection, but not always. Ironically, the same metaphorical repertoires used to reject America and

Americanism reoccur in veritable paeans of praise, presenting America as a liberating counterpoint to Europe's cultural heritage. The creative tension between these two extreme positions has served to set the particular receptive mode for the Americanization of Europe.

If You've Seen One, You've Seen the Mall

Oculists must have a word for what I have set out to do in this book. Looking at the cultural crossbreeding between America and Europe through the eyes of the parties involved requires a higher form of mental squint plus a bent for cultural voyeurism. The obvious problems of focusing that this entails are further compounded by the fact that the angles of observation keep changing. As I will show, it is a matter of many Americas as seen—and invented—by Europeans, as well as of a host of Europes stalking through the American imagination. What title to give to the results of such cultural exploration?

At one point, tongue in cheek, I considered opting for *Occidentalism*. It might have been taken as a reference to *Orientalism*, the title that Edward Said gave to his classic study.[1] It is a connection that in my case would have helped to conjure up connotations of colonialism, which Said explored in his book. Nonetheless, the associations should have been taken lightly, with irony. Of course, there are aspects of colonialism in the cultural exchanges between America and Europe, literally so during America's colonial history but also metaphorically, as in the wistful complaint by the German filmmaker Wim Wenders that Hollywood has succeeded in "colonizing the European subconscious" or Albert Camus's playful impression "that only the Negroes give life, passion, and nostalgia to this country [the United States] which, in their own way, they colonized."[2] Once colonialism becomes a metaphor, cultural interplay becomes the stuff of wordplay. America's colonization of Europe then turns into Europe's Coca-colonization. Beyond the pun there is the diagnosis, not unlike Wim Wenders's. It is the lure of American mass culture, the temptation of its implied pleasure principle, its presentation of fantasies and dreams as "the real thing," that has colonized the European subconscious.

But for much longer the reverse has been the case. For centuries the European subconscious colonized the Americas, even before their discovery, projecting its dreams and fantasies on the "silver screen in the

West," as C. Vann Woodward calls it.[3] The notion of America became an emotionally charged, symbolic invention made in Europe. America was turned into a metaphor made to serve in the context of essentially intra-European debates.

In that sense a separate history has evolved of America as a European repertoire of myths and symbols, beyond the borders of the United States, beyond any manipulative American intent or control. Ironically there are clear parallels to the semantic history of the notion of America within the United States. On both sides of the Atlantic, therefore, there seems to be a continued need for a "myth and symbols" approach. The terms may vary, people may prefer to speak of "icons" rather than "symbols," of "metaphors" rather than "myths," yet clearly a semantic reading of America as a meaningful construct is at the heart of the approach.

As regards my own analysis of Europe's imaginary Americas, I have chosen to emphasize their metaphorical quality. In every European country, at every level of discourse from everyday stereotype to highbrow observation, people use metaphors to express the otherness of America as measured by European yardsticks, producing repertoires that at first glance are of bewildering variety. At the same time, however, these manifold metaphors can be shown to fill a metaphorical space themselves, a space that, like any Euclidian space, can be reduced to three organizing dimensions. Thus, one repertoire can be shown to play on spatial metaphors, where America, in contrast to Europe, is seen as flat and flattening, swayed by vectors that are all horizontal, subject to forces that tend to level the verticality of European life, with its sense of cultural and social hierarchy. A second repertoire draws on temporal metaphors, where America is portrayed as lacking a European sense of history, of the past as a critical ingredient in the makeup of the present. The third repertoire rests on the underlying metaphor of America as lacking the European sense of organic cohesion and integrity, where America is seen as a country of blithe bricolage, irreverently taking apart and recombining at will what to Europeans appears in the light of wholeness, if not holiness.

These three dimensions form the discursive formation of Europe's "occidentalism," the underlying structure of meanings, as Raymond Williams called it, spawning an endless number of meaningful sentences and individual utterances ranging from the highly subtle and nuanced to the coarsely stereotypical. The examples that I give to argue my case throughout this book are drawn from a number of national settings and historical periods, yet they are no more than examples, a sample that could be expanded endlessly. Readers can do that for themselves.[4]

Does this notion of "occidentalism," as a structure of meanings, transcend history? Do not the manifold conjunctions of time and place affect it? The logic of the exercise leads me to say, no, they do not. Clearly the repertoire of metaphors explored in this book ranges across time and national setting, drawing on a varied assortment of writings by travelers, cultural critics, and intellectuals. These authors all may have had their particular concerns and motives when writing about America, yet I contend that the motifs they use are resonant of repertoires that are more widely shared among the larger public and are of remarkable historical stability. Nevertheless, as I already suggested and as I will argue at length later, the use to which people put these metaphorical repertoires can change depending on the larger argument these repertoires are meant to illustrate. They can conjure up images of America that range from praise to rejection. If they imply, as they always do, a comparison between "Europe" and "America" as metaphorical constructs, it is not always "Europe" that sees the balance tilt in its favor.

■ ■ ■

Yet in the end, *Occidentalism* was only one title for the book that I toyed with for a while but then discarded. I opted for the present title because it better conveys both the lightness of touch that I hope characterizes my approach and a sense of the underlying structure of meaning of European "occidentalism." Like any pun, it has a double referent. Evoking a standard saying, it seems to capture well the European sense of American culture as capable of producing only spurious variety, subjecting as it does all cultural production to the leveling logic of America's democratic ethos and its capitalist organization. The mall, in that context, is the contemporary icon of such larger, anonymous forces. The mall is the site where American culture appears in its most commodified, commercial, and consumerist form. As a title, however, the joke refers to only part of what the term *occidentalism* covers. I am aware of that. If the title, however, were to mislead readers into assuming a parti pris on my part, I hasten to say I do not have it, as I hope the following chapters will amply show.

IF YOU'VE
SEEN ONE,
YOU'VE
SEEN THE
MALL

American Culture in European Metaphors

| THE WEST AS WILL AND CONCEPTION |

Europe's reception of American culture has been going on for centuries. It began even before Europeans put America on their maps. As one witticism has it, America was invented before it was discovered. Europe had already produced many fantasy worlds, many utopian counterimages of itself. They could be places of hope, such as a lost paradise or an imminent redemptive millennium, or uncivilized, barbaric places of darkness and doom.

People in classical antiquity and in the Christian era prior to the discovery of America lived with the image of a tripartite *orbis terrarum,* an *oecumene,* that in its old form comprised Europe, Asia, and Libya, representing the North, the East, and the South, respectively; an inaccessible West was screened off by the unfathomable river Oceanus. The image appears in a number of different guises. It shows up in the work of Herodotus and in the Old Testament view of the three sons of Noah, each of whom inherited and populated one of the three known parts of the world. Similarly, the three Magi who gathered to honor Jesus as a newborn king represented the threefold order of the world as it was known then.

Yet there always have been rival stories to this self-enclosed view of the world. From early times the human imagination has been drawn toward the west with all the magnetic force exerted by the unknown and forbidden. In the myth of Atlantis as told by Plato, it is a lost country, a proud kingdom that, following military defeat (at the hands of forebears of the Athenians?), was swallowed by the sea. Nothing remained of it other than an extensive mudbank. The story is reminiscent of other versions, as told in Genesis, of a lost paradise and an all-engulfing deluge. The human inquisitiveness is not so easily satisfied, however. Many mythical seafarers set sail for the forbidden West. The Celtic hero Bran, whose feats are told in an epic poem from about A.D. 700, told of a happy land in the West "without grief, without sorrow, without death." In the larger repertoire of myth Bran returned some three hundred years hence as the Christian hero and saint Brendan (or Brandan), whose peregrinations were told in the *Navigatio Sancti Brendani*. The land in the West, without sorrow or death, assumed the Christian guise of the lost paradise, the land of promise that had been forbidden to postlapsarian humanity. Having landed on its shore, not even Saint Brendan would be allowed to penetrate more deeply into its interior. Here the West appears in the light of prophecy, of a promise of redemption, in either its Christian or pre-Christian versions. Thus, in his *Medea* Seneca tells of a time "when Oceanus will break the bounds that have contained us, when a vast expanse of land will be revealed and Tethys will unlock new worlds, and Thule will no longer be Ultima Thule, the farthest land."[1]

The fear and horror this forbidden land inspired in humans, their sense of blasphemous infringement of a divine ordinance, perhaps come out most clearly in a work written on the eve of the Americas' discovery and steeped in the prevailing late-medieval view of the world: Dante's *Divina Commedia*. The tripartite cosmology of the day still defined Dante's view of the inhabited world as much as it did his view of the hereafter, with its hell, heaven, and purgatory. Nonetheless, not even Dante could resist fully the horrible temptation of infringement. With Dante it is another mythical seafarer—Ulysses—who transgresses the bounds of the self-enclosed medieval world. Once he arrives at the bounds of the inhabited world—the pillars of Hercules, erected as a sign to humans not to venture beyond them—Ulysses calls on his men to collect themselves. He urges them to follow the sun and holds forth the prospect of "a world without people." They then leave the Orient behind and turn "their oars into wings to carry them on their mad flight." It is an act of madness—Dante leaves no doubt about it—an enterprise bound to end in disaster, but Ulysses and his crew are allowed a brief sublime vision. Against the starry sky of "the other Pole" land emerges in the distance, an island surging high into a mountainous mass. It is the island of purgatory, with the terrestrial paradise towering high above it. The elation of Ulysses and his men is short-lived: a whirlwind strikes, and their ship turns around its axis three times, to be engulfed by the sea the fourth time around. "The sea closed again over our heads."[2]

What to Dante, the medieval man, was still a sin, an act of hubris not unlike the one that had expelled humanity from paradise, became a positive force in the Renaissance. The closed, self-contained world of Europe exploded into the unknown. It was as if people freely chose their own expulsion, a self-inflicted exile, a freefall off the known world. Not everyone could witness this without a feeling of horror; there is Masaccio's famous Florentine mural, literally a sign on the wall, depicting Adam and Eve's expulsion from paradise. Rarely has the horror of facing the unknown been expressed so grippingly as by this Renaissance artist. In spite of the fears and trepidation of some people, however, others engaged in the indomitable quest for the unknown. It produced the one voyage of exploration that, in epic concentration, holds all the symbolism of this quest: Columbus's voyage toward the west.

The symbolism is so strong that it may appear at times as if Columbus himself is an invention and rather belongs to those hallowed ranks of mythical seafarers, like Noah, Ulysses, and Bren/Brendan. Reminiscent of Noah, who sent aloft a dove in search of land, here setting sail from Europe was a man whose very name—Columbus—meant dove (It., *colomba*). Like Noah's winged messenger, he returned bringing news of the discovery of land across the ocean. Of course, in spite of such mythical connections and connotations, Columbus stands squarely in historical time, at that critical juncture between the Middle Ages and modern times when people began to have a sense of being the masters of their own fate. They made their own world by making the world their own. The earth, in this novel view, changed from a flat disk (where human beings were to avoid the edge lest they fall off) into a globe where the West blended naturally into the East. That was how Columbus chose to represent his discovery to his royal patrons. He had unlocked not a mythical West but the passage to an equally mythical East, conjured up in names like "Cipango" and "Cathay."

This version, adopted by Columbus himself, is in tune with the rationality of the newly emerged modern view of the world. Nevertheless, there are indications that Columbus also conceived of his venture in terms of the repertoire of European fantasies concerning the West as the site of the terrestrial paradise. In his famous letter to his sovereign masters he refers to the Orinoco, whose mouth he had found, as being in fact the river Gihon, which is one of the four rivers that the Bible says flow outward from Eden. The fresh water that the river poured into the sea "could very well have come from Paradise." Like a latter-day Saint Brendan, Columbus took himself to have explored the outer reaches of the terrestrial paradise. Prior to his voyage, when still engaged in raising funds for his enterprise, Columbus had already referred to stories that old sailors had told him about the West. Already at that stage his fantasy had been fired by the same mythical repertoire that had inspired Dante's Odyssey. And again, later in his life, Columbus returned to this theme. In his *Libro de las Profecias,* dedicated to King Ferdinand and Queen Isabella, Columbus invoked biblical prophecy as foretelling the God-willed success of his voyages of discovery.[3]

Later on Columbus's son Ferdinand weighed in on his father's behalf in a lengthy defense intended to show that Columbus had been fully aware of discovering America. Ferdinand reminds his readers of Seneca's prophetic lines concerning the time when Thule would no longer be Ultima Thule. He goes on solemnly to conclude that beyond a doubt "this prophecy was fulfilled in the person of the Admiral [i.e., Columbus]."[4] This may be so, but whether Columbus was aware of this will probably remain a matter of conjecture.

Whatever the case, it does not really matter much. Whether Columbus thought of himself as having reached the West or rather the outer reaches of the East, the point is that Columbus, in the way he conceived of his achievement, relied on a blend of truth and fiction, of reality and fantasy. As he reported to his royal principals, he was deeply convinced of having reached the terrestrial paradise. Traditional stories and old lore colored his perceptions and gave them their sense and cohesion. That is truly the interesting point, for things have never been much different in the European conception of America. The conception of what soon became known as "the New World" always tended to be cast in a mold of preconceived ideas, fantasies, and dreams that all had their origins in the Old World.

This is not to say that the mold always made for a snug fit. Reflections on the terrestrial paradise, such as those by Saint Augustine or Dante, had taught that it was a "mondo senza gente," a world without people. The opposite proved to be the case, however. It came as a dual shock to old Europe: not only did it have to learn to live with a cosmology consisting of four parts, but it had to allow as well for human be-

ings who out of the blue imposed themselves on the European imagination. What kind of people were they? Were they human? Did they
have souls? Did they share in humanity's sinful state? These and similar questions occupied both ecclesiastical and secular circles. The highest councils of the Roman Catholic church and the Spanish court
weighed these two critical options: should the inhabitants of the New
World be converted and made Christians, or could they, lacking souls,
be made slaves? In his passionate discussion with his opponent Juan
Ginés de Sepúlveda, the Spanish priest Bartolomé de Las Casas wrote
his famous plea on behalf of the American Indians as fellow human
beings, whose souls must be saved. His plea was all the more urgent
because Las Casas was convinced of the imminent end of time. As he
saw it, the conversion of the American Indians was a precondition for
the redemption of all mankind. The debate had a lasting effect on the
European view of America. Not only did the Spanish crown order that
the indigenous population be protected from slavery, but also the very
considerations underlying the royal order—that the American Indians
were born free and should live in freedom—were later to reverberate
in images of America as "the land of the free" and of Americans as
"born free." Ironically the later inhabitants of North America appropriated these rhetorical forms and applied them uniquely to themselves.
Only a few among them realized that the honorific title initially applied
to the indigenous people.[5]

Outside the Church people were concerned not as much with the
American Indians' lapsarian state as with their anthropological place.
What kind of people were they? The wildest fantasies were in circula-
tion. In the European view American Indians ranged from kindhearted
beings, moving about in a state of paradisiacal nakedness, to man-
eating Caribs (from which the word *cannibal* is derived). Columbus had
already referred to man-eaters and to the variety of names by which
they were known (ranging from "Carib," to "Calib," to "Canib"), but
he never managed to find them.

The European imagination, feeding first on these and similar stories
told by voyagers and explorers and slightly later on the physical appearance of Indians brought to Europe, ranged from an early modern
awareness of anthropological relativism, as in the work of Montaigne
("Chacun appelle barbarie ce qui n'est pas de son usage"—People call
barbarism whatever is not their wont),[6] to the mad projection of everything forbidden and taboo that lay submerged in the European subconscious, as in the case of Shakespeare's Caliban. The uncivilized, brute

force of the savage, regardless of whether he eats men or rapes women, makes him into "a devil, a born devil, on whose nature nurture can never stick,"[7] as Shakespeare has Prospero reflect on Caliban. This image of the untamed savage as the embodiment of all the forces of evil, in compact with the devil and to be subdued only by force, long endured as a view of America. In the early days of settlement whites were haunted by fears of scalping and ravaging Indians. Later the white upper stratum of European origin projected such images on a slave population that was African instead of American Indian. Interestingly these repertoires of projection already freely mingle in Shakespeare's *Tempest*: older fears of African blacks blend into fantasies about the American Indian. Caliban, who in the list of *dramatis personae* is described as "a savage and deformed slave," combines a number of fantasies concerning the non-European "Other." Not only is he black, and not only does his mother come from "Argier" (the Moorish Algiers), but his mythological makeup shows as well traits of New World peoples, of "Cannibals" from the Caribbean, of Patagonian giants that Magellan had seen, and of inhabitants of the Bermudas. Although Shakespeare sets his story in the Mediterranean, Caliban's island is referred to as one of those "Stormy Bermoothes" about which the author must have read. At the symbolic level a similar blend turns Caliban into an image of the monstrous: he represents every force opposed to Christianity and civilization. At the same time, however, he represents the dreams of freedom that people tend secretly to associate with the infringement of cultural rules. In a flush of cultural revolt the drunken savage breaks out in song: "'Ban, 'Ban, Ca—Caliban / Has a new master, get a new man. / Freedom, high-day! high-day freedom! freedom, highday, freedom!"[8]

   The Tempest is an early example of European fantasies about America after its discovery. It displays a rejection of America and Americans as diametrically opposed to civilization and culture—a rejection that would continue for centuries, even long after "the American" was no longer an Indian savage but a transplanted European. At the same time, however, Shakespeare's imagination also gave form to the vibrant, carnivalesque element of cultural revolt, the element of liberation that is to be found in the shedding of old Europe's civilization. Generations after Shakespeare have chosen to highlight that side of America and the possibilities it offered of becoming "a new man." In all such fantasies America once again becomes paradise, the fount of rejuvenation, the wondrous melting pot that turns servants and slaves into free beings:

"Highday freedom!" Clearly there is an ambivalence in the European attitude toward America, a rejection that always borders on attraction. As for Shakespeare, such ambivalence perhaps nowhere comes out more clearly than in the words that, at the end of his play, he puts into Prospero's mouth. Referring to Caliban Prospero says, "this thing of darkness, I acknowledge mine."[9]

America as a Tabula Rasa

Shakespeare set his imagination to work when British settlement on the American continent had yet to begin. He could still fantasize about the monstrous hybrid forms living on the mud flats of old Atlantis. Tellingly, Caliban is half man and half fish, a savage monster "on whose nature nurture can never stick." By nature uncivilized and uncivilizable, he represents the danger of barbarous nihilism. When Caliban revolts in a state of inebriation, Shakespeare lends the act the wider contours of a "revolt of the masses." Sinister companions, which we might well conceive of as the rabble of the Old World, the riffraff of Europe, tell Caliban that he can break his master's power by getting at its source, his master's books. "Burn but his books," they tell him. In his depiction of Caliban as a hooligan Shakespeare clearly is inspired by old European fears of the nihilism of the lower classes, seen as a reservoir of chaos and destruction. He then projects these fears onto America as a place of uncouth savages.

That central image, of civilization and culture as a threatened enclave in a savage surrounding, endured even after the first white settlers built a precarious existence for themselves on American soil. It shows up most clearly in the case of the early Puritans in New England. To a large extent their life was cast in the light of a mission, a divine assignment to a handful of chosen people to build the New Jerusalem in America. The wilderness against which they had to secure their enclave was seen as the terrain of diabolic stratagems, of trials and tribulations invented by the devil to obstruct their divine mission.

Much as the New Jerusalem may have resembled a harrowed little outpost encircled by the evil forces of the wilderness—and the stories of women being abducted, surprise attacks, and armed clashes all tend to confirm this picture—in the end a different view of the settlers' enterprise prevailed. As the colonists in New England consolidated their control, and their environment lost its threatening features, events seemed to bear out their initial sense of a new beginning. America had offered them the chance to start anew. They had left behind a Europe mired in sin and deviousness. America to them was the clean slate on which they could record their history in the light of scriptural prophecy. Less than a century after first settlement this view of providential history culminated in Cotton Mather's *Magnalia Christi Americana*, an account of Christ's wondrous works in America. In Mather's view America took center stage in the course of providential history; New England's Puritans appeared as the chosen remnant, anxiously awaiting the Second Coming in their New Israel. America was transformed from a far corner of the world into its center, a beckoning beacon poised as a counterpoint to Europe. In anticipation of the end of times, the Puritans in New England made a fresh start, the beginning of the end.[10]

Such daring claims, made by Cotton Mather and others, carry the old European dreams about America as the land of promise, the terrestrial paradise, the place of redemption. Only through settlement by white Europeans would America come into its own and be able to fulfill its dormant potential. Only then and there would the circle of providential history come to a close. America would be the New Jerusalem. For all practical purposes America might as well have been a "mondo senza gente," for it could fulfill its destiny only once it was touched by Europeans. Ever more clearly, in the view of Europeans and their descendants in America, America would become a tabula rasa, a blank page that they could fill as they saw fit. In the 1720s the Irish philosopher and Anglican bishop George Berkeley gave forceful expression to this tendency to weave America into the pattern of European expectations concerning the course of history. Inspired by ideas that extend back to the Roman poet Virgil concerning the westward shift of the center of the world (to Virgil, Rome had been the new point at which this movement had come to rest, whereas to later medieval minds this *translatio imperii* had reached northern and western Europe), Berkeley wrote his famous lines:

> Westward the course of empire takes its way;
> The first four Acts already past,
> A fifth shall close the Drama with the day;
> Time's noblest offspring is the last.

"Westward the course of empire" would assume the force of a slogan in the conquest of the American West in the period from 1840 to 1870, although people tended to forget that Berkeley had something different in mind. He wrote his poem in conjunction with his plans for the founding of a college in Bermuda aimed at the conversion and education of American Indians. The native people, in his view, still had their natural place in an image of the New World as a pastoral Garden of Eden, as "the seat of innocence, Where nature guides and virtue rules . . . , Not such as Europe breeds in her decay."[11] It is not without a touch of irony that his name has become linked to an American institution of learning, one moreover that fittingly lies at the continent's western rim.

Still later, on the eve of the American Revolution, this theme of the *translatio imperii,* of the "westward course of empire," was taken up by a Frenchman, a descendant of the lower landed gentry in Normandy who after several peregrinations settled in New York. Posing as an "American farmer," this man, Michel-Guillaume Jean de Crèvecoeur (whose nom de plume was Hector St. John), wrote a series of letters to a friend in England that later acquired fame as an early statement of the identity of "the American." Like Mather and Berkeley, Crèvecoeur held the view that history would come to completion in America: "Here the circle will come to a close."[12] He linked the idea to other traditional views of America as a magic fount. In his chapter entitled "What, Then, Is the American, This New Man?" he reminds his readers of the rebirth that awaits everyone coming to America from Europe. Servitude and subjection, rank and status, all fall away in America. "Everything has tended to regenerate them: new laws, a new mode of living, a new social system; here they are become men."[13] An almost Anabaptist enthusiasm transpires from such lines, which Americans made their own. More than a century later Frederick Jackson Turner, in his famous frontier thesis, echoed Crèvecoeur's views. As Turner saw it, the conditions of life on the frontier experienced by generations of Americans constituted the true fount in which they had undergone their baptism and from which they emerged reborn.

Once again, in Turner's work America is woven into a web of older European dreams. Once again, in contrast to Europe, America is seen as a tabula rasa, a new beginning. In that sense America presents itself as a void. It is devoid of the burden of Europe. Crèvecoeur was one of the first to list the European forms that America had cast off or abjured: "Here are no aristocratic families, no courts, no kings, no bishops, no ecclesiastical dominion, no invisible power giving to a few a very visible one."[14] In the early nineteenth century the German poet Goethe put it thus:

Amerika, Du hast es besser
Als unser Kontinent, das Alte,
Hast keine verfallene Schlösser
Und keine Basalte.
Dich stört nicht im Innern
Zu lebendiger Zeit
Unnützes Erinnern
Und vergeblicher Streit.[15]

In Goethe's words Europe appears as a place of frozen forms (*Basalte*), useless remembrance, and vain struggle, a prey to forces of decay. America is free from all this. "It has it better"; it is empty. In the early twentieth century another European, H. G. Wells, reiterated this recurrent view: "There is no territorial aristocracy, no aristocracy at all, no throne, no legitimate and acknowledged representative of that upper social structure of leisure, power, State responsibility."[16]

Although American authors provide such catalogs of absences as well, their tone is generally different. James Fenimore Cooper, Nathaniel Hawthorne, and Henry James all echo Crèvecoeur, but their words read like so many litanies. America may have had the opportunity to start with a clean slate, yet what could American artists possibly write on it? Herman Melville, in his poem *Clarel,* voices this despondent mood: "Columbus ended earth's romance: / No new world to mankind remains!"[17] To Melville, America cannot even be cast in the role of expediter of Europe's dreams. It is no longer the realm of fantasy and imagination: it has been discovered; it is known; it stands empty-handed. James Fenimore Cooper put this sense of disenchantment in different words. To him, the absence of European forms constitutes an American loss. There is, as he put it, a "poverty of material." The American void, in him and others like him, called forth a yearning for the ornate riches of the European scene. It is not hard to see their dilemma: on the one hand they felt called on to give America a literature all its own and to see to the republic's emancipation from European tutelage in cultural as well as political respects, yet on the other hand their standards of success in this endeavor were still the high points of European culture. Thus their cultural nationalism was infused by a sense of inferiority toward Europe.

Europeans occasionally reminded Americans of this state of affairs. As early as the second half of the eighteenth century certain ideas that testify to a cultural anti-Americanism had gained currency in Europe.

In a sense they were echoes of Shakespeare's Prospero, who in reference to the monstrous Caliban says that nurture will not stick on his nature. With the added semblance of scientific argument, French authors in particular, like Georges Buffon, Corneille De Pauw, and Guillaume Raynal, proffered theories concerning the climate and geography of America that would doom all cultural transplants from Europe to wilt on arrival. Just as humans were of stunted growth in the American clime, likewise culture would never come to full bloom there. Against the cocky nationalism of the young American republic, Europeans smirkingly pointed out the absence to date of the likes of Shakespeare, Homer, or Dante. The Abbé Raynal, for instance, wrote in 1770 that "it is a cause of amazement, but until today America has not produced one good poet, not one skilled mathematician, not a single genius in any art or science."[18] A trap was set into which Americans naïvely walked.

John Trumbull, an early cultural nationalist and one of the so-called Connecticut Wits, consequently prophesied the advent of an American Shakespeare, thus holding up a European standard for Americans to emulate. This compelling European standard of cultural success has maintained its discouraging sway in America until the present day. Each time Americans wondered whether their national culture really measured up, they had to admit to their lagging behind Europe. In 1917 Theodore Dreiser, already an established novelist, wrote the following lament in the cultural journal *The Seven Arts*: "it is a thing for laughter, if not for tears: one hundred million Americans, rich . . . beyond the dreams of avarice, and scarcely a sculptor, a poet, a singer, a novelist, an actor, a musician, worthy of the name."[19] The same complaint emerges in Sinclair Lewis's 1930 Nobel Prize address, and as late as 1981 George Steiner reiterated the complaint in *Salmagundi* with facetious glee.[20]

Europe as the counterimage to America may have burdened Americans with a lingering sense of inferiority, yet they also had sufficient ingenuity to compare themselves to Europe in a more positive light. After all, the European repertoire of fantasies about America consists not only of images of darkness and decline. There is a whole gallery of images glowingly depicting the land in the west. The ingenuity of Americans vis-à-vis these latter views has consisted of their casting themselves in the role of historical expediters of all such positive dreams. Indeed, they have done more than that: they have managed to appropriate the more general dreams concerning "the Americas" and to redefine them as applying uniquely to the United States. The very word *Americans* as

I am using it here testifies to this act of appropriation. Whenever the inhabitants of the United States refer to Americans, they are referring to themselves, and Europeans—with the possible exception of those in the Iberian Peninsula—follow their example. It is an act of linguistic arrogation, as well as of arrogance, indicative of the extent to which "Americans" deem themselves to be the rightful and exclusive heirs of all those European dreams that see America as the "Land of the Free" and the "Promised Land." Even Columbus, a quintessentially Mediter-ranean man and the historical link with Latin America, eventually be-came woven into the pantheon of U.S. national heroes as almost an honorary Yankee. In an early burst of nationalist rapture the American poet Joel Barlow dedicated his epic poem *The Columbiad* (1807) to Columbus, the visionary, the man able to foresee the later glory of the American republic. Thus, Columbus was cast as the precursor of that long line of explorers and pioneers who, with a visionary sweep of the arm, invited Americans to fulfill their manifest destiny and to conquer the American West. Nineteenth-century representations sometimes portray Columbus in this symbolic guise, but he more often appears transformed into the goddess Columbia, the American counterpart to the British emblem of Britannia. Her precise origins are unknown. Per-haps Barlow described her when he wrote of the angel that appeared to Columbus in his captivity, to whom he addressed these words:

> Unveil . . . my friend, and stretch once more
> Beneath my view that heaven-illumined shore;
> Let me behold her silver beams expand,
> To lead all nations, lighten every land,
> Instruct the total race, and teach at last
> Their toils to lessen and their chains to cast.[21]

Here is the familiar vision not simply of America as the Western hemi-sphere but more specifically of the American republic as the shining ex-ample to the world. Also apparent are the features of Columbia as the Statue of Liberty. After all, the view of America as a beacon to the world did not inspire only Barlow and his contemporaries; it set responsive chords reverberating in Europe's republican circles as well. We must not forget that the Statue of Liberty was a gift from the French people to the Americans as a symbolic expression of America as "Liberté éclair-ant le monde" (Liberty enlightening the world). In that particular guise, as an echo of Columbus, Columbia roamed through the iconographic imagination of nineteenth-century America. In a famous John Gast painting popularized through engraved reproductions and simply entitled "Progress," Columbia is airborne, a guardian angel directing the westward march of the Americans. In a clear reference to progress as technical progress, Columbia holds a roll of telegraph wire in one of her hands.[22]

It took a while longer for Columbus to reach a similar iconographic status. He was truly adopted into the national pantheon in 1893, at the time of the great Columbian Exposition in Chicago, celebrating the fourth centennial of the discovery of the Americas. Since that time his proud statue stands in front of the white Union Station building in Washington, D.C., not far from the Capitol. The latter building may still have Columbia rather than Columbus for its pinnacle, yet Columbus has made it into the very heart of the District of Columbia.

Metaphorical Dimensions of the European Critique of American Culture

So far I have considered an America seen as a tabula rasa, a blank projection screen that both the European and the American imaginations filled as they wished. Yet its emptiness was not simply the precondition that allowed free rein to the powers of imagination; emptiness itself—America as a void, a vacuity—was a potent metaphorical ingredient in the production and projection of images from outside. One version of that image of emptiness presents itself as a new beginning, a clean slate. It is the hopeful version that looks on America as offering the possibility of a renewal, a rejuvenation, to a European culture that is old, weary, and decadent. A different version sees the emptiness in a negative light, as a loss, a void, the denial of Europe's rich cultural heritage. This latter version, as I mentioned, is current in Europe as well as in America. I now consider a number of recurrent metaphors that Europeans, in their critiques of America, have connected with the central image of America as an emptiness.

A separate cultural history could be written about the language that Europeans have developed for their rejection of America. There is a standard repertoire of views that are never more than mere stereotypes. We all know them and in unguarded moments undoubtedly have used them. As regards their content none of these views is of any great interest, yet collectively they can teach us a few things. People normally use them as if they were making factual statements about America, yet in fact they are speaking in metaphors. The repertoire of stereotypes about America is also a repertoire of metaphors. Some are clichés, whereas others are strikingly fresh and inventive. Taken together they can be seen as filling a metaphorical space of great variety and richness, yet like any space, this one can be reduced to its main dimensions.

In making such an attempt I should point out first that much of the European imagery about America is really a matter of a comparison, often made tacitly, between Europe and America. Whenever Europeans call Americans shallow or superficial—arguably the most common stereotype about Americans—in the same breath they are also saying that Europeans are neither. Later on I will explore exactly what people mean to say when they use such worn clichés; here it suffices to say that they are measuring Americans by a yardstick that will always show them in contrast to Europeans. Calling Americans shallow or superficial implies a view of Europeans as naturally probing beneath the surface, or looking up from it, appreciative both of depth and elevation. Europeans apply to America many metaphors that can be reduced to such a high-low vertical dimension.

A second dimension along which to order this metaphorical space is a temporal axis. Statements referring to America as "young" or "new"— irrespective of whether they are meant to disparage or praise—or as a country lacking history or historical awareness conjure up a contrast to Europe in terms of time as a sociocultural variable. A third yardstick that Europeans apply to Americans measures a contrast in mentality; according to this measure, Americans lack the European sense of organic cohesion, of a cultural gestalt. This contrast normally translates into European language in terms of the contrast between quality and quantity. Whenever Europeans blame Americans for being obsessed with dollars and the price of things, they in fact blame Americans for ignoring the intrinsic qualities of objects that Europeans value for their uniqueness while ruthlessly reducing the objects to the one-dimensional standard of their exchange value in dollars. Americans "value" things differently and more literally than do Europeans. The American approach toward the heritage of Western civilization displays a literally analytic touch that dissolves the context and cohesion of individual objects and leaves Europeans wringing their hands in dismay and disgust. In the eyes of Europeans Americans rush in where the initiated fear to tread.

All these examples serve to show that Europeans, in their views and conceptions of America, use the imagery of metaphors. They have created a metaphorical space to visualize the contrast between America and Europe. The varied images and metaphors that inhabit this space can be studied by reducing them to these three main dimensions. I already reviewed them rapidly, and I will return to them shortly, but first there is one more general point I need to make.

European metaphors about America do more than simply express the quintessential "otherness" of that country, preferably in terms of a perceived contrast between Europe and America. In every critical argument about America there is usually a second element. It is an old habit of Europeans to recognize the features of their own future in America. At times the country assumes the tonic quality of a beckoning horizon, for example, when it is seen as the harbinger of a world of democracy, freedom, and equality. Many in Europe and America have chosen to look at the country in this light, as a guide and promise. Even when America did not quite measure up to Europe, Europeans often had the ominous sense of seeing their own future in it. When they saw cultural erosion and the demise of values and norms in America, they often tended to connect this to processes of social change that were at work in Europe also.

We should, therefore, keep two European undertakings separate. Sometimes, in their metaphors about America, Europeans try to express what strikes them as peculiarly American, as a cultural modus operandi that has its own logic distinct from Europe's. As an exploration of what is truly unique to American culture, this venture does not reflect back on Europe and can therefore be done with relative equanimity, in a spirit of intellectual curiosity. This is not the case when America is seen as foreshadowing Europe's future. Then, whatever the findings of one's forays into America, they inevitably will be measured in terms of European anticipations. Different as these two forms of discourse concerning America and American culture are, they often tend to mingle. The metaphorical imagination of America then takes place in a European context of cultural concern and discontent. "America" then tends to turn into a figure of speech, a code word that stands for decay and corruption in Europe, even in the absence of an empirical link or parallel. Ironically, though, even in cases where America is wrongly adduced as the root of a particular evil in Europe, it may well be that people have correctly sensed some of the inner working of American culture.

LIFE ON THE SURFACE

Many metaphors about America present the country as a place of cultural erosion, leveling the contours of the cultural landscape that Europeans know and appreciate. European observers who express themselves in such terms tend to show the duality that I have just described. Only rarely do they state the transatlantic difference with intellectual detachment; more commonly there is a tone of unease, as if people have the ominous sense of America being the harbinger of Europe's future. America then appears as the country that corrupts and perverts European values and cultural standards, eroding the complex outline of Europe's cultural landscape. Not only does America have this effect on cultural transplants from Europe, but it similarly affects culture in its European setting. The locus classicus of this view is Alexis de Tocqueville's analysis of cultural life under conditions of social equality. Tocqueville develops this argument in the second part of his study of democracy in America, the more somber part where America serves as the illustration of Tocqueville's more general reflections about equality as the main organizing principle of social life. Liberty and the problem of its preservation—the classic preoccupation of political philosophy— are Tocqueville's main concern in the first part of his study (the part that came out as a separate volume in 1835 and was joined by the second part a full five years later). Not until this second part would equality become Tocqueville's central concern. Only then, in a remarkable foreshadowing of others' much later cultural and political critiques of mass democracy, does he present his famous exposé concerning *individualisme* (a word that he invented) as a form of hidebound conformism or his thoughts about political apathy. Tocqueville's concept of equality begins to resemble French sociologist Emile Durkheim's later concept of anomie. It is seen as an erosive force that leads to the complete leveling and flattening of the political and cultural landscape. As Tocqueville puts it, "The greater the extent of equality, the more insatiable the taste for it becomes."[23] It is not so much that the range of human desire has widened but that desire itself has changed in shape and essence. "When people have become roughly similar and follow the same route, it is hard for any single one among them to walk fast and to leave behind the uniform crowd that surrounds and presses him on all sides."[24] Not only is there a collective force that works to obstruct individual distinction, but the very concept of distinction has been reduced to a narrow range of marginal differentiation. "No matter how democratic the social state and the political constitution of a people, one can be sure that every single citizen will always see near him some points that rise above him. One may expect that he will fix his gaze on precisely those points."[25] Such an individual will do this, moreover, with a view to leveling such differences as have caught his or her attention. People may still have an eye for distinction, as well as an urge to distinguish themselves, yet the impulse has become self-defeating. People not only no longer aspire to rising above the multitudes; worse than that, they no longer aspire to rising above themselves. People have been turned into thoroughly socialized animals, meekly following the marching order of the crowd around them. Similarly, such leveling can be observed in matters of cultural taste and cultural standards. As Tocqueville argues, the production of literary work no longer follows the traditional rules of composition and form. Literary tradition or a sense of the historical genesis of other forms of art no longer plays a role. History has contracted into the ephemeral here and now. Surface effects have taken the place of *profondité,* of depth. The leveling proceeds from both sides: heights are eroded, and depths are filled in. All that remains is the emptiness of horizontal space as the last haunt for the unstoppable leveling spirit.

In his critique of America seen as the ideal type of egalitarian democracy, Tocqueville ushered in a repertoire of metaphors that would recur in later critical writings on mass society and mass culture. In their evocation of pairs of logical opposites—flatness versus height or depth, constraint versus boundlessness, an expanse of time versus the single moment, the group versus the individual—the underlying antithesis is always between the ways of Europe and those of America, or in more historical terms, between societies in an aristocratic mold and the emerging type of the democratic society.

It was not until the traumatic advent of mass democracy in Europe, in the turmoil of the immediate post–World War I period, that this rhetorical repertoire gained currency among a generation of conservative European critics of culture. Once again America provided them with the material for their case. Once again they looked toward America with the ominous sense of watching Europe's future. People like Oswald Spengler in Germany, Georges Duhamel in France, and Johan Huizinga in the Netherlands are among the better-known examples from this era of cultural pessimism in Europe. Theirs was an anguished awareness of the erosion of cultural standards ushered in by the age of mass consumption and mass culture. To the extent that America was the harbinger of this modern world, the country inspired in them mostly a sense of decline and loss. Interestingly, at the same time others in Europe welcomed America's modernity. These were mainly on the political Left, in the trade union movement or left-wing political parties, or they were leading intellectuals, like Antonio Gramsci in Italy or Hendrik de Man in Belgium. What intrigued them was not so much the culture of mass consumption as the power of mass production. To them, America represented the breakthrough from the realm of scarcity and poverty toward the realm of affluence, with consumption open to everyone. Gramsci was the first to use the word *Fordism* to describe this quantitative leap in society's production potential.

Nonetheless, whatever the precise tone of European reflections on America in this period, whether it was a cultural pessimism or an anticipation of progress, both groups looked toward America as representing Europe's future. Few were those that chose to look at America in any other light. One was a man who is usually mentioned as one of the leading cultural pessimists in the interbellum, the Spanish philosopher José Ortega y Gasset. He had no use for America in his critique of cultural trends in Europe. To him, America did not foreshadow Europe's future. As he saw it, America had only just entered history, and Europe could learn nothing from its experience. America was still at a primitive stage, albeit in the camouflage of the latest inventions. In his "Preface to French Readers," which in 1937 he added to *The Revolt of the Masses* (1929), he expresses the satisfaction of having been proved right by history. America was mired in depression. Against all those who in the twenties had looked hopefully from a stagnant Europe toward an America wallowing in prosperity, he had maintained that America, far from holding out the prospect of the future, was in fact a distant past, a primitivism. But he was an exception.

As regards the others, such as Spengler and Huizinga, who did discuss America in their critiques of culture, let me analyze in greater depth what metaphors they used. An interesting case from the Netherlands is Menno ter Braak. I will discuss him again later on, but here my focus is on one particular essay that he published in 1928: "Why I Reject 'America.'"[26] At the time of writing the author was a budding twenty-six-year-old intellectual. One should not misread the title, or for that matter the entire piece. The America that is so curtly dismissed really is an America in quotation marks, "America," a construct of the mind, a composite image based on the perception of ominous trends that are then linked to America as the country and the culture characteristically—but not uniquely—displaying them. Nor is it only outsiders who are struck by these trends and reject them. Indeed, as Ter Braak admits, he is willing to acknowledge as a European anyone sharing his particular sensibility and intellectual detachment, "even if he happens to live on Main Street." Ter Braak illustrates this attitude with the striking parable of the young newspaper vendor whom he saw one day standing on the balcony of a prewar Amsterdam streetcar, surrounded by the pandemonium of traffic noise yet enclosed in a private sphere of silence. Amid the pointless energy and meaningless noise the boy stood immersed in the reading of a musical score, deciphering the secret code that admitted entrance to a hidden inner world. This immersion, this loyal devotion to the probing of meaning and sense, to a heritage of signs and significance, was to Ter Braak the ingredient of Europeanism. To him, it constitutes the quintessentially European reflex of survival against the onslaught of a world increasingly organized around the tenets of rationality, utility, mechanization, and instrumentality yet utterly devoid of meaning and prey to the forces of entropy. The European reaction is one that pays tribute to what is useless and unproductive, defending a quasi-monastic sphere of silence and reflexiveness amid the whirl of secular motion.

This reflex of survival through self-assertion was a current mood in Europe during the interbellum, a Europe in ruins not only materially but spiritually. Amid the aimless drift of society's disorganization and the cacophony of demands accompanying the masses' advent into the political agora, Americanism as a concept had come to focus the diagnosis of Europe's plight. The impulse toward reassertion—toward the concentrated retrieval of meaning from the fragmented score of European history—was therefore mainly cultural and conservative, much as it was simultaneously an act of protest and defiance.

Huizinga's is another name associated with this mood of conservative apologetics. On his return from his only visit to the United States, at about the time that Ter Braak wrote his defense of Europeanism, he expressed himself thus: "Strange: among us Europeans who were travelling together in America . . . there rose up repeatedly this pharisaical feeling: we all have something that you lack; we admire your strength but we do not envy you. Your instrument of civilisation and progress, your big cities and your perfect organisation, only make us nostalgic for what is old and quiet, and sometimes your life seems hardly to be worth living, not to speak of your future"[27]—a statement in which resonates the ominous foreboding that "your future" might well be read as "our future." Indeed, what is only implied here comes out more clearly in Huizinga's more pessimistic later writings, when America became a mere piece of evidence in his case against contemporary history losing form. Thus, Huizinga makes the following sweeping indictment in *The Shadows of Tomorrow* (1935): "The number, so it was said, washed across the individual; the mass dragged the individual along, defenseless, and lowered him to a level that always was the lowest common denominator of the more simple and coarser features, while leveling and washing away the more complex and 'higher' expressions of the individual. New regimes could stimulate these coarsening trends and use for their own purposes such negative feelings like rancor, vengefulness and cruelty."[28]

Huizinga and Ter Braak may have inveighed against an obnoxious Americanism, against an "America" in quotation marks, but neither could be mistaken for a mouthpiece for vulgar anti-Americanism. Both were too subtle minded for that, forever aware of the counterargument, of ambiguity; both were also too open to the real America as a historical given to relinquish the mental reserve of the quotation marks. Ter Braak thus concluded his piece as follows: "'America' I reject. Now we can turn to the problem of America." The Huizinga quotation, which comes from a book of travel observations and was already full of ambivalence, continues, "And yet, it is *we* that have to be the Pharisees, for theirs is the love and the confidence. Things must be different than we think." With both authors, what strikes us in their rejection of what Europe was wont to call Americanism is their intellectual sense of wonder, of admiration even, and—especially in Huizinga's case—of an affinity with and appreciation for that other variety of Americanism, that heritage of high-minded ideals that inspired much of American history.

It is of interest to note that Americans produced a similar critique of their own culture. When one reads Ter Braak, one cannot help being reminded of the refined American aesthete Henry Adams, who in a certain way appears to be an American version of Ter Braak's newspaper vendor. Adams's quest was for the "useless" and highly private transcendence of the aimless noise and whirl of his contemporary America, which represented for him nothing but mere entropy, a pointless, senseless waste of energy. There were others like him, sharing his view and attitude, even though few European critics were aware of this at the time. In general it is safe to say that Americans are second to none in their anti-Americanism. It is almost a constant of American culture, although this tends to escape European critics. At regular intervals American intellectuals indulge in self-criticism and self-rejection that do not differ greatly from European critiques either in sharpness or in use of metaphors. In one such period, at the time of World War I, James Oppenheim, the editor of the cultural journal *The Seven Arts,* wrote, "For some time we have seen our own shallowness, our complacency, our commercialism, our thin self-indulgent kindliness, our lack of purpose, our fads and advertising and empty politics."[29] The statement is characteristic of a renewed and acute sense of the barrenness of America's cultural landscape. Van Wyck Brooks, one of the leading cultural critics of the time, referred thus to the concept of Americanism as it had gained currency in Europe: "for two generations the most sensitive minds in Europe—Renan, Ruskin, Nietzsche, to name none more recent—have summed up their mistrust of the future in that one word; and it is because, altogether externalized ourselves, we have typified the universally externalizing influences of modern industrialism."[30] Brooks thus provided an early, concise version of Ter Braak's and Huizinga's later indictments of Americanism, of an "America" in quotation marks. As Brooks saw it, American culture was only one early version or type ("we have typified") of what the universal forces of industrialism threatened to bring elsewhere as well.

In spite of these similarities, however, European cultural critics may seem to have argued a different case: their main concern was the defense of a European culture that they saw as threatened from without, even though the actual threat may have been endemic to their own society and culture. Rallying to the defense, they chose to take the offensive, rejecting America. In that sense Europe's alleged cultural superiority was the ultimate offense vis-à-vis an America that clearly had the upper hand militarily and economically. Oswald Spengler, in his *Jahre der Entscheidung* (Years of decision), really rubs it in: "Life in America revolves solely around its economy and lacks depth, the more so as absent from it is the element of true historical tragedy, of true fate, which has deepened and educated the souls of the European nations."[31] Huizinga made much the same point in a 1941 essay about contemporary history losing form,[32] yet Spengler's choice of words, emphasizing *Tiefe* and *Seele* (depth and soul), as well as the element of true historical tragedy, is more telling. Spengler merges two metaphorical dimensions, the spatial and the temporal, into one: he connects the shallowness of life in America to its lacking a sense of true *historical* tragedy.

Others would have a similar hunch. Albert Camus, following his 1946 visit to the United States, made this observation: "The afternoon with students. They don't feel the real problem; however their nostalgia is evident. In this country where everything is done to prove that life isn't tragic, they feel something is missing. The great effort is pathetic, but one must reject the tragic *after* having looked at it, not before."[33] At about the same time Jean-Paul Sartre made similar observations on the absence of a tragic sense of life in America. The country, for all its blithe optimism, struck him as tragic in a rather pathetic way precisely because of this absence.[34] Spengler, Camus, and Sartre, who looked at America in two different postwar situations, illustrate the general tendency toward cultural self-elevation in societies that have seen themselves forced into a defensive posture by stronger rivals. The latter, for all their strength and dominance, are seen as cold and shallow cultures, if not actually dead ones,[35] the very antitheses of the cultures under threat, which are warm, vibrant with life, deep, and full of soul.

In his classic study of the process of civilization in Europe, Norbert Elias gave an early illustration of this strategy of cultural defense. In the late eighteenth century the German bourgeoisie, in its social ascent, came up against the oppressive radiance of French culture. In their defense of Germanness they opposed French *"civilisation"* to German *"Kultur."* The first they saw as a superficial veneer; the latter, as deeper, warmer, and more authentic. Something similar occurred in a movement of nationalist emancipation in Latin America in the late nineteenth century. In his book-length essay *Ariel,* which he wrote in 1900, Uruguayan author José Enrique Rodó contrasted the cold rationality of the imperialist North American civilization with the deeply felt *"alma"*—the soul—of Spanish American culture. Once again, cultural sublimation was the answer to the defiant sway of the United States. And even today—to give a very recent example—Leonard Jeffries, a black teacher at the City University of New York, has made an international splash not only with theories that present Africa as the cradle of Western civilization but—more relevant in the present context—with his views opposing "the destructive white race of cold, materialistic ice people" to the intellectually superior black race of "warm humanist sun people."[36]

■ ■ ■

The critics that I have mentioned so far, Europeans and Americans alike, generally tended to connect their critique of America to technical and industrial developments. If these critics viewed America as having surfaced as the nation that had advanced farthest on the road toward a culture of mass consumption, it had surfaced in a highly metaphorical sense. Not only had it reached the surface; it had become mere surface. It had produced a national culture that was quintessentially superficial, a surface phenomenon whose main cultural vectors were all horizontal. Huizinga, unwittingly echoing Van Wyck Brooks, spoke of an "exteriorized culture." In its conformism, in its peer-group emulation, in its consuming quest for ever-changing thrills and satisfactions, it presented a picture of all drift and no mastery. In the great Tocquevillean tradition, Georges Duhamel, in his *Scènes de la vie future,* described the Americans as slaves, held thrall to the social dictates of a consumption society in spite of their hallowed rhetoric of freedom and individualism. He saw film, then a new form of mass entertainment, as "le plus puissant instrument de conformisme moral, esthétique et politique" (the most potent instrument of moral, aesthetic, and political conformism), as a wave of destruction coming from America and hurling itself across the intellectual landscape of France. He argued that film had the power to entertain, even at times to move an audience, but never did it incite individual consumers "de se surpasser"—to rise above themselves—as any true form of art should.[37] Never did American culture challenge the individual to pause and reflect, to find coherence and meaning, to consummate rather than merely to consume. In this connection Albert Camus made this astute observation: "At the corner of East 1st Street, little bar where a loud juke box smothers all the conversations. To have five minutes of silence, you have to put in five cents."[38]

In much the same vein Marnix Gijzen, a young Flemish poet and novelist born in 1899, wrote a preface to his 1927 collection of travel impressions entitled *Ontdek Amerika* (Discover America), which had earlier been published separately in the Belgian newspaper *De Standaard.* "Almost to a man we undergo the levelling influence of the American film *de quatrième zône* [fourth rate]: its adaptation to every conceivable audience has been pushed so far as to eliminate its inner meaning. . . . Yet the American film exerts its influence on our thinking and behavior: by systematically ignoring anything problematic it creates an atmosphere of intellectual indifference, it is a factor dissolving our stabilized popular life." Nor was film the only carrier of such harmful influences:

> The cheap car and the mobility it provides are slowly changing our society in ways that we cannot always fathom precisely but whose advanced state I had every opportunity to study in America. The car as a commodity rather than a luxury object is an American conception: it left its imprint on a society that almost in its very essence could be called nomadic. In this nomadicism, in the extreme mobility that characterizes America, the car is the main element. It plays a main role in public indecency, it further weakens the already fragile ties of family life, it allows youngsters a freedom that without exaggeration we may deem too great. The time that the car helps save in certain respects it otherwise causes to be lost in pure feverishness: it contributes to "superficializing" life, it exteriorizes it in large measure.[39]

Gijzen also looked on America as a country preceding Europe on the road toward cultural decline and social decomposition. To present his case he employed the same metaphors of surface, of horizontal motion, of a loss of depth and meaning.

■ ■ ■

Whatever the precise case that people may be making against America, more often than not they tend to come up with variations on the theme of a vertical dimension missing in America. Whether they see America as cold, efficient, conformist, or unstoppably energetic, they always refer to aspects of a national mentality that is seen as being on the surface, never probing the depths of its innermost stirrings, never rising above the immediate here and now. Tocqueville sought the central explanation of this life on the surface in the prevailing egalitarianism of the culture. Many later critics tended rather to blame the new culture of consumption. The two cannot really be seen in separation, however. In fact many of Tocqueville's observations can be seen to suggest an interconnection that later authors like Thorsten Veblen (in *The Theory of the Leisure Class*), David Riesman (in *The Lonely Crowd*) and W. Lloyd Warner (in his 1950s studies of social status, taste, and consumption behavior) further developed. If competition is the central motive force in the area of production, "invidious distinction" and "marginal differentiation" (to use Veblen's words) become the engines of a consumptive frenzy. Freud referred to it as the "Narcissism of marginal distinction." The role played by rules of etiquette as markers of social distinction in Europe's stratified societies came to be played by the socialized dictates of "good" taste in the context of America's more egalitarian ethos. As the new guideline serving to direct the many decisions that individual consumers have to take, taste now determined the social game of marginal distinction in a larger setting of overall conformity. Taste became the marker in a game of reference-group behavior indicating with which groups people wanted to be associated and from which they wished to be differentiated. As a result "taste communities" arose, what Daniel Boorstin called "consumption communities." Their order is one of a horizontal criss-cross rather than of a hierarchy of high versus low.

Thus, the horizontalization and leveling that Tocqueville connected to the American ideal of equality was later seen as related to America's being the first country to assume the contours of a consumption society. The behavior of individual consumers in mass society now formed the new terrain for the hidebound conformity that Tocqueville had already observed. Individualism in the sense of distinctive behavior still occurred, but it had undergone a transformation compared to its traditional form in Europe, where good and bad taste had long been seen in connection with the socially high and low. Culture there was normally seen as vertically differentiated into high and low forms. In America sociocultural distinctions fanned out horizontally, linked as they were to the variety of peer groups that had a keen sense of mutual difference, but not in terms of any implicit hierarchy.

When Tocqueville reduced the contrast between Europe and America to one between a proud and self-reliant individualism with a loathing of social dictates and a hidebound conformism that took its cues from its social environment, he was of course overstating his case. Traditional European distinction behavior always betrays elements of social conformism, of a conformation to standards of behavior set by hierarchically ordered social strata.

The contrast, however, particularly in its overstated version, has tempted many later observers and has become a staple of the European critique of American mass culture. In 1955 the English writer and broadcaster J. B. Priestley published his grand denunciation of the mass-production-for-mass-consumption society, which he termed "Admass" and which was inspired more or less directly by the American experience: "This is my name for the whole system of an increasing productivity, plus inflation, plus a rising standard of material living, plus cultural democracy and the creation of the mass mind, the mass man. . . . Most Americans (though not all; they have some fine rebels) have been Admassians for the last thirty years; the English, and probably most West Europeans, only since the war."[40] Even many Americans voiced this contrast; in *The Lonely Crowd,* for example, Riesman set in opposition two forms of reference-group behavior, a contrast reminiscent of the antithesis of individualism and conformism. In the consumption society of postwar America he observed the emergence of "other-directed man," who was forcing out his historical predecessor, "inner-directed man." The latter character type had thrived in the relatively stable social hierarchy of stratified societies in which parents equipped their children with a sense of social bearings that would be their compass for the rest of their lives. A rapidly changing society like America's made this character type obsolete. Like an anachronistic Rip van Winkle, inner-directed individuals would wander aimlessly in a world utterly beyond their grasp and comprehension. Rather than use a compass, people now needed radar to catch the constantly changing signals emitting from their surroundings. Their behavior and attitudes were in need of constant fine tuning in a process of ongoing socialization. In Riesman's view, however, this other-directed personality was not merely the slave of the collective "other," not simply a fish that meekly followed the movements of the school. Riesman had a keen eye for the more picaresque side of this new social game and for the rivalry of a social "one-upmanship" with all its tactical moves and calculations. The "other-directed man," as Riesman saw him, was not simply the dedicated follower of fashion.

Many non-American critics of mass culture chose to see things differently. Their inspiration came from Marx and Freud rather than from Tocqueville. Their astute sense of the erosive impact of capitalism on such central pillars of the liberal worldview as self-interest, individual needs, and more generally, the rationality of individual behavior made them explore capitalism's massive false consciousness, or what Herbert Marcuse called its repressive tolerance. A striking example of this, once again from France, is Simone de Beauvoir's travel report, *L'Amérique au jour le jour* (America day by day). Traveling in America a few years after the last world war, she felt torn between excitement and rejection. Repeatedly she found herself carried away in raptures by the pace and variety of American life, yet always there was a reprimanding voice reminiscent of both Marx and Tocqueville:

> In this profusion of dresses, blouses, skirts, and coats, a French woman would be hard put to make a choice and not offend her taste. And then one begins to notice that underneath their multi-colored wrappers all chocolates have the same taste of peanut, all bestsellers tell the same story. And why choose one toothpaste rather than another? There is an aftertaste of mystification in all this useless profusion. A thousand possibilities are open: yet they are all the same. A thousand choices allowed: all equivalent. Thus the American citizen will be able to consume his liberty inside the life that is imposed on him without so much as noticing that such a life itself is not free.[41]

This indictment invokes a familiar repertoire: taste in its refined European form versus its false imitation in America, European elitism versus an uncouth American egalitarianism, hierarchy versus flatness, and above all, the European recognition of the aspect of slavery in the vaunted rhetoric of American freedom.

This same repertoire emerged again in the liberationist rhetoric of the late-1960s counterculture. Other contributions to such relatively short-lived international consensus came from the neo-Marxist Frankfurt school in Germany or from Marxist sociologists like Jean Baudrillard in France. Again the pattern is familiar: capitalism was the main theoretical target, but for all practical intents and purposes the critical arrows were mostly aimed at America as the tangible embodiment of everything that is wrong with capitalism. In both the European and the American varieties of the counterculture, anticapitalism and anti-Americanism seamlessly blended into each other. The critique of what was seen as the leveling and shallowness in American culture derived from the more general critique of the culture of capitalism. What capitalism had done to America, it would in due course do to cultures elsewhere. In this critical context America once again emerged as the harbinger of Europe's future. In this critical onslaught no one paused to reflect whether American culture might have a logic all its own, whether Huizinga was right to muse that "things must be different than we think."

In conclusion to this section on metaphors that in one way or another see the contrast between Europe and America as a matter of a vertical dimension missing in America, I once again quote Huizinga. Not only did he publish a collection of "miscellaneous observations," as he called them, following his only journey to the United States, but he also kept a diary that was not published until 1993. There, as an entry for Thursday, April 29, he wrote the following reflection: "In the morning from Philadelphia to Baltimore. The landscape has something light, something *ingénu, sans conséquence,* lacking depth, as if one dimension were missing [note the metaphor]. At times everything here makes that impression. As if, orbiting in a sphere around the essence of things, one is suddenly moved out to a more distant, wider sphere, at higher speed but more remote."[42]

THE METAPHORS OF TIME AND COHESION

Metaphors of high versus low, of depth and flatness, form only one dimension in the metaphorical space where America is imagined. Other images refer to time, the sense of time, and the passing of time; they could be grouped along a second dimension. A third, closely related dimension refers to what we may call the combined effects of space and time, producing the historically unique and organically coherent. I now analyze these metaphors in greater depth.

It is an old American claim to be beyond European history. The American republic constituted a new beginning, or as the U.S. national seal has it, a *Novus Ordo Seclorum.* At an early stage of their history, Americans already talked of a new world order. President Bush was not the first to do so. Americans love historic watersheds. They love to proclaim the end of historical periods and the beginning of new ones. If there is not a "New Era" to be proclaimed, there is instead a "New Deal," a "New Frontier," or a "New Nixon"; books continually appear with titles like *"The End of Ideology,"* or even *"The End of History."* Being a proper historian in a country that likes to conceive of itself as being outside history creates its own problems. The American historian David Noble has written an interesting little study about this quandary: *Historians against History.*[43]

This remarkable attitude has not escaped Europeans. If they want to be congratulatory, they patronizingly call the country "young," even if this is mostly inapposite. In many respects the country is old, or even old-fashioned. Its Constitution and its political parties are among the oldest in the world. County lines were drawn in such a way that people could reach the county seat in one day with a horse and buggy. In most cases, however, Europeans have something different in mind when they speak of differences regarding time.

Again Tocqueville is a good early observer. As he explained it, the public discourse in a mass democracy will tend to focus on the immediately appealing. If politicians want to address the citizenry across all lines of social and regional difference, they would be ill advised, in the clamor of rival voices, to read a well-crafted historical essay. On the contemporary political stage, which is dominated by television, the political message has reached ultimate condensation into what is known as the sound bite, the catchy, quotable slogan that one may hope will linger in the heads of the zealously zapping television audience. This is not a new phenomenon, however. Tocqueville already mentioned the loss of tradition and historical depth in favor of special effects and cheap thrills. In his observations on the topic the metaphors get mixed, perhaps unavoidably so. His analysis of the shallowness and loss of depth could not but imply the loss of a sense of history and historical depth. Huizinga, as I have shown, made similar observations. When in America he longed for things peaceful and quiet, he added in the same breath, "things old." What he must have meant was a sense of the presence of the past, an awareness of historical growth and continuity. What struck him in America was the opposite attitude, the tendency to fetishize the news. He had this to say about American journalism: "The great newspapers, even if their number is legion, can actually be seen as one, as one loud call that is repeated daily across the land. . . . [The European traveler] hates this daily flood of loud stories, telling of crimes, political scandals, marriage break-ups and weddings, those colored and fragmented bits of political news, that lack of information about what is truly happening in the world (he really means the old world, forgetting he finds himself in the new world)."[44] The word *fragmented* is the crucial one. In Huizinga's view the news has broken into disparate tidbits, without line, continuity, or context. Of course there was nothing particularly new or American about this. There is the well-known anecdote of King Frederick the Great of Prussia, who one day ran into the philosopher Immanuel Kant and asked, "Well, Mister Kant, what's new?" Kant appositely responded by asking, "I assume, Sire, that you know the old already?" In the view of many Europeans this need for news for its own sake, clearly not unknown in Europe, has assumed excessive proportions in America. Even Huizinga, in spite of all his mental reserve and open appreciation, was led to conclude that

American journalists aim at reducing the intellectual challenge to their readers while simply trying to catch their attention, however fleetingly. Longer articles are printed in fragmented form ("continued on page 4"), which, according to Huizinga, hinders the reader from looking up the sequel to even the most thrilling paragraph. The newspaper aims at the reader simply "picking up a few bits here and there." The approach tends to reduce printed matter to the lowest form of equivalence: the small news, the big news, the advertisements—all have been taken out of context and cohesion and have become mere morsels of information, miscellaneous messages.

The question today, of course, is whether these observations about America can still make outsiders frown. The techniques Huizinga described have become commonplace in all contemporary media—the press, radio, and television—wherever we live; European countries offer daily illustrations of an attitude and an approach that could have struck Huizinga as peculiarly American. What remains of interest, though, is that these trends did strike Huizinga as American, that apparently in his day and age there was a more marked difference between Europe and America than there is today. If so, it would illustrate a more general phenomenon: what people see as crucially different in America, if not as "typically American," is only a matter of difference of phase in developments otherwise parallel. The question then remains of whether trends occurring in Europe later than they did in America, even if they were due to indigenous forces of development, could not still have received a prior American "coloring."

As Huizinga saw it, the fragmenting of the news, the separation of current events from their historical context, and the reduction of the news to, as he put it, "slogan, the brief, catchy phrase," all constituted "a regression of culture." They all resulted from America's being a mass democracy and would therefore, in due course, come to other mass democracies as well, a clear case of parallel developments, with Europe following closely on the heels of America. Interestingly, however, Huizinga also connected these trends as observed in America to a strictly American background factor, the "anti-metaphysical cast of mind" in that country. This mentality was the lasting heritage of an Enlightenment rationalism that had entrenched itself more firmly in America than anywhere else. Huizinga asked, "Do we not feel as if placed back in the eighteenth century?" He then continued, "the anti-metaphysical cast of mind naturally implies an anti-historical one. In spite of a flourishing and superbly organized practice of history [as an academic endeavor]

America's mind is thoroughly anti-historical. A historiography that in the march of humankind wants to see purely the theodicy of progress, is not the true kind." Or, as he put it elsewhere, the American is directed toward the present and the future too much to be open to the mystery of the past.[45]

Many others have tried to put into words this particular aspect of American culture. Time and again they tried to evoke the image of a nation that lacks the European sense of history, that is without memory, cut adrift from the passage of time, bobbing along with shifting tides and currents. Spengler pointed to the absent element of true historical tragedy, *das grosse Schicksal*. He too mixed two metaphorical dimensions: lacking a sense of historical tragedy, the American soul had never had a chance to deepen. Spengler connected the superficiality of American life to the lack of "real" history. To Ortega y Gasset, America had only just entered into history; it was at a primitive stage or was a primitivism itself.

These metaphors have retained their currency. In 1986 Jean Baudrillard published a thin volume entitled *Amérique*. America's lack of a history is one of the many contrasts between America and Europe that Baudrillard aphoristically conjures. Like Ortega y Gasset, Baudrillard calls America primitive, unburdened by Europe's historical heritage. In America he finds the triumph of oblivion over remembrance. America, to him, is "la seule société primitive de l'avenir, . . . celle d'un fait métasocial total aux conséquences imprévisibles, dont l'immanence nous ravit, mais sans passé pour la réfléchir, donc fondamentalement primitive" (the only primitive society of the future, . . . a society that is totally metasocial, with unforeseeable consequences, whose immanence delights us, but which has no past to reflect it—a society, therefore, that is quintessentially primitive). It is a society that never pauses to reflect on itself, "beau dans sa diversité superficielle" (beautiful in its superficial diversity). Complex and diverse, yes, but superficially so. The true immanence of America, therefore, "la vérité de l'Amérique," can be fathomed only by Europeans; only they tend toward reflection. For their eyes only can the surface come to reflect deeper layers, hidden from direct view. They are able to envision what is not there to be seen. Consequently, only Europeans can conceive of life at the surface in America as a "perfect simulacrum," the mere reflection of deeper meanings. This perception will always escape Americans. Engaged in forming the ghost images of their collective existence, they are like the bathing beauties in a 1950s Esther Williams movie, unable themselves to see the figurations that together they form. Baudrillard puts it thus: "Les Américains, eux, n'ont aucun sens de la simulation. Ils en sont la configuration parfaite, mais ils n'en ont pas le langage, étant eux-mêmes le modèle." (The Americans themselves have no sense at all of the simulation. They are its perfect configuration, but they are unable to describe it, because they themselves constitute the model.) Europeans know the raptures of analytic thought. They are the excited audience watching from the side. Americans lack this reflective attitude. They live in "une actualité perpétuelle des signes" (a perpetual present of all signs), a continuing story without history. Americans have no sense of historic roots; they are uprooted.[46]

■ ■ ■

Whoever lives totally in the present has no sense of historic meaning and context. Nor will such a person have a sense of organic cohesion. Indeed, anything that can be conceived in terms of internal coherence has a historical dimension, or a historicist specificity in its configuration of constituent elements. This leads to a third metaphorical repertoire that Europeans have used to express what they saw as American cultural defects. Once again Huizinga provides a telling example. When introduced to the Dewey decimal system, the system for filing library holdings that was being adopted in America around the time when Huizinga wrote, he recognized a quintessentially American impulse at work. As he saw it, time and time again living, organic connections in the body of human knowledge were sacrificed to the need for classification. The human mind had been made subservient to the tyranny of the decimal system. It confirmed his intimations concerning the Americans' antimetaphysical bent and their inclination toward subjecting the spiritual realm to the dictates of technical organization.

Many are the areas in which Americans were seen to display this lack of reverence for the organic cohesion of things. Production constitutes one such area. In his early writings about the alienation of industrial work, Marx concentrated on preindustrial artisans, who could still express their individuality in the products they made, but America offered a more radical illustration of the ominous trends toward fragmentation than Europe did. At about the time that Marx was writing, a transformation of industrial production was taking place in America that would become known as the "American system of manufactures." It centered on the idea of "interchangeable parts"; henceforth industrial products would be conceived as a set of components separately produced and separately replaceable. The idea had first taken hold in the manufacture of arms and had been introduced there by Samuel Colt. In his case there would be no Marxian alienation; his name became synonymous with the guns leaving his factory. Nonetheless, his productive innovation spelled the end of the individual artisan. Henceforth no finished product would display the individual skill of its maker. Individuality as a unique, organically coherent ensemble of characteristics had fallen prey to America's antimetaphysical spirit.

Americans themselves would probably call it good old Yankee ingenuity, and they would be thinking of the slightly eccentric spirit of non-conventionality deemed characteristic of New England but to be found elsewhere in America as well. It is a spirit of blithe bricolage and thrives on the assumption that cultural entities will reveal their inner secrets if you disassemble them into their component parts. Once you have taken that liberty, why not be as irreverent when reassembling the parts? There is the example of Charles Ives, a successful businessman and composer and one of the great musical innovators of our age. As he remembered it, his father, "half in fun and half seriously," let him form chords by piling thirds, one major, one minor, on top of one another. As if seeing himself through his father's eyes, he wrote, "This boy's way—of feeling, if you can have two 3ds, major or minor, in a chord, why can't you have another one or two on top of it, etc.—[is] as natural to a boy as thinking, if three bases in baseball, why not four or five . . . —it's an obvious and natural way of having a little fun!" This is the fun of the artisan who has just invented a new contraption. Ives must have been aware of the comparison. He mentions a concert of his music where young Sally Whitney was present and goes on to say, "Sally's grandpa, Eli, invented the cotton gin, so Sal was used to invention!"[47]

America's attitude toward Europe's cultural heritage has always shown this spirit. When faced with the aura of holiness, historicity, individuality, and local setting that envelops European culture, Americans characteristically displayed the happy irreverence of the uninitiated. They found themselves not inside European history but facing it from the outside, like tourists in a museum. An entire historical heritage presented itself to them in the light of contemporaneity. Henry James, another famous son of New England, had this to say: "It seems to me that we are ahead of the European races in the fact that more than either of them we can deal freely with forms of civilization not our own, can pick and choose and assimilate."[48] Americans, according to James, have an eclectic freedom that allows them to select elements from European culture at their own will and whim and to rearrange them in the same spirit. The American modernist Ezra Pound is another, more extreme case in point; he showed how the American imagination, free from European traditions, could make something new from its separate elements, something that could appeal equally to Americans and Europeans.

Ives, Pound, and James are highbrow examples. They all followed a high artistic calling. Nevertheless, this fragmenting, antiorganic attitude of the Americans appears on a more everyday level as well. If, for example, the skyscraper is a uniquely American contribution to international architecture, its originality is due not only to its sheer size but mostly to its sovereign infringement of traditional rules of stylistic unity, proportion, measure, and scale. The skyscraper lacks all the ingredients of organic closure. Another story can always be added, in any style. It represents an architecture that is quintessentially composite, lacking any compelling logic of cohesion or closure. H. G. Wells, in *The Future in America*, had already addressed this issue in 1907. Entering New York harbor he saw the skyscrapers of Manhattan rise up before him, "the strangest crown that ever a city wore." He went on to say, "They have an effect of immense incompleteness; each one seems to await some needed terminal." Comparisons with St. Peter's in Rome or St. Paul's in London forced themselves on him: "These are efforts that have accomplished their ends. . . . But New York's achievement is a threatening promise, growth going on under a pressure that increases." In the next line he termed it "mechanical, inhuman growth."[49]

The skyscraper might be called the middlebrow illustration of what I have in mind. It illustrates the antiorganic spirit of Americans as it affects the realms of engineering and technical design. Examples abound as well in the area of lowbrow mass culture. In *Travels in Hyperreality* Umberto Eco provides a tongue-in-cheek description of America as "the last beach of European culture." Whereas cultural heritage is slowly crumbling in Europe, in America we can find the complete collection, copied a thousand times over, enlarged or reduced, in every material conceivable. If America is a land without castles, no problem: America will buy them in Europe, take them apart, and reassemble them in random order. Hearst Castle in California, in its many rooms, offers the visitor a tour through European periods and styles. When the French protest against the opening of Euro-Disney on their hallowed ground, Disney's director, Michael Eisner, is truly amazed (or feigns to be). How can people say that Disney would have no eye for older cultures? There is an entire section in Euro-Disney devoted to the discoveries and fantasies of Da Vinci and Jules Verne. "Culture?" Eisner asked: "Sleeping Beauty is culture, and that's French; Peter Pan is English, Pinocchio Italian, Snow White German."[50] What are these Europeans complaining about?

I could go on in this vein. Clearly, in their way of dealing with history, tradition, and organic closure, Americans show a characteristic talent for cultural dissolution mixed with an ingenuous nonconventionality that strikes many a European observer as a cultural deficiency. Europeans can never simply take American culture as an intriguing variant of Western culture in its own right and explore its unique characteristics; they always want to sit in judgment. And more often than not the judgment is negative, cast in words that testify to a virulent anti-Americanism. A striking case in point is Sigmund Freud. In Peter Gay's biography of Freud, the latter appears as a rabid anti-American—"Yes, America is gigantic, but a gigantic mistake"—full of scorn for the dull, coarse, and gullible American, who is able to understand only one language, that of money. In endless variation Freud expounded on the American dollarmania. As Gay points out, Freud was far from original in this. He was using clichés that were a century or more old. Charles Dickens, in his *Martin Chuzzlewit,* had already produced a biting caricature of the Americans using essentially the same ingredients. The Americans, or so we are told in Dickens's novel, preach freedom but live in fear of public opinion; they talk about equality, yet they hold slaves. They are snobs and money grabbers. Conversations with Americans "may be summed up in one word—dollars. All their cares, joys, hopes, affections, virtues, and associations, seemed to be melted down into dollars."[51] The worldly wise Wells was equally aware of the currency of such views in certain social circles. When he attempted to characterize the form of the American social and economic process, he concluded, "An English Tory will tell you promptly, 'a scramble for dollars.' A good American will tell you it is self-realisation under equality of opportunity. The English Tory will probably allege that that amounts to the same thing."[52]

Many others in Europe have used similar language to describe Americans. As early as 1913 Italian author Guglielmo Ferrero felt he could confidently sum up the difference between Europeanness and Americanness as one between a qualitative versus a quantitative sensibility.[53] The language is highly telling. The reference in the Dickens quotation to the melting down into dollars is perhaps the central metaphor for America's antiorganic, decomposing cast of mind. What has a greater dissolving effect on the nature and identity of things than money does? Money is the central instrument for reducing the endless variety of the intrinsic value of things to their one common aspect: their exchange value. Everything has its price; everything can be bought and sold. Money is the ideal instrument for what Freud called "the American pattern of replacing quality with quantity."[54] Many Europeans do picture the American as the individual who, checkbook in hand, has reduced European culture to a garage sale, who has dissolved its context and discarded its aura.

The Attraction of the Void

Europeans have created their own imaginative space for America. They have filled this space with images and metaphors meant to express a sense that, in comparison to Europe, America has been found lacking. As Huizinga put it, "We all have something that you lack." Sometimes, as in the cases of Crèvecoeur and Goethe, the lack was viewed positively. Most often, however, the evaluation is negative, implying a critique, if not a rejection, of American culture. At times the criticism is delivered dispassionately, when observers are able to see American culture as a separate entity, unrelated to Europe. More often America is seen as a threat, as a force of corruption affecting cultures elsewhere. The metaphorical dimensions of space, time, and organic cohesion that I have introduced have on the whole served in a discourse of critique and rejection.

But there are exceptions. This same metaphorical repertoire has sometimes been used to describe America as a rapturous counterpoint to European civilization. In much European resistance to American culture there is often a submerged fascination, a repressed Freudian pleasure principle, that works to make the public discourse more vituperative, if not abusive. Sometimes temptation wins out, however. Then, suddenly, Europeans are able publicly to appreciate forms of American culture, at times even sooner than their American counterparts. American jazz music, the "hard-boiled" detective novel, and the Hollywood B-movie are all examples of American "low culture" first raised to mainstream status by Europeans as an act of cultural rebellion in their national setting. It was always a matter of younger generations rebelling against the entrenched cultural order and turning values upside down, embracing American forms of culture not for what they lacked but for what they offered in terms of vitality and energy.

A good recent example of this can be found in Jean Baudrillard's *Amérique*. I referred to it earlier to illustrate the repertoire of metaphors that Europeans use to imagine America. Baudrillard, however, gives the metaphors a radically different twist. Baudrillard wishes to evoke America as a place of rapture and liberation precisely because it lacks the ingredients that made Europe so oppressive. His is a rhapsodic view of America, yet it draws on the same metaphoric imagery that others have used to reject America. Baudrillard in a sense is flattering America with not faint but ironic praise. He must have followed quite an existential trajectory to reach that stage, shedding a number of intellectual fashions along the way. Varieties of Marxism and neo-Marxism provided French intellectuals with their frames of reference until well into the 1970s. Whatever they derived from those structures did not usually include an open Americanophilia. The demise of the infatuation with the many Marxisms made feasible a reappreciation of America and American culture.

Baudrillard was no longer a young man when he wrote his *Amérique*. Nonetheless, the book has all the aspects of a cultural revolt that one tends to associate with the young. Moreover, as in the case of so many French people before him, America becomes the central expression of this revolt. French intellectuals, as I pointed out earlier, have a collective history of infatuation, secretly or not so secretly, with America. I remember watching a film years ago—it must have been about 1960—made by a young French documentary filmmaker, François Reichenbach, entitled *L'Amérique insolite* (Uncanny America). I was reminded of it by Baudrillard, who mentions the title in the course of his argument. Reichenbach gave us a view of America as a sustained theatrical effect, as a case of Brechtian alienation; his film is like a report on life on a distant planet, alien yet strangely seductive. Baudrillard undertakes a similar voyage through space, traveling a universe of pure and absolute freedom in a successful escape from the gravitational pull of Europe—a Europe that has become mired in its heritage of intellectual rituals, caught in rigid conceptual frames, decadent, incapable of an unmediated, direct confrontation with reality. To Baudrillard, America offers the liberation from that conceptual imprisonment. "What we lack is the inspiration and courage for what one might call the zero degree of culture, for the power of non-culture. . . . We will always remain nostalgic utopians, torn between the ideal and our reluctance to realize it. We declare everything to be possible while never proclaiming its realization. Precisely the latter is what America claims to have achieved." "It is we who think that everything culminates in its transcendence and that nothing exists without first having been thought through as concept. Not only do they [the Americans] hardly care for that at all; they rather see the relationship in reverse. They are interested not in conceptualizing reality, but in realizing the concept and implementing the ideas."[55]

Old echoes resound in this statement. Baudrillard is not the first to hold that America has had the audacity to implement what had been thought out and dreamed up in Europe. It has shed the old Europe, which was burdened by history and caught up in unreal structures of thought. Thus, America could have become the authentic expression of modernity, whereas according to Baudrillard, Europe will never be more than its dubbed or subtitled version. But there is more to Baudrillard's argument than this. In a sense he seems to return to the 1960s, hankering for the libertarian rapture, the sense of instant gratification, unmediated by the intellect, that to many at the time was the appeal of the counterculture. Even though he was on the Left in the 1960s, he was an ideologue in the French manner, challenging the established order and seeking conceptual guidance from China and the Soviet Union rather than from America, so he missed out on the excitement of the moment. It took the disenchantment of the French Left during the 1970s, and their sense of ideological bankruptcy, for Baudrillard to become susceptible to the lure of American culture.

Once again, before our eyes, a romance unfolds, a game of cultural adultery in which so many French intellectuals have indulged. They have a keen eye for all that is banal and vulgar in America, yet at the same time more than anyone else they are tempted by the élan vital, the shameless authenticity of American culture. These romances always have one basic plot. It is always a case of a tired, elderly European turning toward America in the hope of regeneration, if not rejuvenation. America is unspoiled, primitive, youthful. It is unaware of itself. It is just there. It is Eden before the Fall. Europeans have tasted the forbidden fruit—they are obsessed by knowledge and reflection—yet hope to lose themselves in America. Baudrillard is in a sense a twentieth-century Crèvecoeur, reaffirming America's regenerative potential.

In Baudrillard's *Amérique,* and similarly in Umberto Eco's *Travels in Hyperreality,* a remarkable twist is given to the familiar arguments of many critics, American or European, of American mass culture. Whereas critics from Henry Adams on have deplored America's forsaking its historical spirituality, whereas they have seen the signs of a fall from grace precisely in the mindless entropy of consumerism, Baudrillard and Eco testify to a sense of exhilaration. Cities, highways, traffic—all are as meaningless as America's deserts, but the impact is at the same time liberating. It is all utterly devoid of significance. It is just there, but in a rather complex way. Both Baudrillard and Eco speak of hyperreality. Reality has spawned its own replicas. Surrounded by phantom images one can no longer tell which is the real thing. America becomes Disneyland. Whether it is vulgar or sublime no longer matters. Those are European categories better left behind. One should experience America as it presents itself, the only truly primitive society of our age, a utopia become reality.

In Eco's view of America as the last beach of European culture, everything will still be there when the real heritage has crumbled to dust in its countries of origin. For America to fulfill its salvage mission, it has to treat Europe's culture in a highly modernist, if not postmodernist, fashion, treating all of it as one large *objet trouvé*, recasting, duplicating, multiplying, crossbreeding, and mass-marketing it. On the whole, Eco's tone and choice of words are slightly more critical, quoting Louis Marin on Disneyland as degenerate utopia. In this world of the fake, "what is falsified is our will to buy, which we take as real, and in this sense Disneyland is really the quintessence of consumer ideology."[56] Baudrillard is well beyond such criticism and seems to revel in alienation. Floating freely through America's universe, an escapee from European gravity, he offers a reader's guide to America's phantom images. With great metaphorical virtuosity he moves from image to image. At one point he calls America a "special effect," which leaves the reader slightly puzzled. Who is behind the effect? The French book cover does not help. It gives us two names: "Amérique" and "Jean Baudrillard." Is it Baudrillard who allows us to perceive America in its many phantom images, or is it the other way around? I tend toward the latter option. America becomes a wide projection screen for Baudrillard's fantasies of self-liberation. In one ongoing stream of aphoristic, often highly imaginative, but totally noncommittal snippets, he takes us on his psychological journey. Strangely, however, he still seems entrapped in habits he pretends to have abandoned. With all his metaphors and associations he is still busy weaving America into an argument and a structure of concepts. He is still quintessentially European, taking America into the world of European intellectual preoccupations. Enjoying life "on the surface," sucked along in the slipstream of American life, Baudrillard as well testifies to the European sense, expressed by Huizinga and others, that "we have something that you lack." But Baudrillard's point is precisely that Europeans cannot be too sure that they should cherish that "something."

"L'Amérique, mais c'est la déconstruction!"

Europeans have woven America into a web of images of their own making. Meanings have become attached to America that truly belong to a European history of critical self-reflection. America has become a constituent element of the history of European ideas. Rarely, therefore, are Europeans able to approach America free of all preconceived ideas. It is always themselves they are likely to see reflected there. They are apt to see the country as an unsettling counterpoint to their own cultural conventions and to translate the "otherness" of America into contrasts that more often than not tend to reflect America in much the same way a distorting mirror would. We can all produce our own lists of such contrasts. Europe values quality; America knows only quantity. Europe has a keen sense of authenticity; America adores the fake and phony. Europe appreciates things old and quiet, it has "depth"; America dissipates its energies in shallow pursuits. Europe experiences itself as meaningful and finds in America what is pointless. Europe knows and appreciates individuality; America subjects it to ruthless standardization. In America individuality turns into spurious diversity, producing ten breakfast cereals that all taste like cardboard. With almost no effort one can reduce these contrasts to the metaphorical dimensions explored before. Always America is molded and made subservient to the purposes of a European discourse, to European categories and preoccupations. America becomes a construct of the European mind.

Yet one intriguing question remains. Could it be that in this rich repertoire of images about America there is more than prejudice and stereotype? Could there be kernels of truth and astute perception? In every image that I have reviewed there is always a mixture of evaluation—mostly negative—and of observation. When could we say the balance between the two is such that observation prevails over evaluation and that the image can be seen truly as an intimation of the real inner work-

ing of American culture? I am inclined to say that the imagery representing America in terms of spatial and temporal metaphors does not
really teach us much about America. The element of evaluation far
outweighs observation. Rarely are such images more than the ready
stereotypes that travelers tend to take along as part of their luggage.

The balance is different, however, in the case of those images that tend
to see an antiorganic streak in the American cast of mind. It appears that
the deep structure, or the matrix, of American culture obeys a number
of transformation rules that work to dissolve into its constituent elements
everything that to Europeans appears as an integral whole, to be appre-
ciated only in its entirety and integrity. This is a cultural inclination that
may have to do with America's historical eccentricity. The country has
long been at the margin of the older, European cultures. Everything cross-
ing the Atlantic to come to its shores, immigrants from every European
country and cultures from every European country and cultural period,
always suffered a loss of historical context and meaning. Europe has
never existed in America in any form other than disassembled into its constituent elements. That perhaps is what has allowed American culture its
remarkable freedom at rearranging that which had undergone historical
growth and gestation in Europe.

The recent intellectual fashion of deconstructionism in the United
States provides one ironic illustration of this tendency. Transplanted
from France and derived from theoretical views developed by Lacan,
Derrida, Foucault, and other French philosophers, deconstructionism
proved to be a wonderfully apposite instrument for giving intellectual
shape to the militant emancipation of minorities that had been going
on in America since the late 1960s. This emancipation—of women,
blacks, gays, and American Indians—provoked a new awareness of one
particular instrument of oppression: entrenched forms of hegemonic
discourse. The inferiority of minority groups had been encoded into
linguistic conventions and thus had been made to appear as "natural,"
as part of a natural order of things. Once cast in this light, emancipation came to be seen as a battle for linguistic control. Every construction that language allowed people to give to reality, all conceptual conventions that had entrenched themselves in everyday language, served
to perpetuate established views of minority positions. Consequently, it
was concluded that emancipation movements must squarely confront
such linguistic conventions and aim to deconstruct them. Language and
linguistic conventions, as tools of oppression, were ruthlessly taken

apart into their component elements and rearranged as tools to give voice to those who had been ignored by the reigning discourse. Although the philosophical insights inspiring this approach were novel and fashionable—which to a certain extent could account for their intellectual snob appeal—they could effortlessly blend into a game long familiar to Americans. Derrida for one must have sensed some of this when he pondered the question as to why his views could have gained such fashionable currency in America. Writing in 1986 he proffered the following hypothesis with a little facetious smile: "L'Amérique, mais *c'est* la déconstruction!"[57]

High and Low

THE QUEST FOR CULTURAL STANDARDS IN AMERICA

One of the metaphors that Europeans use to visualize America represents it as a country of leveling, erosion, and shallowness. Europeans are able to come up with any number of illustrations even if—or more likely, especially if—they have never been to America. Unhampered by firsthand experience, they profess to *know,* as if it were a matter of divine revelation, that Americans are superficial in their social interactions. Americans tend to act as if they have known you for years but will forget about you an instant later. Their style of social intercourse suggests a closeness and informality that strike these worldly wise Europeans as fake and inauthentic. On occasion not even the more sophisticated visitors are above such cheap shots. Camus, in his *American Journals,* quotes a spokesman as informing him that "human relationships are very easy here because there are no human relationships. Everything stays on the surface. Out of respect and from laziness."[1] It never occurs to such outsiders that conventions of social interaction in America follow their own codes, which the uninitiated can crack only with some effort and openness of mind. Nor does it occur to them that different codes are not necessarily inferior to their own.

In contrast to Americans, Europeans tend to pride themselves on a firm sense of cultural hierarchy, the sense of high versus low, of the sublime versus the vulgar. Americans, according to such European stereotypes, lack this sense and are unable to distinguish the high from the low, the genuine from the fake, art from kitsch. The European cultural landscape, these critics tell us, has undergone a ruthless flattening in America.

Whether in the area of social interaction or of cultural standards, Europeans should really be asking themselves whether the differences they perceive are not the result of underlying, systematic rules of transformation. They should feel duty bound to move beyond the facile stereotypes. Tocqueville would have had a ready answer; he would have pointed to the reigning democratic ethos of social equality in America. Every stylized form of social intercourse in Europe, every hierarchization of cultural standards there, always betrays its aristocratic origins. The display of deference and distance in European social interaction is the remnant of earlier codes of social distinction that have survived the demise of Europe's older stratified social orders. They have become conventions that people experience as natural. The same holds for cultural standards, for people consider their conceptions of what is refined and elevated as natural and innate, forgetting that their logic derives from the quest for distinction among the older elite strata in their societies. Again, all such conceptions have survived the democratization of European societies.

In America the relationship is reversed. Regardless of historical social distinctions and differences, there is the lasting, compelling, and self-evident code of democratic equality. It is a code that people simply follow in their views and actual behavior, irrespective of any social differences between them. Roosevelt and Bush may be examples of patricians in politics, yet their public behavior could show no trace of their background. The kind of folksy colloquialisms adopted by George Bush were his tribute to the populist tone of democratic politics. As he told reporters afterward, he had enjoyed his television debate with Geraldine Ferraro: he had "kicked a little ass."

No matter how much Americans may take this ethos of democratic equality for granted, they have always been aware of the complex relationship between democracy and the world of culture and the arts. They found themselves in a curious dilemma. Should Americans attempt to overcome their sense of cultural inferiority by beating the Europeans at their own game? Would Americans have to produce their own Shakespeare? That is how some Americans saw it. Others saw America's task as responding to the European challenge with a truly American answer. If America were to produce art, it would have to be democratic art, an expression of America's democratic ethos rather than a watered-down version of European art. The jury of peers would have to be the entire American people rather than an elite assembly of European art mandarins. Underlying this latter approach is an element of democratic revolt and artistic emancipation that has produced a truly American canon of culture and the arts, where we can look for the rules of transformation that have given the American way with cultural forms its particular twist, whether in the area of human interaction or of artistic production. There lies the crucial difference that transcends questions of inferiority or superiority.

Walt Whitman's work illustrates this point. Although Europeans may have hailed him as America's Homer or Shakespeare, he hardly seems to fit into such a pantheon. He appears to represent a break rather than a continuity; his democratic art was a break with tradition, with established formulas, with views concerning proper subject matter or a poetic vocabulary. In one broad sweep of democratic catholicity he embraced all and everything: the sublime and the mundane, the high and the low, the holy and the profane. He transcended all such antitheses in one continued song in praise of the democratic unity and cohesion of creation. He is the democrat as mystic, a visionary with a "democratic vista." Yes, his approach is leveling, yet at the same time it achieves a sublime transcendence. His verses have the soaring freedom of skyscrapers and are as quintessentially American.

Whitman illustrates one way in which Americans have coped with the tension between their democratic calling and the European heritage of cultural hierarchies. His way was a highly personal one, however, and certainly did not bring a lasting emancipation from the European model. The nineteenth century exhibited trends toward a closer approximation to the European standard rather than movements away from it. In an interesting study tellingly entitled *Highbrow/Lowbrow: The Emergence of Cultural Hierarchy in America*,[2] Lawrence Levine shows how, in the course of the nineteenth century, entire fields of a democratic enjoyment of art were removed from direct popular control and made subject to the dictates of cultural elites. Forms of popular art became enshrined as high art. Levine shows how drama, music, and opera were turned into cultural forms for the "happy few" and how in practice such art—by Shakespeare or Beethoven, for example—became the exclusive domain of the experts and the professionals. Earlier in the century this had not been the case. For instance, Shakespeare, in a great variety of hybrid versions, had been common, popular property. His plays were performed in adapted versions to fit particular occasions; people drew on them for commercial messages, for public addresses, and for parties and other festive functions. Shakespeare belonged to everyone, and no one was willing to let others touch "his" Shakespeare. Loudly, and with the aid of sundry projectiles, audiences vented their rage at performances that displeased them. The public was critic and director at the same time. Gradually, however, Shakespeare was "cleaned up" and enveloped in an aura of sacredness. No longer was he the common property of the common folk. Winning out against the vulgar joys of democratic cultural consumption was the rival view that high and sacred art existed only for the enjoyment of the cognoscenti. It took breeding and education for people to be counted among the initiates.

This trend clearly brought America closer to European conceptions of art. A hierarchization of publics had occurred that, according to Levine, had not been there earlier in the century. Yet it did not mean an end to the debate about a democratic and truly American art. The debate tended to touch on other domains and other forms of art. A recurring theme in this debate was the question of whether artistic standards are inherently incompatible with the desire for the equal, democratic sharing of art. If a work of art has the irreplaceable aura of uniqueness that the traditional European view claims for it, how can it lend itself to democratic consumption? The question became all the more urgent with the advent of mechanical techniques of reproduction, such as lithography, photography, and phonography, which could render countless copies of what, according to some, was irreproducible. The invention of chromolithographs, or chromos as they were called in America, in the second half of the nineteenth century heightened the debate. Welcomed by some as a form of "democratic art," chromolithography was seen by others as pure cultural decay. Edwin Lawrence Godkin, the editor-in-chief of *The Nation*, used the influential weekly to make himself into the spokesman for this kind of Victorian elitism. He coined the word *chromo-civilization* to describe the more general cultural decay and loss of a sense of cultural standards in the America of his time. The culture of copied art could never be more than a pseudoculture. It could lead only to "a society of ignoramuses each of whom thinks he is a Solon. . . . The result is a kind of mental and moral chaos."[3]

The debate in no way hindered the new medium's popularity. In many an American household one could see framed chromos that reproduced not only works by the masters in the pantheon but also landscapes, cityscapes, and renditions of historical pageants that had been made especially for the new medium. Each succeeding revolution in the techniques of reproduction served to expand ever further America's store of replicas. The country increasingly came to strike Europeans as a replica of itself, although lacking the mark of authenticity.

America as the site of imitation and kitsch, devoid of the sense of critical distinction, remained a favorite stereotype of Europe's cultural snobs. They could not get over their amazement at the baseness of the American citizen's democratic cultural enjoyments. Let me turn again to Georges Duhamel. In a chapter sarcastically entitled "Le Divertissement du Libre Citoyen" (The entertainment of the Free Citizen), he recounted his experiences in an American movie theater, the example par excellence of mechanical reproduction. When his eyes wandered from the silver screen up to the ceiling, he saw "a sky where stars are twinkling and light clouds are drifting past. Of course, it is a false sky, with false stars, and false clouds. It serves us a false impression of freshness. For indeed, everything here is false. False is the life of the shadows on the screen. The world is false. Perhaps I myself am no longer more than a simulacrum of a man, an imitation of Duhamel." The sense of alienation continues:

> Already I can no longer think as I wish. The moving images substitute themselves in place of my own thoughts. The music . . . Right! The music! What is this music? One hears it without listening. It moves like a breeze, it goes by like a breeze that you don't feel. Come on! Let's try to protest. Let me listen to this music. I want to! I want to! I want to listen to this music and not only hear it. It is as I already thought: it is false music. Preserved music. . . . They call it "records." It is canned music.[4]

In itself this litany was not new. Europeans had felt that American culture was inauthentic and fake even before the advent of mass culture and the mass media. Nor had they been truly surprised at the ready welcome given in America to the means of mechanical reproduction; the country in a sense had been predisposed toward them. Duhamel and other European guardians of culture voiced their observations in tones of denigration, but they did have a point. America had been more open to new techniques of cultural distribution than any European country had been, precisely because of its democratic and egalitarian calling. Characteristically America developed new technical inventions in the direction of mass production, whereas in

Europe such inventions tended to be seen as products for an elite. America thus brought photography within the reach of the many with the development of its simple Kodak box, cheap and user friendly. America turned the automobile into a mass-transportation product when in Europe only the elite could afford one.

At the same time, however, Americans were never unaware of the tension between "high culture"—a culture, made in America, that could vie with the best of European culture—and "democratic culture." American culture would have to be democratic, yet how could it hope to avoid the vulgarity that Europeans always tended to connect to the masses? In what follows I focus on one particular group of American intellectuals and their reflections on their national culture as published in the short-lived cultural journal *The Seven Arts*. I will pay special attention to photography as one of the new forms of art in the age of mechanical reproduction. My central concern will be the question of how intellectuals regarded photography as a form of art in relation to the great democratic dilemma of their times: the integration into American society of the immigrants that flooded into the country on an unprecedented scale.

Face Value: Photography, Immigrants, and Cultural Critics

One recurrent theme in the intellectual history of the American nation is the debate about immigration. Of course, intellectual reflection was never the sole response to the large-scale and heterogeneous flow of immigrants into the country, which was seen as a continued challenge to accepted notions of American nationhood. There was always the more visceral response of xenophobia and nativism, but these tended to add urgency to the debate among intellectuals about the contours and inclusiveness of the American identity. Generally the debate can be seen to have oscillated between the extremes of a narrow Anglo-Saxonism and a cosmopolitan cultural pluralism, centering on a homeostatic midpoint of "melting-pot" conceptions that tended to combine an openness of access for a wide variety of aliens with fairly rigorous standards of assimilation into a mainstream American mold.

Rather than review the broad outlines of this history of self-definition, I propose to focus on one group of intellectuals who briefly, and brilliantly, coalesced around *The Seven Arts* in 1916 and 1917. With all the fervor of intellectual young Turks, a generation of cultural critics appeared in this short-lived cultural journal, urged on by such pressing existential concerns as the state of American culture, America's entry into World War I, and the emancipation from their intellectual fathers, especially John Dewey. Their varied arguments encompass several intersecting lines exploring new developments in the arts and the potential for a rejuvenation of American culture. Photography as a new artistic medium was one topic for discussion; the immigrant as a potential source for cultural renewal was another. But what links, if any, between the two did the critics of *The Seven Arts* perceive? Before I address this central question, let me define briefly the place of this group of critics in the context of American intellectual history.

Occasionally a group appears on the stage of intellectual history that is later recognized as an intelligentsia, as more than a mere intellectual elite. Only in hindsight does one recognize that such a group, in its internal debates and on a basis of shared intellectual affinity, has given shape to the central issues of its age. A recent example of this is the generation of the "New York intellectuals," "the Family," which came of intellectual age during the 1930s but which was only later recognized and studied as a distinct intellectual band. The *Partisan Review* was its intellectual forum, then and later, providing a focus to an ongoing debate on American democracy and American culture.

The "New York intellectuals," however, were not the first instance of an intelligentsia in the modern sense of the word. Earlier the group publishing in journals such as the *New Republic, The Nation,* and more particularly *The Seven Arts* functioned as an intelligentsia not only in the eyes of later historians but in their own view as well. At the time the notion of the intellectual as someone who performs the role of social critic was of relatively recent vintage. The word *intelligentsia* itself was of rather recent Russian origin, and the word *intellectual* in its specifically modern sense was a new arrival from France. Of course, Marx had been among the first to point to such a group's historical role in its capacity to transcend its narrow class perspective. Later Alfred Weber and Karl Mannheim, using a felicitous metaphor, would speak of a *"freischwebende Intelligenz"*—a free-floating intelligentsia.

The individuals in the group that I have in mind here, including Van Wyck Brooks, James Oppenheim, Waldo Frank, Walter Weyl, Walter Lippmann, and Randolph Bourne, had quite a few shackles to cast off before they could float, free and unhampered, over the cultural and political stage of their time. There were the fetters of a narrow and provincial "genteel culture," the hollow optimism of a commercial spirit, and the bigoted nationalism that wished to close the gates to any more unassimilable aliens. Those were the antiquated molds obstructing the renewal of thought that a changing American society needed. And the changes had been many.

The growth of the industrial trusts, the rise of the labor movement, and the growing dominance of organizations over individuals undermined the historical foundations of individualism. The trend toward monopoly and the corporations' demands for state intervention in the economy made classical liberalism obsolete. The emergence of the United States as a world power appeared to require a new foreign policy, one that repudiated earlier traditions of isolationism, opposition to standing armies, and limited government. The "new immigration" from southern and eastern Europe seemed to require a reassessment of the nation's identity and culture. These were among the urgent issues to which the social critics addressed themselves. One of these issues—immigration—is my particular concern here.

What, according to this intelligentsia, was the place of the immigrants in American society? What could they contribute to the cultural future of the country? Needless to say, the intellectual approach to such questions was completely at odds with the anguished calls for measures to stem the influx of "inferior" races. One feature of the intelligentsia's worldview was its cosmopolitanism, an attitude that ill accords with the nationalistic impulse—or so it may seem at first glance. In fact, a closer look at the proliferation of essays uncovers a complex relationship between their cosmopolitanism and a certain streak of nationalism. Indeed, one of their guiding concerns was the definition of a truly national American culture, one freed from the dominance of the British cultural standard and its domestic New England keepers.

Ironically, it was an English intellectual, Bertrand Russell, who in a piece contributed to *The Seven Arts* developed a number of arguments that, in one form or another, were echoed by kindred American contemporaries. In the October 1917 issue, at a time when World War I signaled the devastating potential of European nationalism and America appeared to hold out a promising alternative to precisely such nationalism, Russell's piece was published under the fitting title "Is Nationalism Moribund?"[5] As Russell saw it, there were various reasons to doubt whether, in the next one hundred years, nationalism would still be the "dominant form of herd instinct"; America in particular could demonstrate this. He noticed "certain broad and obvious facts," such as the massive immigration of people of "many different races." At the time of its revolution America had still formed a true nation, "bound together by love of liberty, by traditions, and habits brought from England." Even after the Civil War one could still conceive of the victorious North as a nation. But now things had changed. A large part of the population still harbored sentiments of European nationalism: "Such people cannot have toward the United States that kind of intimate, passionate, narrow sentiment that they have towards the nations from which they have come. No doubt their children as a rule lose much of their European nationalism, but I gravely doubt whether they would be found to have acquired a new American nationalism at all comparable in force to that which they have lost."[6] In view of later outbursts of a truly American patriotism, Russell may appear to have been proved wrong on this count, but that should not concern us here. In 1917 he could still find America, in its internal composition, to be the epitome of a "family of nations." Thus it could lead the world, showing the way toward internationalism rather than nationalism—in other words, toward the formation of a supranational government. "The mixture of races and the comparative absence of a national tradition make America peculiarly suited to the fulfillment of this task."[7]

Conceiving, as Russell did, of America as a "family of nations" or as a "nation of nations" was not in itself new. Whitman had earlier expressed this view. What should strike us in his argument is the link that he perceives between the theme, traditional in itself, and the great expectations prevailing in his own time concerning America's potential role as a force for renewal on the world stage. Other European intellectuals shared these hopeful feelings. Romain Rolland, who wrote the opening essay to the first issue of *The Seven Arts* (Nov. 1916), expressed himself thus: "You have great advantages over the European nations. You are free of traditions. You are free of that vast load of thought, of sentiment, of secular obsession under which the Old World groans. The intellectual fixed ideas, the dogmas of politics and art that grip us, are unknown to you. You may go forward, unhampered, to your future."[8] He called on America not to be a slave to foreign examples. "Your true model is within yourselves."[9]

Again, as with Russell, there is a resonance in these words of an older American idea, the idea that America is "born free," released from the incubus of European history. But this America must shoulder a new burden. As Rolland put it, "It is to establish from all these free-moving personalities within your States a tie that shall be as a bloodbond. . . . Their voices are unconscious and spontaneous and discordant.

Compose from them a Symphony. Think of the rich foundation of your country. It is made up of all races; it has flowed into you from all continents. May this help you to understand the essential spirits of these peoples whose sum must be America."[10] It is America's historic assignment to create its own American culture, a culture that also—and here we have a parallel to Russell's global expectations of America—should provide the model for a new world culture: "The hour has struck for mankind to begin its march towards the ideal simply of Humanity. . . . And the Thought of the future must be a synthesis of all the world. To achieve this fertile union should be the work of Americans. . . . You must harmonize all of the dreams and liberties and thoughts brought to your shores by all your peoples."[11] A formidable assignment indeed! Nevertheless, Rolland was rather casual about it: "Behind you, alone, the elemental Voice of a great pioneer, in whose message you may well find an almost legendary omen of your task to come, your Homer: Walt Whitman."[12] The word *alone* here is unintentionally discouraging, for there were other voices clamoring, a far cry indeed from Walt Whitman's cosmopolitan boosterism, a narrow-minded cacophony bespeaking a different America altogether. "Away with the immigrants, the radicals, the socialists, the strike breakers, the bastard peoples!"

Caught in the midst of this din America's intellectuals had to blaze their own trail, inspired by America's high-minded traditions yet at the same time aware of the forms of vicious nativism that these traditions could assume. What then, in their assessment of the options and dilemmas of American society and American culture, was their view of the immigrants? The picture is rather varied. In the case of Van Wyck Brooks, what emerges is an impression of continuity in his critical reflections on American culture, a tendency to conceive of the American people in the light of an unbroken Anglo-Saxon tradition extending back to the Puritanism of New England. He saw this tradition as a historic burden that obstructed a truly creative national culture. He enviously referred to Europe, where the national impulse had brought such an impressive flowering of national cultures. At the same time, however, he realized that Europe was different: "It is vain to look for anything quite like this in America. . . . For we are not a race to begin with; we are incongruous at once in blood and in culture." Nonetheless, with the unshakable confidence of the youthful rebel, he clearly perceived "the certain visible sign of some prodigious organism that lies undelivered in the midst of our society, an immense brotherhood of talents and capacities coming to a single birth."[13] Americans had been too occupied by their pursuit of material success, their emotional lives stifled by Puritanism, for them to be able to give artistic expression to their inner lives and historical experience. This applied equally to the native-born American and the immigrant: "It is a commonplace that immigration from without and migration within the Republic have prevented the formation of any structure in our society for literature to build a nest in. No sooner has the nucleus of a living culture begun to take shape than the tides of enterprise and material opportunity have swept away its foundations."[14] This disparaging assessment is in stark contrast to Russell's and Rolland's sense of anticipation. Americans often seem to need a foreigner's perspective for a balanced view of what goes on in their own country. Another illustration of this can be found in the January 1917 issue of *The Seven Arts*. In an article reviewing the enthusiastic travel impressions of the itinerant Danish author (and later Nobel laureate) Johannes V. Jensen, Paul Rosenfeld in seeming disbelief wrote, "[Jensen] tells us of the romance of our existence, of the poetry of our big business, of the young sound strength of it all . . . and beauty follows strength . . . in all human creations made for use, in steamships and locomotives, in bridges and steel constructed buildings. [Jensen] tells us that the architecture of America, the skyscrapers, the grain elevators, the collieries, embody the essential architectural style, and will one day be considered beautiful."[15] Waldo Frank, one of the editors, clearly was of a different opinion. In the same issue, in a piece entitled "Vicarious Fiction," he wrote, "we have lavished our forces altogether on the immensities about us, turned our genius into steel and stone, and to these abdicated it. . . . We find ourselves smaller than our buildings, and yet we know that until we are greater than the vastest of these, we shall be no true nation." As if echoing Brooks, he wrote, "To an astonishing degree, we have objectified our lives. And we have failed to hold within us the power to experience what we have put forth . . . buildings crush us . . . laws are shackles . . . traditions weigh upon our heads."[16] Diverse as their perspectives may be, that of the Dane and that of the American, both men apparently overlooked one aspect, one way of looking up at America's buildings: that of the immigrant. Indeed, it was immigrants who erected the America of "stone and steel," immigrants who "lavished their forces." One may be reminded of the moving vignette in Louis Adamic's autobiography *Laughing in the Jungle*. At one point Adamic reminisces on the return of an emigrant from America, emaciated and decrepit, his health wrecked, to the village where Adamic lived as a young boy, in what until recently we knew as

Yugoslavia. Little Louis sat listening to the old man's stories about work in the mines and the steel industry and looked at photographs that the man had brought home with him. Some of them were photographs of New York: "'The day before I sailed home I walked in these streets'— he pointed at the picture—'where the buildings are tallest—and I looked up, and I can hardly describe my feelings. I realized that there was much of our work and strength, frozen in the greatness of America. I felt that, although I was going home . . . I was actually leaving myself in America.'"[17] If Americans were to abide by the exhortations of Waldo Frank—"to hold within them the power to experience what they put forth"—the experience would certainly have to comprise an awareness of the trials of the immigrant population. But the young intellectuals writing in *The Seven Arts* were far too impetuous and restless for that. Storming the stuffy bastions of America's stagnant, provincial culture, they had no time left for the careful documentation of life as it was lived by the strangers in their midst. Yes, in their various assessments mention was made of the immigrants, as I have shown, but in a more abstract, strategic sense. In the immigrant origins of the American population they saw the strategic alternative to the pressing weight of an Anglo-Saxon, if not British, cultural mold, a strategic opportunity for the fashioning of a truly national culture, and perhaps even an international one.

Consequently Randolph Bourne, in a review of Mary Antin's autobiography *The Promised Land*—a veritable paean of praise to the American "melting pot"—could decide to take issue precisely with the melting-pot ideology. In an analysis broadly reminiscent of his contemporary Antonio Gramsci, he discerned in the melting-pot ideology of his day the hegemonic strategy of an established cultural elite out to fashion the immigrants after its image of "the American." He leveled his critique at that "ruling class, descendent of those British stocks which were the first permanent immigrants," a ruling class that, as he saw it, dictated the conditions of Americanization without hearing those to whom these conditions applied.

Bourne nevertheless shared with his intellectual allies their sense of living in a time of potentially great change. In his eyes this potential for change was linked crucially to the strategic options that were open to America in its position vis-à-vis the war that was raging in Europe. In America's policy of official neutrality preceding its intervention in the war, he had already discerned the hypocrisy of a double standard, betraying the innate pro-British reflex of the establishment. Not only would the self-conscious adoption of a true neutrality toward the European conflict safeguard America's role as an intermediary; more important, it would also provide the country with the opportunity of emancipating itself from the quasi-colonial dominance of a culture in the British vein. Bourne's continued opposition to U.S. intervention in the war led to the demise of *The Seven Arts*. The outside financial support that had kept the journal afloat was withdrawn.

A supplement to the April 1917 issue, coming at a time when the dice had been cast and America was soon to intervene in the war on the Allied side, was devoted entirely to the theme of American independence and the war. The choice of words is telling. The piece, editorial in form, presents arguments commonly used in Bourne's contributions. Participation in the war on the side of England meant a war for a "world as we have known it." Many in America, the *New Republic* among them, enthusiastically endorsed such action. A fault line appeared dividing American intellectuals against one another. *The Seven Arts* refused to go along; it refused to believe, as did so many others, that "any other kind of world would not be inhabitable." For what had that beloved prewar situation looked like? "Internationally, as a nation among nations, . . . we [were] to a large extent dependent on the strong arm of England. But we are colonial in a deeper, a more insidious way: all that part of our life, which for want of a better word, we must call spiritual, derives from the Mother Country. Through that hidden, uncut nexus come those emotions, those habits of thought which betray us as provincials in everything we do and say. . . . We must overcome that which is England in us."[18] In that same piece, which as likely as not sealed the fate of *The Seven Arts,* there follow two passages that summarize what had inspired the journal and its contributors all along:

We have been fortunate, it now appears, in our immigration policy, for beyond a doubt our strength to break free has increased with the influx of Continental immigrants. They have leavened the English lump with other traditions and other bloods, and if for the time being, they have divided us against ourselves, in that very inner conflict lies the hope of our freedom. Out of this added blood has risen some of our most characteristic expression, with the promise of a genuine American art. For our dominant expression was New England, and the words themselves give away the case. *New* England was *Old* England transplanted, and weakened in the transplant.

America faced a critical choice: to choose England's side and remain indefinitely on England's leash or to break free and go its own way. The latter was the more risky, involving as it did a break with the known and familiar. The second passage reads, "It is, however, the sort of risk that any man must take if he is to be true to himself and wants to be strong enough to stand alone."

Here, in summary form, are the main features of *The Seven Arts*. The journal gave vent to the rebellion of a generation of young intellectuals; it expressed a generational conflict in terms of a national and cultural emancipation. It displayed the courage of its convictions not only in its stand against the war but also in its attitude toward America's immigrant population. At precisely the time when the world conflict found its reflection in lines of division and conflict ostracizing America's immigrant groups, *The Seven Arts* chose to vest the hope of America's freedom in them. It refused to go along with the defamation, persecution, and repression of non-Anglo-Saxon minorities, with the spirit of nativism that was about in America. It chose to abide by the high-minded calls from congenial foreign minds such as Russell's and Rolland's.

The Seven Arts thus kept alive a spirit of cosmopolitanism in an age of narrow nationalism. It also preserved an openness of mind toward America's ethnic diversity at a time when people closed ranks around a diffident Anglo-Saxonism. It kept the immigrants in full view when many were busy narrowing their focus. In its short, almost feverish life, however, the journal never got around to fleshing out its view. It never made clear, other than in very general terms, precisely how the immigrants could contribute to America's cultural renewal. It may have been that this intelligentsia, free-floating as it was, was simply flying too high, moving in a sphere of abstractions and programmatic precepts. Even when these intellectuals hovered, pausing to consider the new art forms of their time, such as film and photography, the standards they applied were those of the cultural highbrow, in disregard of Van Wyck Brooks's exhortations to search for the "genial middle ground" between highbrow culture and lowbrow life. To the extent that they did get the immigrants in view, these were seen in the light of a high cultural calling.

A telling example of these highbrow preoccupations is an essay on photography by Paul Strand, later a famous photographer himself. He argued that in the work of American photographers something had happened of which no one had been fully aware, "namely, that America has really been expressed in terms of America without the outside influence of Paris art-schools or their dilute offspring here." Between 1885 and 1910 a group of people had been at work "with honest and sincere purpose," "without any background of photographic or graphic formulae, much less any cut and dried ideas of what Art is and what it isn't." In such innocence lay their strength. Whatever they wished to express could be conveyed only in ways that they had discovered on their own: "In the same way the creators of our skyscrapers had to face the similar circumstances of no precedent, and it was through that very necessity of evolving a new form, both in architecture and photography, that the resulting expression was vitalized." Here again, however, the yardstick is that of the highbrow: "They will be the masters no less for Europe, than for America because by intense interest in the life of which they were really a part, they reached through a national, to a universal expression."[19] To illustrate his argument Strand cites the names of Alfred Stieglitz, Clarence White, Edward Steichen, Gertrude Käsebier, and Frank Eugene.

Although interesting and lucid, the argument betrays a blind spot to events on other levels, an inability to see that the high artistic standard could apply as well to the lowly area of the documentation of common people's daily lives. It may be true that few immigrant autobiographies had as yet been written and that ethnic America had yet to establish itself as a milieu for the novel, yet the case of photography is different. Documentary photographers whose names now figure in the pantheon of American photography had already been at work well before 1910. Like the photographers hailed by Strand, they were self-taught and had to acquire their mastery while practicing their art. At the same time, however, they had all along been giving expression to America "in terms of America," unaware that they were simultaneously creating works of art. We may think of Jacob Riis, Lewis Hine, or Arnold Genthe, but there were many others whose works are now collected by museums. These individuals may have had different creative impulses. In the case of some there may have been a reform impulse, a sense of social commitment; others may simply have needed to document social life as they saw it in the cities, the small towns, and the countryside. In the case of Genthe, it may have been a bent for the exotic, willfully indulged by Genthe's retouching hand in the laboratory. Their work was not unknown; it was published in journals and in books and was shown as lantern slides illustrating lectures. It remains unclear, however, why it did not receive the attention of an intellectual avant-garde calling for a new American culture as an expression of America in terms of America—an avant-garde, moreover, that repeatedly vested its hope in the fact that America was a land of immigrants. In the store of immigrant experiences, expectations, and emotions, America harbored a reservoir of potential cultural renewal that Riis, Hine, Genthe, and others drew on for their work. It may be that their work was too exclusively documentary, too pedestrian and simple, to be included in the canon of a new American art. It appears to have fallen victim to the snobbery of highbrow conceptions of art.

■ ■ ■

Perhaps there is a different explanation, however. Art with a capital A often implies a conception of autonomous art; at any rate, it has done so at least since the nineteenth century. Like the intellectuals who had begun to constitute a social stratum of their own, transcending the narrow ideological perspective of a social class, artists as well had won a similar sphere of autonomy for themselves. The autonomous artist moved in a sphere with guidelines and a sense of calling all its own, a bohemia that had consciously turned away from society. This much is clear: "Art," with its pretense of being autonomous, is not what people like Hine, Riis, and others like them set out to produce. Their photography was inspired by a sense of social service. It was an instrument in the service of that broader moral impulse that gave the period its name, the "Reform Era." Riis, himself an immigrant who had known all the hardship of immigrant life, never tired of documenting with pen and camera how the "other half" lived. Hine, who photographed the immigrants on Ellis Island or in the industries of Pittsburgh and child labor elsewhere in America, was well aware of his documentary impulse. In a speech before the annual meeting of the National Conference of Charities and Correction, he explained his motives. It is a highly personal manifesto whose general drift is apparent in its title: "Social Photography: How the Camera May Help in the Social Uplift." People like Hine saw it as their particular calling to allow their contemporaries to look across the ever-greater gulfs emerging in the society of their time. America no longer was a land of small, tightly integrated communities. The camera might help to restore a clarity of vision in a society that had expanded beyond people's traditional horizons. Confronting anguish about the hordes of aliens invading the country, people like Riis and Hine restored to the aliens their individual dignity, showing their faces, their expressions, and their emotions.

While visiting Ellis Island Henry James, a refined aesthete and autonomous artist if ever there was one, was unable to get much beyond an impression of hordes, of crowds of people. In his book *The American Scene* he wondered what effect this "visible act of ingurgitation" would have on the American national identity. What could it mean "to share the sanctity of [the] American consciousness . . . with the inconceivable alien?"[20] One proof of the artistic sensibility of Hine and Riis is that they were able to imagine the inconceivable aliens, presenting them in their photographic images to the more shortsighted among their compatriots.

They did it with the miraculous new means of photography. They made history in more than one sense. They kept time by freezing it. The whirl and transience of events, the milling crowds, came to a halt in their pictures; the roar of machines and the noise of the streets vanished from them. There is a double stillness in their photographs, of movement and of sound, compelling the viewer to pay attention.

At the same time, however, neither Hine nor Riis was content to leave it at that. Both were aware of the extent to which an accompanying text can determine the reading of a photograph. Riis combined image and text in his articles, books, and lectures. Hine experimented with collage. Both were engaged in reestablishing a ruptured communication. In that sense both produced the democratic art that Whitman had urged on American artists. The fact that the young intelligentsia around *The Seven Arts* had made Whitman's entreaties its own makes it more difficult to understand why its constituents had no eye for the work of great contemporary photographers like Riis, Hine, and Genthe.

Twenty Years Later: Documentary Photography and Democratic Art

There is an ironic paradox in the cultural crusade of Van Wyck Brooks, Randolph Bourne, and others like them. They constituted a group of cultural nationalists who wanted to breathe new life into the sterile, inbred culture that characterized the America of their time. The diagnosis, according to Brooks, was clear. Two traditions, those of the pioneer and of the Puritan, opposing practical ingenuity to an introverted cast of mind, had developed in relative isolation, without mutual contact or influence. They constituted two separate spheres of life, those of the highbrow and of the lowbrow. The latter lived in a world of "catchpenny realities"; the former, in a wilted sphere of spiritual life that never reached beyond the pieties of an outdated Puritan heritage. Brooks pleaded on behalf of a "genial middle ground" where the two would meet and could revitalize each other.

There was a measure of polemical overstatement in his cultural diagnosis that a more mature Brooks would later renounce. In the 1940s, using an almost filiopietistic tone, he evoked the cultural worlds in which a number of great American authors had moved. By then he had developed a keen eye for the fusion of the individual creative imagination and the social life that surrounded it, for precisely the middle ground where reality and imagination merged. He acknowledged Whitman's case in particular as a successful fusion of a democratic fervor and an artistic imagination.

Brooks's later work was in keeping with the spirit of the time. The artistic rediscovery of an America in its common, everyday appearance had already begun in the 1930s. The artistic imagination now returned home, whereas previously it had turned away in a spirit of cultural revolt from an America that was seen as oppressive, narrow, and provincial while seeking to express its feelings of cultural alienation in modernist experiments. There was a sense that the America that had been rejected had not really been understood. During the 1930s there was a vibrant revival of a democratic enthusiasm that would critically affect the relation between artists, art forms, and society. Elsewhere as well, outside America, there was a felt need for art that would be closer to the people, for artistic production as a public act with a clear social resonance. In the totalitarian regimes of the time, such as those in Germany, Italy, and the Soviet Union, this social relevance was imposed from on high, while art in the modernist vein was officially branded as *entartet,* degenerate. Nonetheless, artists clearly did not need the prodding of totalitarian dictates to leave the ivory tower of modernist experiment and to turn toward a more public aesthetics. When the Soviet Union saw fit to ordain a socialist realism as the new artistic orthodoxy, it was strangely in line with trends that elsewhere, under democratic conditions, were sustained by artists of their own volition. This does not mean, of course, that we should ignore the role of central governments, including that of America. Indeed, in the 1930s, for the first time in American history, the government acted as a public sponsor of the arts, commissioning individual artists in the context of public arts projects. Thus the New Deal gave a touch of central orchestration to the more general democratic enthusiasm and conferred on it the feel of a collective endeavor. Those works of art in particular that government sponsorship had made possible, in painting (including murals), literature, sculpture, music, architecture, photography, and documentary film, show a return to the stylistic modes of expression of a vernacular art, an art that the common people could understand. Thus, composers like Aaron Copland and Virgil Thompson drew on the repertory of American popular and folk music. Thomas Hart Benton, Grant Wood, and other painters depicted everyday life in the American Midwest. John Steinbeck, a writer, and John Ford, a film director, each in his own way rendering the story of *The Grapes of Wrath,* evoked an image of the misery and heroism of American farmers driven off their land in the Oklahoma dust bowl and searching for a new life in California.

There is something a little odd about this "homecoming," this "looking homeward," of American intellectuals and creative artists. To the extent that they directed their gaze homeward, they tended to see the home in a remarkably homogeneous light, as if there were one commonly accepted view of it, one consensual narrative. It seems as if, in the renewed eulogy to democracy, a tacit agreement was at work as to its visual representation. In creating an iconography for the democratic vistas of the 1930s, artists tended to construct an all-American image whose features, facial and otherwise, are remarkably reminiscent of America's oldest line of descent: the Anglo-Saxon one. The "poor whites" who look at us with guarded pride from the unforgettable photographs of the 1930s, the displaced farmers that Steinbeck described for us and that John Ford showed on the silver screen, are all descendants of the earliest immigrants. The folk tunes that Copland and Thompson quote in their music are in a line of musical descent that goes back to the British Isles. The man whom Copland eulogizes in his *Lincoln Portrait* as the central icon of the American democratic ethos is Abraham Lincoln, whose stark features form a prototype for all those tormented portraits of poor whites in the 1930s. Copland in particular may make us aware of the underlying tension between identification and representation. He was a son of immigrant parents, a Jew, who in his construction of the American epic chose to focus on that one long line of Anglo-Saxon continuity rather than on the fault lines of America's ethnic geography. At the same time, however, the 1930s were a period in which ethnic Americans fully came into their own. Their life became the stuff of ethnic novels, sociological monographs, and Hollywood gangland movies; they were a coveted constituency in the Roosevelt coalition. In spite of this, however, when it came to designing an iconography to represent America's proud and unbending democratic tradition, the gene pool tended to be reduced to the Anglo-Saxons.

There is a further element to the "homecoming" of America's intellectuals and artists that I want to consider. In a certain sense their return to the American fold was an act of repudiation as well. As Thomas Hart Benton put it, "We objected to the new Parisian aesthetics which was more and more turning art away from the living world of active men and women into an academic world of empty pattern. We wanted an American art which was not empty, and we believed that only by turning the formative processes of art back again to meaningful subject matter, in our cases specifically American subject matter, could we expect to get one." Almost as if echoing Randolph Bourne, he went on to say, "we felt that we were on the way to releasing American art from its subservience to borrowed forms. In the heyday of our success, we really believed we had at last succeeded in making a dent in American aesthetic colonialism."[21] Unlike Bourne, though, Benton wished to repudiate not the old mother country of England but rather the slavish imitation of whatever the high priests of highbrow art in Paris had ordained.

We who have the wisdom of hindsight might find this rather ironic. We now know that in those years a new artistic rebellion was hatching, a movement *against* the aesthetics of a democratic art, *away* from the genial middle ground toward the high points of an American modernism, which would break through triumphantly in the late 1940s as "abstract expressionism." Paris would be beaten at its own game: in the area of avant-garde art as well America had now become the world leader. New York, not Paris, was now the international center of modernism.

This later development made much of the cultural revolt of the 1930s look dated. It now appears to have been out of step with long-term international trends of artistic renewal; it was instead a throwback to outmoded forms of realism. In hindsight what strikes us in the artistic production of the 1930s is a documentary impulse that was of great political and social relevance at the time yet an artistic dead end. The enthusiasm for the middle ground produced "middlebrow art" at best, not a contribution of lasting importance to the development of an international artistic idiom for the twentieth century.

Nor had this awareness entirely escaped contemporary observers of the artistic scene. Already in the 1930s a debate had been gathering momentum in the United States concerning mass culture and popular culture, especially in the circle of a young, radical intelligentsia of Marxist inspiration centered on the *Partisan Review.* A classic early statement is a 1939 article by Clement Greenberg entitled "Avantgarde and Kitsch." Greenberg wrote the article at the behest and with the collaboration of one of the journal's editors, Dwight Macdonald. The article was a frontal attack on kitsch, on the banal aesthetics of the culture of the Popular Front and the demagoguery of a mass culture that Greenberg observed in the Soviet Union, Nazi Germany, and Italy, as well as in the United States. Against the fake populism of that type of culture Greenberg spoke on behalf of modernism and the avant-garde as the only true carriers of a cultural revolution. The article was an opening shot in a debate about mass culture that would fully come into its own after World War II.

■ ■ ■

But is there not a different way in which we can look at the period? Could we not argue that this constellation of critical views was in a way similar to the one encountered in the case of *The Seven Arts?* Did not critics such as Greenberg once again, in their prescriptions of what American "high" art should be, tend to overlook what had been produced in terms of an authentic American artistic idiom? Let me, in order to answer these questions, once again take the example of photography.

Our image of the 1930s in America is to a large extent formed by photography. Some of the photographs taken in those years have acquired the hallowed status of icons of their age. They have become the central images of what America went through in those years. There is the photograph of a father, leaning against the storm, enveloped in clouds of dust, trying to reach the safety of a sagging shed. One child is near him; a second, a mere toddler, lags behind, blinded and astray, as if he has lost touch with the others. There is the photograph of a "migrant mother," old before her time, lines of fatigue marking her face; she sits with a distant look, her head not quite at rest in her hand. Two children stand leaning against her, seeking her protection. These are photographs that keep returning to haunt us on posters, on dust jackets, and in documentaries about the Great Depression. They are only two examples of the treasure trove of photographic material produced in the 1930s under government auspices. The Farm Security Administration (FSA) produced the largest body of such photographs. Under the strong-willed leadership of Roy Stryker, "his" stable of photographers, including Walker Evans, Dorothea Lange, Arthur Rothstein, Ben Shahn, Russell Lee, Jack Delano, and John Vachon, gave visual expression to an America facing up to the trials of the depression with a mixture of resilience and stubbornness. They captured mostly, though not exclusively, America outside its great cities. Stryker instructed the FSA photographers to document poverty. It was their task to give visual form to the more abstract problem of rural poverty with which the FSA had to cope. In the cases of the Rural Electrification Administration (REA) and the Tennessee Valley Authority (TVA), photographers had to show the face not of the problem but of the solution. Their work shows towering cranes, high-rising dams, and men with safety helmets, all shot from low camera angles. The message is clear: America is rising up from the depths of the depression.

Taken together these photographs constitute a body of work that ideally suited the democratic pathos of the time. Like the earlier documentary photography of Riis, Hine, Genthe, and others, it was a contribution to restoring a "democratic vista." There is a Whitman-like transcendence in these silent witnesses of a democratic community in a time of distress. Roy Stryker himself expressed this eloquently when he explained why of all the photographs of the FSA project, his favorite was Dorothea Lange's picture of the "migrant mother": "After all these years, I still get that picture out and look at it. The quietness and the stillness of it. . . . Was that woman calm or not? I've never known. I cannot account for that woman. . . . She has all the suffering of mankind in her but all of the perseverance too. A restraint and strange courage. You can see any thing you want to in her. She is immortal. Look at that hand. Look at the child. Look at these fingers—those two heads of hair." [22] One single picture of a woman and her two children allowed Stryker—as well as us—to experience something larger, a sense of communion with a larger community.

That in itself would suffice to rank such documentary photography as American art, an art equal to America's democratic calling. Of course, those who tend to apply further criteria to works of art with a view to distinguishing "high" art from "low" art will want something more. An art that is merely documentary belongs to the outdated mode of realism and could never aspire to the sensibilities of modernism. In this latter vein artistic creation had become a highly self-conscious act. Modernist artists had become aware of the contrived nature of their work, of the artificiality of art. They had cast off established conceptions of the relation between art and reality at a time when modernist conceptions of reality tended to see it as unhinged, if not broken beyond repair.

This revolution of established views had some ironic implications. For example, it tended to explode the established academic views of high and low in art. As part of the radical breakdown of every social and cultural convention, of every accepted rule of assessing value and significance, which were now seen as no more than precarious constructs, the sublime and the vulgar had become inextricably jumbled. In its formal experiments modern art gave radical expression to this. The world was seen to have fallen into shreds and morsels, and modern art reflected this in its use of collage and sampling. Newspaper headlines and popular jingles were the subject of an aesthetic recycling that shamelessly elevated them to the rank of such hallowed images as "windmill in landscape" or "female nude with flowers." Parallel to this shift, the criteria of the connoisseurs of art had changed as well. High art, they now ordained, would henceforth be an art expressing the spirit of the avant-garde revolution. No art form that sought to be documentary in the realist mode could ever hope to qualify.

This may be so—and it is true almost by definition—but does it apply to the flowering of American photography in the 1930s? This much is clear: the purpose of modern art may have been to express a world that had fallen apart, but no such tragic sense of rupture and fragmentation can be found in the photographic view of America in the New Deal years. The pervasive feeling is rather one of a recuperated democratic community, of unbroken human dignity in a time of economic disaster. Whereas modern art thrives on discontinuity, by dint of a rebellion against paternal canons of art, *l'art de papa,* clearly there is no trace of that to be found in the American 1930s. For that matter, earlier American modernists had shown that formal experiments could well go hand in hand with a relatively unscathed image of reality. The great American impressionist painters could express themselves, using the subjective idiom of French examples, without sharing the sense of a fragmented objectivity with their French confreres. Charles Ives was able to combine a radical renewal of musical idiom with a sense of meaningful continuity with the past, with "the things our fathers loved," as the title of one of his songs has it. With them, as much as with the artists active in the 1930s, the impulse is one of restoring continuity rather than of seeking a radical break with the past. Yet my point is that such an impulse need not necessarily produce art whose main or sole aim is to be easily accessible and broadly appealing. Ives admittedly goes to extremes in his farewell to musical conventions, but on a more moderate level, could we not recognize a similar venture in the photography of the 1930s, taking it beyond an impulse merely to document reality?

At first glance we may seem warranted in applying the label of realism to the body of FSA photographs in particular. Those in our day and age who wish to get an impression of what the Great Depression looked like could do worse than to begin by examining these photographs. But it does not take long for any close observer to become aware that the impact of these photographs is not solely the result of their subject matter. A strangely unsettling sense grips us, as if we are looking with eyes not our own. Emerging between the observed and the observer is an intermediary force that seems to direct our gaze compellingly. The observers may feel that they have stepped outside themselves and entered into the realm of the subjective imagination of artists wielding their cameras. Slowly they may become aware of the many creative interventions, of the rearranging and reordering of "reality."

One category of photographs makes use of what we might call the collage as *objet trouvé*. In their explorations of the America of their day, the FSA photographers had a keen eye for the ironic or tragic clash between the faces and fables of their society. In one photograph the viewer looks out from behind two shabby vagabonds walking down an endless road. In the empty landscape a billboard to their right reminds them, "Next time, take the train." Another photograph shows us a wooden shed and tents erected alongside a road—temporary home to destitute farmers on their way from Oklahoma to California. In jarring juxtaposition a huge poster announces the film about their plight, *The Grapes of Wrath*, "opening next week." There are many more examples. The National Association of Manufacturers had erected billboards all across the land proudly proclaiming the "World's Highest Standard of Living" or "There's no way like the American Way." One such billboard, captured in an FSA photograph, depicts a happy "all-American" family in their car, the father behind the steering wheel, the mother affectionately, though a trifle annoyingly, clutching his arm, and the heads of two merry children popping up behind them. Everything else in the photograph—a backdrop of dereliction and decay—contradicts this merry picture. The photograph was reprinted in 1939 in the Netherlands in the socialist journal *Socialisme en democratie,* illustrating an article by J. M. de Casseres as "a specimen of American humor and self-criticism." Yet another example, a photograph by Mary Post Wolcott, shows the trunk of a pine tree in Georgia with three texts nailed to it. The top one reads, "Dost Thou Believe on the Son of God." The lower two read, "International Fertilizers" and "Green Spot—Ice Cold."

Reality produces its own collages. They are not the result of any creative manipulation by the artist. They are truly *objets trouvés*. Nonetheless, the effect would have been hardly different had the artist produced it. All it takes is an observant eye. Zooming in on the contradictory faces and fables, the artist engages in the recycling of the vulgar and quotidian while at the same time adding his or her own reading to the many-layered meaning of reality. It is a form of creatively reprocessing bits of reality that does justice to the democratic equality of the futile and the sublime in the great Whitmanesque manner. At the same time, however, in this recycling of low culture, in this reordering of images and simulacra of reality, we may salute an artistic approach that has characterized much of America's creative production in our century. I amply illustrate this in later chapters.

Apart from the use of collage, there is a more general point to be made about the FSA photographs and their alleged status as merely documentary, or realist, art. Those who, like me, cannot stop looking at these pictures will share my feeling of a strange alienation effect at work. Especially in the work of Walker Evans, but also in that of others such as Russell Lee, Jack Delano, or Dorothea Lange, reality undergoes a strange rearrangement. It finds itself reduced, as it were, to the parallel screens that jointly make up a theatrical stage set. I can think of no better phrase to describe the effect than "parallel planes." The angle in the photographs is mostly straight, in a direct confrontation with the objects. The lighting tends to accentuate the surface rather than the space, bringing out not only the first plane but the second and third planes behind it. Reality is forced into an imposed order of parallel surfaces. All connecting space between them seems to have fallen away. Walker Evans in particular has a keen eye for these interposed voids, empty and silent. The effect is especially striking in the case of lifeless objects—the wooden sidings of a house or adjacent billboards across a hardtop road, shown at a right angle, with the flat facades of America's Victorian architecture rising behind them like so many haunted mansions. But his portraits have this quality as well, with his sitters staring us straight in the face, appearing to be inaccessibly frozen in their first plane, flat forever.

Looked at this way, the alleged documentary nature of 1930s photography appears in a different light. Clearly it is the product of the same disassembling mental mode that, in the first chapter, I suggested may be characteristically American. The work of Evans and his colleagues utilizes that typically antiorganic approach to reality, taking it to pieces and then rearranging the separate parts. The art of Evans and his fellow photographers thus appears far removed from realism as we commonly know it. It follows the transformation rules that characterize American culture more generally. It is art, therefore, in a quintessentially American vein. I leave for others to bicker about whether it is also, in any European sense, high art.

Film as a Mechanical Art

| HOLLYWOOD IN HOLLAND |

Like photography, film is a mechanical form of art. The debate about the status of film as art is inextricably linked to the debate about the mechanization and standardization of culture that was raging in Europe and America during the early twentieth century. Mainly because America was ahead of Europe in what Dutch historian Johan Huizinga called the instrumentalization of life, many were wont to attribute these ominous trends to America. Hardly ever did people pause to consider whether these processes of mechanization and standardization might not have parallel effects in Europe and America, irrespective of their provenance, or whether they might not work out differently depending on historic context and prevailing cultural attitudes. Mostly people tended implicitly to take an intermediate position, assuming that the process of mechanization had already assumed a thoroughly American guise and that Europe would get to know it as such.

It is good, therefore, to recognize that many guardians of culture in America as well worried about the commercialization, mechanization, and standardization of American culture. I have mentioned Henry Adams, scion of a leading American family, and his concern about the loss of spirituality in the culture of his homeland. He had a keen sense of decay and degeneration that he shared with many of his status and

descent. Another "New England eccentric" that I have already introduced, Charles Ives, expressed himself in his diaries as follows: "But the
Camp Meetings aren't the only thing that have gone soft. How about
some of the seed of 1776? There are probably several contributing factors. Perhaps the most obvious if not the most harmful element is commercialism, with its influence tending towards mechanization and standardized processes of mind and life (making breakfast and death a little
too easy). Emasculating America for money! Is the Anglo-Saxon going
'Pussy'?"[1] The quotation is redolent of a fear of the proud Anglo-Saxon
part of the nation becoming effete because of the newly rising culture
of consumption and its facile pleasures.

A chorus of concordant voices in Europe produced similar litanies.
In 1927 the Frenchman André Siegfried had this to say: "For so much
luxury brought within reach of every worker . . . a heavy price is being
paid: nothing less than the transformation of millions of workers into
automatons. 'Fordism,' i.e. the essence of American industry, results in
the standardization of the worker-as-such. Craftsmanship . . . has no
more place in the New World, but with it have gone certain conceptions
of man that we in Europe do consider as the veritable basis of civilization."[2] What Ives still saw as the result of mechanization alone assumes
under Siegfried's hands the proportions of an American/European
clash. Huizinga, for that matter, takes a larger view; he perceives in
America the first signs of a process of civilization that is much more
general in portent: "Organization becomes mechanization; that is the
fatal moment of the modern history of civilization." His broader view,
however, does not make his mood of cultural demise any less acute.
Nevertheless, he is aware that without mechanization, there will be no
civilization at all: "The process of refining culture is inseparable from
that of instrumentalization." The process, however, has two distinct
effects; it has a power to bind and a power to liberate. It appears ("taking America as the most perfect example") as if the balance tends too
much toward the first, toward the subservience and bondedness of the
individual, rather than toward setting the individual free.[3]

Huizinga goes on to ponder the possibility of whether the instrumentalization of life in America might not work out differently in Europe:
"Organization in the sense of standardization means the establishing
of a uniform and well-defined technical nomenclature . . . to the American it constitutes not only an individual need rather than a necessary
evil, it also constitutes a cultural ideal. . . . Everyone familiar with their
sense of conformity and collective identity will realize this. The Amer-

ican *wants* to be equal to his neighbor. He feels spiritually safe only in the normatively ordained, not to mention the fact that the latter also implies 'efficiency.'"[4] Siegfried further sharpens this contrast: "As for the races that are individuals in their work—the Frenchman who insists on thinking for himself and by himself; the Mediterranean with his genius for gardening and love of the soil—they all aggressively assert their individuality as if they could not fit in into the American MACHINE."[5] This takes us back again to one of those classic oppositions that Europeans tend to perceive between themselves and "America": individual heterogeneity versus the uniformity of the mass. The opposition here, as in so many other cases, is a tactical sleight of hand intended to keep the American threat at a safe distance. Europe, according to this view, simply is not amenable to the American way.

Duhamel, for one, had long given up on this hope. As he saw it, America was Europe's future. Mass society would manifest itself in Europe in the forms that it had already assumed in America; from America it would hurl itself like a devastating wave across the Old World. In his apocalyptic vision "le machinisme" and "l'homme-outil" took central place. He too conceived of mechanization mostly in terms of the loss of human individuality and creativity.[6]

The German view of the perils of mechanization reveals this same theme of the machine person—"Chauffeurmenschen," they were occasionally called there. Yet the accent appears to be put a little differently in Germany, on the preservation of the "folk spirit" (*Volksgeist*) and *Kultur,* on the collective rather than the individual aspect. A well-known example from the 1920s is a book by Adolf Halfeld, *Amerika und der Amerikanismus.*[7] It bears the highly charged subtitle *Kritische Betrachtungen eines Deutschen und Europäers* (Critical observations by a German and European). The publisher used the book's dust jacket to lay it on thickly: "Das Gegenstück zu Henry Ford. Wer dieses Buch gelesen hat, ist dagegen gefeit, den Amerikanismus zu predigen!" (The counterweight to Henry Ford. Those who have read this book are safeguarded against preaching Americanism!) The culture of Europe, "insbesondere der deutschen Kultur" (German culture in particular), was destined for annihilation "durch das auf Materialismus und Lebensmechanisierung eingestellte Amerika" (at the hands of an America that is geared to materialism and the mechanization of life). Rationalization in the American vein was the order of the day, "einerlei ob sie den Menschen im Menschen tötet" (regardless of whether it kills what is human in Man). The publisher presented the book as a counterblast to the much more positive view of America that was prevalent in German industrial circles, among both the entrepreneurs and organized labor— the view that saw America as the epitome of rational economic organization. Halfeld and other conservative critics of culture opposed this view, arguing the many negative effects of mechanization and rational organization.

Halfeld, "Deutscher und Europäer" (German and European), came up with the following contrast between Europe and America: a "Europäische Welt der Charaktere, der plastischen Symbole und des im Volkstum wurzelnden Gemeinschaftsgeistes" (a European world of strong characters, of expressive symbols and of a communal spirit rooted in the folk) stands opposed to "ein Amerika der Maschinenmenschen, das aus dem einen Grundprinzip des Erfolges eine Wertordnung von beleidigendster Dürftigkeit ableitet und das Leben seinen ewigen Geheimnisse beraubt" (an America of machine people, which from the one guiding principle of success deduces a value system of the most offensive spiritual poverty and which robs life of its eternal mysteries).[8] Clearly it does not matter much that European observers from Karl Marx to Max Weber, basing themselves solely on European developments, had designed their grand theories about the rationalization and the *"Entzauberung"* (the disenchantment) of the world. Halfeld still felt that he could describe Europe as the continent where the luster and magic of life were still untouched. "Von der höheren Warte unserer abendländischen Entwicklung gesehen, erscheint der Amerikanismus geradezu als ein Versuch, die Zusammenfassung aller gesellschaftlichen Kräfte in moderner Form zu verwirklichen—und zwar durch eine gegen den Geist und seine stets wachen Bedenken gerichtete, einseitig wirtschaftliche Zwecksetzung" (Seen from the higher vantage point of our western development, Americanism appears as the straightforward attempt at realizing the synthesis of all social forces in a modern form— and it does this by setting a goal that is one-sidedly economic, in opposition to the mental reservations of the human spirit).[9]

Other German authors developed variations on this general theme: mechanization and economic rationality seen as a threat to the European spirit. Once again the entire metaphoric repertoire of anti-Americanism is brought to bear. A contribution by Richard Müller-Freienfels to *Der Deutsche Gedanke* in 1927, for instance, makes it clear that, to him, the danger of Americanism for Europe lies not "in der Einführung amerikanischer maschinen an sich" (in the introduction of American machines as such) but "in der Nivellierung des Geistes, die diese in Amerika selbst gezeitigt haben" (in the leveling of the mind that they have produced in America). He distinguishes a general American-ism, a developmental phase that Europe is experiencing as well, from a more specific Americanism that Europe would have to oppose. He sees as elements of this latter form of Americanism, in addition to a spiritu-al leveling, the mindless pursuit of ever-new records, the idolization of sports, and the devaluation of man to a machine. That is what Europe should fend off; in opposition to this, Europe must stress "ihre Wertung der Qualität gegenüber der Quantität, organisches Leben gegen Mech-anisierung, Persönlichkeit gegen Nivellierung" (its valuation of quali-ty as opposed to quantity, organic life versus mechanization, personal-ity against uniformity).[10]

Yet another German contemporary, the philosopher Count Hermann Keyserling, a holist in the Carl Jung tradition, founded his critique of the mechanized society mainly on an ideal type of the total human be-ing. Keyserling too, however, especially in his *Amerika: Der Aufgang einer neuen Welt* (America: the rise of a new world; the book would be published in France as *Psychanalyse de l'Amérique* and would influence the French image of America), connected his more general cultural cri-tique to America. Much like Huizinga, he used a stratagem intended to keep America at a distance: he acknowledged the existence among Americans of a natural socialism and attributed it to the fact that "die sozialen Tendenzen in der Amerikanischen Seele wirklich vorherschen" (the social inclinations truly dominate the American soul). American ideals like "normalcy," "likemindedness," and "standardization" all testify to this. In fact, however, they constitute the relapse from a high-er to a lower level of civilization. Given their cast of mind, which limits itself to "dem Intellekt erfaszbare" (what the intellect can fathom), to the level of practical intelligence and common sense, Americans orient themselves toward the future yet tend to ignore the "unzerreiszbare Zusammenhang von Vergangenheit, Gegenwart und Zukunft" (the inseparable connections between the past, the present, and the future).[11] The human image in America is cast in terms of mechanization and the physical control of the world. In the psychology of behaviorism—ac-cording to Keyserling a typically American view of humanity—human beings appear as animals, rats on a treadmill. All human behavior can be reduced to acquired routines that, in their turn, can be seen as fully determined by external factors and are therefore open to external ma-nipulation and control. Thus Americans appear as a species that is uniquely in tune with the world of commerce, of mechanization, of manipulation through advertising, of rational organization. They are the perfect cogs in the perfect American machine.

I need to make one further point. There is a remarkable consistency in the foregoing arguments as summarized, almost to the point where their validity seems to be reinforced more by their repetition in endless variations than by anything else. Nevertheless, at the hands of other authors this same discourse can suddenly appear in a different light. With the culture critics considered thus far, those Europeans who tended to connect America to secular trends of mechanization and industrialization were willing to acknowledge the rationality and efficiency of America's economic organization; Huizinga referred to America's "perfect organization." Yet there are examples illustrating the contrary view. Consider H. G. Wells, who after his arrival in New York had this to say: "Noise and human hurry and a vastness of means and collective result, rather than any vastness of achievement, is the pervading quality of New York. The great thing is the mechanical thing, the unintentional thing which is speeding up all these people."[12] One day later "the effect remained still that of an immeasurably powerful forward movement of rapid eager advance," but, perhaps because of a good night's sleep, he could also write that "the human being seemed less of a fly upon the wheels."[13] He was now able to perceive more clearly an element of human direction and control, of a collective exercise of will, in what only a day before had struck him as the mechanical, unintentional thing. The image of a machine world, without sense or purpose and in constant motion, yet without "vastness of achievement," may remind us of Henry Adams, who at about the same time projected his metaphor of entropy onto the American scene. Yet Wells was cut of different timber. He was the kind of socialist who saw the way of the future lying in large-scale technology wedded to an equally large-scale spirit of collective enterprise. Sentimentality and nostalgia were alien to him. At Niagara Falls the power turbines impressed Wells the most: "They are will made visible, thought translated into easy and commanding things."[14] In Boston he had already encountered this sense of purpose, of planning and foresight, applied to problems of urban growth. He described his tour of the city as the exploration of "a fresh and more deliberate phase in this great American symphony, this symphony of Growth."[15] Growth excited him, "mechanical things" made him rave rapturously, as long as there was the attendant element of "deliberateness," of intentionality. In that sense he was closer to the enthusiasms of the Progressive movement in America than to the sense of disinheritance and alienation that characterized aesthetes like Henry Adams and Henry James.

Thus, mechanization and its cultural effects could be seen from totally different perspectives: as a threat to tradition and individuality, especially in France; as undermining the *Volksgeist* and *Kultur,* as valued in Germany; as a force of renewal that would bring prosperity and freedom, the view of labor union leaders and socialists in a number of European countries; and finally, as the carrier of a new aesthetics, more beautiful than Niagara Falls. As I will now show, the debate about new forms of mechanical art such as photography and film would alternate among these various perspectives. But from whatever angle this debate was joined, America remained a point of reference.

Film, Hollywood, and Holland: The Interwar Years

The reception of American films in the Netherlands and the critical exploration of their Americanness proceeded on a variety of levels, eliciting the varied critical discourses that characterized each of a number of self-styled communities of cultural guardianship. One such community centered its discourse on the aesthetics of film as a new art form. A group of filmmakers and film critics organized the Film Liga, which aimed at developing a set of aesthetic criteria that would help them to define film as a serious and autonomous art form in the face of a widespread disparaging view of film as a vehicle of mere mass entertainment. This debate among cultural elites, pitting a younger generation of cultural rebels against the guardians of entrenched views of "high culture," forced the advocates of film as a new art form to respond to the arguments of their opponents and to define their own views vis-à-vis the flood of movie productions coming from the American entertainment industry. In a sense they reflected the hierarchical views of their opponents: their own aesthetics critically centered on a ranking of high and low, of the vulgar and the sublime, that led their opponents to reject film in general. To the extent that they developed a critical language for weeding out the low from the high in film production, American film was their characteristic target. Their critique of its commercialism, of the studio system, of the film star phenomenon, and of the industrial standardization of the product betrayed not only their aesthetic concerns but also a set of preconceived ideas concerning American culture that were the common wisdom among cultural elite circles in Europe.

There were other responses of cultural guardianship as well, centering on criteria of morality rather than aesthetics. In the pluralism of the Dutch cultural landscape, with its segmented pattern of denominational and sociopolitical blocs, each bloc developed its own discourse in its exploration of the pernicious impact of film as a new form of mass entertainment. This was only one effort in a larger cultural campaign. Against the new forms of entertainment ushered in by the new culture of consumption and outside the tutelary reach of these subcultural blocs, each bloc tried to develop vibrant and educational forms of leisure activity, drawing on folk repertoires and emphasizing healthy outdoor activities, in order to keep the young under constant cultural surveillance. In what was truly a collective reflection on the viability of morally comforting forms of popular culture, once again one can see wider views of American mass culture affecting the discussion of American films.

THE FILM LIGA: AESTHETICS VERSUS COMMERCIALISM

In the Netherlands during the interwar years the advocacy of film as a new art form always served to promote other objectives as well. Each of these objectives in its own way added a tone of urgency to the debate, giving it the wider relevance of a fight for cultural survival, if not renewal. One context of militant assertion was that of a budding generation of young intellectuals trying to break through the constraints of an established cultural discourse. Their exploration of film's expressive potential was part of a wider search for new modes of expression and a new aesthetics in an age when the established canons of art had been shattered beyond repair by war, revolution, and massive social change. Those who considered themselves to be members of an international avant-garde, such as Theo van Doesburg, founder of the journal for modern art *De Stijl,* welcomed film as a medium able to harness modern technology in the service of his ideas of a *"nieuwe beelding"*— a "neoplasticism."[16] Van Doesburg's incorporation of film into his more general views of an avant-garde, antibourgeois, and antinaturalist aesthetics was not adopted universally by others of his generation, yet they shared with him the urgent quest for a critical language that could do justice to film as a new art form. I will return to them at greater length later.

A second general assertion that was often implicit in critical writings about film was related not as much to a younger generation asserting its cultural views as to the need to reassert a sense of cultural identity in the face of eroding forces. The emphasis in the latter case was more on cultural survival than on cultural renewal. Nonetheless, the two assertive purposes are not mutually exclusive. Many of the younger as well as the older generation can be seen to have argued along both lines, in defense of a cherished but threatened cultural identity and in favor of a radically redefined aesthetics. Thus, in the Netherlands there were people like Johan Huizinga and Menno ter Braak, members of two different generations, arguing the case for cultural defense on behalf of "Europe" versus "America." As I will show later, Ter Braak was at the same time a young rebel in search of a new film aesthetics. He fought on two fronts at once. But so did Huizinga, albeit with less vigor, because of both age and temperament.

Huizinga's views on film are characteristically ambivalent. They reflect the mixed feelings he had about America. At one point in his 1927 collection of travel impressions he went so far as to accept film as an art form for which a new muse or patron saint would have to be found. He instantly qualified this position, however, pointing out that the "movies"—as he put it in his Dutch text—are a mere illustration, albeit the most important, of an ominous shift in our civilization away from reading to watching, away from the printed word toward "ideographic" information. Still, Huizinga again was ambivalent. Pondering the impact of film as he had witnessed it in America, he was aware of its democratic potential. Film was Whitmanesque in its capacity to restore a democratic vista, allowing people a comprehensive, if vicarious, view of the variety of life in their society. At the same time, however, Huizinga's more pessimistic views of the mechanization of contemporary culture qualified these high hopes. As one of the new mass media, film, like radio, aimed at a mass audience, catering to its average taste. Film tended to simplify and stereotype its message. It might widen people's views of society, but only spuriously so, through a flattening of the social and cultural landscape. Film "habituates the nation from high to low to one common view of life. Due to its limited means of expression, its highlighting of what is external, and the need to appeal to a general audience, film shuts off entire areas of spiritual activity. It imposes a limited number of standard views of life that will eventually become the mass view."[17] Thus, film was one of the contemporary forces of cultural erosion that were at work in America. As an art form, visual though it might be, it would never create lasting, self-contained forms, such as sculpture or painting do. No dreams of neoplasticism for Huizinga. In its narrative flow film, to him, was more like literature or drama. Geared as film was to a mass market, it could catch the attention of its audience compellingly yet only transiently, for fleeting moments. Unlike drama or literature, it could never cause the audience to pause and reflect.

Nevertheless, mixed as Huizinga's feelings about film may have been, he managed astutely to define the inner force of a medium in a way that has inspired critical reflection on film until the present day. Even today the academic study of film is centrally involved with the intriguing exchange between the imaginary world of the silver screen and the sense of identity of the individuals watching that world. The moviegoers participate in a process of identification with the shadows on the screen that leads them to step outside themselves. Huizinga made the following perceptive observation:

> [Film] shows the urban dweller country life, or at least an image of it, it shows the countryman urban life, it gives the poor a view of luxury and the rich one of misery, all highly stylized so as to make it easy to appropriate. Thus film rather works to conciliate than to sharpen class resentment. The repeated illusion of the life of the rich affords the poor a certain communion with luxury and refinement; its fantasy image becomes a part of their daily existence. In the hero the audience exalts itself, and, beyond this, film stars off the screen offer it a new model for emulation, a novel assurance of options open to everyone.[18]

Of course, these are but one individual's idiosyncratic views. They are the armchair musings of a man who was never centrally involved in the raging debate about film. As a leading cultural critic, however, he lucidly pointed to a number of social and cultural trends that served as a framework for the discussion of issues that a younger generation was addressing. Unlike Huizinga, though, many of his younger contemporaries shunned his characteristic caution and ambivalence. They tended to hail the advent of new art forms, such as film and photography, that harnessed techniques of mechanical reproduction for purposes of reaching a mass audience. Where Huizinga had perceived, in the mechanization of culture, a tension between the promise of a democratic art and its fake realization as mass culture, the younger generation's advocacy of film centered precisely on the technical conditions of film production. To them, film promised a restored union between the worlds of technical invention and artistic creation, between culture and the machine, which had for so long been disconnected. During World War I the machine had visited its destructive potential on the world of European culture. At the same time, however, in the huge collective endeavor of the belligerents, a new appreciation of the machine had arisen as the harbinger of a new technical civilization. No longer could intellectuals, in their role of cultural critics and guardians, afford to ignore the novel sense of exhilaration, of nervous speed and energy, that technology had spawned—and film to them was the perfect new medium to convey this novel existential awareness. Instead of rejecting film as a mere technical contraption unable ever to provide more than shallow entertainment to the masses, or continuing the spurious division between a highbrow sphere of cultured life and the lowbrow realm of the engineer, the younger intellectual generation made film the object of critical reflection. These critics were aware that film had not yet realized its full artistic potential. Their responsibility, as they saw it, was to nurture this fledgling new art form, to create a new critical language, develop a new aesthetics, and educate the larger public.

Theirs was always a struggle on more than one front. There was first of all the aspect of a generational struggle, of a younger generation defiantly challenging the dominant forms of discourse in the marketplace of ideas. Whereas Huizinga and people of his generation and cast of mind still tended to cling to a dichotomous, if not Manichaean, view of the life of the mind in a mechanized world, many of the younger generation radically had adopted the machine as a powerful ingredient of contemporary culture. This position was generational rather than ideological. There were young writers across the political spectrum defending film against its many detractors.

Thus, for example, in *Communisme,* the theoretical journal of the Dutch Communist Party, G. de Waal argued a position that was no doubt ideologically correct but that at the same time reads like a highly original defense of industrial film production. Against all those who held that film was doomed by the industrialization and standardization of its production, he argued in favor of large-scale, industrial production as the only mode compatible with prevailing forces of production. Against the elitists who favored films made for a happy few in small artisan shops and ateliers, he used essentially the same argument, pointing out that their views represented an outdated stage of development. What was wrong, according to him, was not the mode of production but its capitalist auspices. The profit motive as the main force behind film production prevented film from realizing its full potential.[19]

Others not as far to the left were equally sanguine in their views of film as a mechanical art. Thus, Leendert J. Jordaan, a socialist and one of the early film intellectuals in the Netherlands, saw technology as the most crucial characteristic of his time. It had deeply affected the conditions of everyday life, yet it had been ignored as an object for cultural reflection. Film incorporated precisely the spirit of the age of technology and, like technology, would be there to stay. In a piece full of martial metaphors—and tellingly entitled "The Struggle for the Silver Screen"[20]—Jordaan called on the intellectuals to take film seriously and to provide critical guidance to the general public through the press. The forum that Jordaan chose for this plea was the short-lived cultural journal *NU* (Now), which, not unlike *The Seven Arts* ten years earlier in the United States, was meant as a call for the revitalization and rejuvenation of cultural life. As one of its two editors, the socialist Adrianus M. de Jong, put it in the introduction to the first issue, art could no longer be the private act of single individuals: "The watchword of the new age: 'Brotherhood!' echoes around the world. It is the call of a young, passionate breed, ready for every sacrifice not for their own greatness but on behalf of the common weal."[21]

The clash of generations was one of the recurrent features of the debate about film, but there was always a second battle line. If the advocacy of film as a new art form was the issue, then to emancipate film from the sway of older forms of art, one needed a negative yardstick, as well as a new critical language and a new aesthetics, for the proper appraisal of film on its own terms. Many of film's early supporters agreed that the proper defense of film required them to disavow its low, mass-entertainment forms. The implicit elitism of their position translated into the polemical rejection of "Americanism." It was a position that they shared with many of the older breed of cultural critics and that served to bridge the gap that otherwise kept the generations apart.

Thus Jordaan, in the previously cited piece, pointed out that the struggle for the silver screen ("one of the most urgent problems of our time—of NOW!") not only meant a struggle with outside opponents but should imply an inner purge as well. "It means, among many other things, a struggle against 'Americanism'—against the senseless and mindless transplant of the insipid, childish mentality and the overflowing energy of a young, and newly marketed culture onto our old, experienced and weary state of mind."[22] In a later issue of *NU* Jordaan took up the theme once again and made it his central argument; the piece is entitled "Americanism and the Film." "We, children of the old Europe, do not like the Americans. . . . We do not like them because the best in us rebels against this: our culture and our tradition." "To us this white brother 'over there' remains a boisterous, narrow, conceited, arrogant and very vulgar upstart. Altogether a relative whom we wish well, as long as he does not force himself on us. Precisely this, we are sorry to say, has been happening in recent years, in most emphatic ways, through film." At the very moment when film, "in its nobler forms" (needless to say, Jordaan was thinking of German, French, and Russian films), was beginning to gain acceptance among the more educated classes and when it was becoming a cultural force in its own right, the American film industry had gained hegemonic control of world film production. By cornering the market the U.S. film industry exported its mentality worldwide; Europe was flooded with structures of thought "made in America." "Now this is fatal, absurd, intolerable!" Europe, to Jordaan, was a house, "old, decrepit perhaps, but venerable," illuminated by the luster of Rembrandt, Bach, Beethoven, Dante, and Shakespeare, that is invaded by a stranger "who, shamelessly, pins 'pictures' of soapbox beauties on the walls and fills the rooms with the blare of the Charleston and the Dirty-Dig." Not only were the masses held in thrall, a case of "chronic mass poisoning," but intellectuals with an interest in film had to endure this deluge as well.[23]

Jordaan's attack was one of the more unsubtle blasts in the chorus of anti-Americanism in the 1920s. In early 1925 the literary and cultural monthly journal *De Stem* surveyed Dutch intellectuals about their views on film. The editors set the tone by calling film a wicked witch, "swollen by all the evil juices of our civilization." Not surprisingly, the negative replies were many, stressing film's mechanical, naturalistic, and standardizing elements. American films were the main culprit. The young poet Jan Slauerhoff was willing to give film a chance on condition that the importation of American films be stopped for the next twenty-five years. In the same year, 1925, at a conference on "the movie theater problem" organized by the VCSJ, a Christian youth organization, H. C. Verkruysen, the director of an art school in Haarlem, denied the possibility of film ever developing into an art form. Again, his arguments were mainly aimed at American films.[24] As J. Scholte, founding member of the Amsterdam Film Liga, put it in the group's 1927 manifesto: "Once every hundred times we see: film. For the rest we see: movies. The herd, the commercial regime, America, kitsch."[25]

Another cofounder of the Amsterdam Film Liga, Menno ter Braak, also had his less-subtle moments. In a piece that he wrote as editor of an irreverent Amsterdam student weekly, *Propria Cures,* his rallying cry was "Europe for the Europeans." With true crusading zeal he called for the culture of old Europe to be defended to the last breath. "Mind bestows life, Americanism kills." "Americanism makes man into a senseless machine, . . . a coin gone smooth. It penetrates everything, erodes everything, depraves everything to the core."[26] In 1930, as a film critic for one of the leading Dutch quality papers, he wrote a piece entitled "'Americanism' in the Film World."[27] His tone was more Olympian in the later piece, but his judgment was equally harsh. It was the lasting achievement of American films, naively unaware of rival art forms and produced simply for the entertainment of the masses, to have stumbled on the basic rules of cinematic movement "when Europeans were still clumsily training their lenses on the Comédie Française or were pinning their hopes to eerily expressive decors." Without the naïveté of Americans (Ter Braak presents them here almost as noble savages), without their lack of inner conflict, film as art, "which is so dear to the more complicated Europeans, would have foundered on the rocks of other art forms." For the further development of a serious film culture, however, America had become an encumbrance—or more precisely, not America but Americanism. Americanism as a mental habit had extended far beyond the geographic confines of a particular country. In the far-flung standardization of film production in America, "it may have reached its most threatening heights, yet as a mentality it can be found elsewhere." It is the mentality "of the commonplace, of the cliché."

What is remarkable in all this fevered elevation of American culture as the central threat to everything that these authors held dear is not the cultural survival reflex itself. It is rather the language in which they cast the main contours of the conflict. It is not Dutch culture that is threatened by Americanism; it is European culture, Europeanism. There is much irony in this. If one of the most potent effects of the rising challenge of American culture was the reactivation of a variety of national discourses in Europe, using Europe rather than their varied national contexts as their frame of reference, then European critics of America have much for which to thank America. Yet this point is usually overlooked.

It was not just the smaller national cultures in Europe that tended to cast their critique of America in European terms, although it may have been more frequent there. Among the leading critics of Americanism in Germany and France as well, the main contrast as they construed it was between "America" and "Europe." Nonetheless—and this is not without irony, too—the Europe invoked in French writings (e.g., by Duhamel or André Siegfried) or in German writings (e.g., by Spengler, Halfeld, or Keyserling) is always cast in either a characteristic French or German light. French authors tended to project typically French views of a creative individualism onto the larger European screen to highlight the contrast to the American standardization of production, which aimed at the average tastes of the masses. German authors tended to argue in terms of the collective *"Seele"* (soul) of the *"Kulturvolk"* as the central defining element of the civilization of the *"Abendland"*— the West. That, in their view, constituted the central European antithesis to Americanism.

Not only did these writers often cast the image of Europe in characteristically national terms, but "Europe" often served them as no more than a flimsy rhetorical veneer. More often than not it could hardly paper over the fault lines between the various national cultures. An amusing example of this can be found in André Siegfried's writings. In 1927 he wrote the preface to a study by André Philip about labor conditions in America entitled *Le problème ouvrier aux Etats-Unis*. It is a study about the place of the worker in an industry that had become organized around the tenets of Fordism, Taylorism, standardization, mass production, and above all, *"le machinisme."* Siegfried lauds Philip as a "bon européen" (a good European) who had set out to measure American labor conditions by a European yardstick of humanist values. He remembers how he himself had become aware of "le monde européen comme un ensemble" (the European world as a whole) only after having gone to America. It is only in America that "on prend conscience d'une réalité qui nous échappe ici, c'est qu'il existe un esprit européen, dont l'esprit américain est souvent la parfaite antithèse" (one becomes aware of a reality that escapes us here, namely, that a European spirit does exist, one to which the American spirit often stands as the perfect opposite). From a moral point of view America, new as it is, has been cut off from Europe's twenty-centuries-old traditions by the hiatus of emigration across the ocean; it no longer shares much with the old Europe that is still in direct communion with Rome, Greece, and even India. Clearly up to this point Siegfried conceives of Europe "comme un ensemble," as an integral whole. He soon begins to add individual detail to his picture, however: "Parmi les peuples européens, le français est celui qui a eu, le plus, la conscience de ce qu'est un individu, un homme" (among Europeans, the Frenchman is the one who has had the clearest sense of what it means to be an individual, a man). France clearly takes pride of place in the European ensemble, embodying some of the core values of Europeanism. But Siegfried does not leave it at that. He goes on to single out one other country from the European whole, describing it as an America in Europe: Germany. "Les Allemands, si semblables à tant d'égards aux Américains modernes, se sont jetés dans la standardisation avec une sorte de passion, comme ils font toutes choses. Il n'est point d'Allemand, aujourd'hui, qui ne chante avec conviction l'hymne de la 'rationalisation'; celle-ci répond évidemment à leur génie de discipline, avouons-le aussi, à leur manque de personnalité." (The Germans, so similar in so many ways to the modern Americans, have hurled themselves onto a course of standardization with a kind of passion, as they always do. There is no German, today, who does not with conviction sing the praise of "rationalization"; the latter clearly accords with their mind for discipline, and, let us admit it, their lack of personality.)[28] So much for the European ensemble.

Skin-deep as the rhetorical veneer of Europe may have been, it remains a noteworthy fact that in many European countries people chose to conceive of their opposition to America in such terms. Be that as it may, every national context also produced specific references to the survival and defense of the national culture. In the Netherlands, though, they are few and far between. For the period of the silent movies I have found none. When films began to talk, however, the strictly national contours of the debate about film came more clearly into focus. Film lost its transnational character. It could no longer transcend linguistic barriers, as it had done before. Films now had to be dubbed or subtitled. The larger European countries all opted for dubbing. As the more expensive of the two, dubbing was not commercially attractive in the smaller language areas. Ironically, in the Netherlands film distributors briefly toyed with the idea of using German-dubbed versions, which does not seem to indicate an acute awareness of a threat to the Dutch national language and culture. Interestingly, however, when the Haarlem-based Dutch newsreel producer *Polygoon* announced the introduction of Dutch soundtracks in 1931, its director, D. Hamburger, deemed the occasion sufficiently newsworthy to make an appearance on the screen. He proudly made the point that henceforth the use of the Dutch language would be a potent means of defense against "the array of alien intrusions into the Dutch language for which the American sound film in particular stands indicted." Later in the decade, in the socialist monthly *Socialisme en democratie,* H. Brugmans reviewed a Dutch full-length feature film. He did not find much ground for praise, but he did appreciate the attempt. "Without a doubt, it is a national interest that within our language area we create our own film industry. Just as surely as it was a boon to the artistic level of films shown in the Netherlands when France broke the stranglehold of America . . . it is unmistakeably a gain when the Netherlands acquires a certain independence in this area."[29] There must surely be more examples like these, yet in the debate about film, the defense of an independent Dutch culture has on the whole played a relatively minor part, certainly when compared to the heated discussion concerning an independent film aesthetics.

This latter discussion can be summarized as follows: in their struggle for an independent film aesthetics, a group of young Dutch film enthusiasts, publishing widely but clustering around the Film Liga and its journal, were battling on two fronts simultaneously. In their explorations of the young medium they tried to establish a canon of pure film, assigning it its rightful place alongside other art forms. At the same time they had to defend their canon against forces of standardization and routinization in film production, which they typically tended to identify with the American film industry, or more generally, with a pernicious and pervasive Americanism.

Their critical standards were typically highbrow. Their dual battle for the emancipation of film from its humble beginnings may have made them overly elitist in their approach toward film as a mass medium. Until the late 1920s very few American films met with their approval; those that did were seen as clear exceptions to what had become their established view of European film versus American film, epitomized by Fritz Lang's *Nibelungen* and Cecil B. DeMille's *Ten Commandments,* respectively. Among Ter Braak's film reviews only one is really appreciative of an American film, James Cruze's *Jazz*. As L. J. Jordaan related it more than ten years later, in an obituary for the revered German filmmaker Walter Ruttmann, Ruttmann had surprised all those present by openly praising Cruze's film during a speaking engagement for the Amsterdam Film Liga. More surprisingly, Ruttmann, "the great innovator," spoke about Hollywood without the usual anger, recognizing those few who never compromised their principles in that great film metropolis. During the 1930s film critics gradually began to take a more balanced view of American films. A. (Janus) van Domburg, in a collection of film essays published in 1936, was one of the first to rank D. W. Griffith among film's avant-garde innovators for his creative use of montage. More generally, Van Domburg argued, European filmmakers and film critics tended to overstate their rejection of anything American in their attempt to protect film as an autonomous art form. Guided by the best of intentions, their rejection was understandable but ill-considered. Not only was there a need for a greater sense of balance, but the level of film criticism in the Netherlands needed to be raised. "All too rarely do we learn what makes a good movie; which are the characteristics that make film art an autonomous form of expression; why film should not consist of a series of photographs but rather of a dynamic-rhythmical ordering of movement and why movement on the screen has nothing to do with film while movement outside the screen has everything to do with it." There are echoes here of Ter Braak's earlier reflections on the aesthetics of film, the same use of temporal-spatial metaphors from music and ballet as adjacent but different art forms. But there is no longer the tone of the militant manifesto. Van Domburg's musings read like accepted wisdoms.[30]

■ ■ ■

To the extent that there was still a sense of a battle to be waged, the line of confrontation was different. As Van Domburg put it, addressing his fellow Catholics in the Netherlands, "In general, Catholic film criticism, as it appears in the press, has been over-zealous in its focus on the moral side of film."[31] Not only among Catholics but also in other segments of Dutch society that were held together by a common faith or philosophy, a critical reaction toward film had developed that tended to see film as an ethical problem rather than as an aesthetic promise. There indeed lay a third field where the advocates of film had to act. Whereas previously they had tended to see themselves as witnesses for the defense of film as art, they now were called to meet the prosecution in a different case. If film was still threatened, it was by those guardians of morality who saw film as a moral threat.

Dutch *Verzuiling* and American Films: The Debate about Ethics

In the interwar period a process of segmentation of Dutch social and political life that had begun in the late nineteenth century reached fruition. It is described variously as a reaction to industrialism and its socially uprooting effects, as a reaction to the secularization of society, as an attempt at countering the appeal that socialism exerted on the emerging working class, or as the answer to the advent of mass democracy. A reaction it certainly was, and of a self-reinforcing nature to boot. Older collective identities that had served to set the lines of conflict in Dutch society for centuries—of a liberal, free-thinking urban elite versus the guardians of Calvinist orthodoxy, of Calvinism versus Catholicism—were being reactivated under the impact of forces of modernization. Groups of a later coinage, such as workers in industry, had little choice but to adopt the organizing logic of the society's older segments and emerged as rival blocs, or "pillars" (zuilen), as they were called in the Netherlands. These blocs contended for political power in the newly opening area of mass democracy, organizing as political parties. They also chose to seek their strength in relative isolation, cordoning off their respective constituencies against outside social and cultural influences. This aspect of cultural isolation is particularly relevant to my analysis.

Among the carriers of unwelcome views were traditional media, such as the press, or newer ones, such as radio and film. The natural inclination for each of the sociocultural segments was to take control of the media and the flow of information. This is what happened with the press and radio. There were liberal and socialist newspapers, as well as Calvinist and Catholic ones. Also, in the late 1920s the airwaves were channeled along the various segmental lines. Both the production and broadcasting of radio programs were fully controlled by corporations set up under the organizational aegis of the various pillars.

With film things were different. For one thing, the pillars never succeeded in carving up the market for the distribution of films, mostly because they were economically incapable of producing the goods. The market was dominated by imported films; in the early 1930s German and American productions shared this dominance equally, and after 1933, following Hitler's takeover of power, the Americans controlled the field by themselves. In 1938 and 1939 the American share of the market hovered around 60 percent.[32]

Unable to control either the production or the distribution of films, each of the various sociocultural segments of Dutch society had to devise a response to the challenge of an independent film-entertainment market. Sometimes, with a view to legislative regulation, they managed to join forces. One concern that they all shared was the so-called movie-theater problem (bioscoopvraagstuk). In 1926 their joint support helped to pass a "Movie-Theater Act" that was meant to "counter the moral and social dangers of the movie theater." The act set up a national review board that had the authority to examine all films prior to their public release, to set age-related standards for admission, or even to ban films that violated public morality.

Clearly this was no more than a minimal common defense in the face of a threat that to many appeared to call for a wider cultural counter-offensive. Traditional frameworks of cultural guidance had been exploded, ironically, by precisely those changes that many had welcomed as progress: reduced working hours, increased disposable incomes, and a wider range of choice for the individual consumer. Consumption and leisure were new areas that had grown outside the established frameworks of cultural control. In response, each of the various sociocultural blocs in Dutch society frantically tried to devise strategies to gain control over the new culture of consumption. Trying to orchestrate the consumption of culture within their respective constituencies, their common point of negative reference was always the reality of commercial entertainment, offering cheap thrills, consumption rather than consummation, and oblivion rather than the uplift of education.

As the socialists saw it, the aim of a socialist cultural policy should always be education for a better world to come. They provided their own alternative frameworks for socialist youths to spend their leisure time and for socialists in general to spend their holidays (often by enjoying nature) and to sharpen their sense of distance toward the surrounding capitalist culture. Ironically, as socialist observers like W. A. Bonger pointed out, what happened was no more than a replica of the cultural emancipation movement under liberal bourgeois auspices earlier in the century.[33] The aversion felt toward the cultural erosion brought by the characteristically American entertainment industry was more widely shared than many socialists tended to think. Nevertheless, their choice of language and arguments in setting their views of a socialist culture against a capitalist culture, typified as that produced in America, gave the socialist cultural offensive its distinctive flavor. It formed part of that wider international discussion among socialists concerning the contours of "socialism as a cultural movement," as the leading Belgian socialist theoretician Hendrik de Man put it.

In addition, one strategic option for moral guardianship considered by socialists was typical for them and could never have come from liberal-bourgeois circles: the option of socializing film production and distribution, along with the communalization of movie theaters. A proposal in that general vein was presented in 1922 in *De Socialistische Gids,* in an article by Dirk van Staveren, who would go on to become the long-standing chairman of the national film review board. By then he had moved far from his early radical views, but in 1922 he could still write, "The root of our present plight is in the fact that the film industry and the movie theater enterprise are capitalist, run and organized with a view to making profit. It follows naturally that the primary concern is not: What is good? What has the greatest educational value? But rather: What films will allow me to draw the largest crowds?"[34]

In addition socialists may have had their own, ideologically inspired resistance toward film as an entertainment industry. These latter-day students of Karl Marx may have seen a contemporary "opiate of the masses" in the imaginary world of the silver screen and the darkness of the movie theater. In a 1931 article about Marlene Dietrich published in *De Socialistische Gids,* Hendrick G. Cannegieter put it thus: "indeed the movie theater, this opium den of the West, is the refuge protecting the mind from the erosive assaults it has to sustain in real life. Here, free from self-control, people dream away, carried by the reflections of their own desires and moods in the shape of moving shadows on the screen. This is the true, spontaneous, natural process of grasping all that the rational intellect will not acknowledge."[35] Apart from the sneering reference to the opium den, the statement is remarkably perceptive and may remind us of Huizinga's earlier observations concerning the imaginary world of the movie audience.

In the case of the Dutch Calvinists there were similar attempts at controlling the leisure-time activities of their constituency. As in the case of the socialists, there is a distinctive element in their endeavor. Unlike the other sociocultural blocs, which all in one way or another had accommodated to film as a form of art and a medium of entertainment, the Dutch Calvinists tended mostly toward a wholesale rejection of film. Ever since the Reformation their tradition had been averse to visual imagery. They were the people of the Word and of the Book. They were mostly critical of what Huizinga had described as the shift toward an eidetic culture, moving away from printed words to visual images. For example, as late as the 1930s, in the religious-socialist journal *Tijd en Taak,* Tjeerd Lichthart referred to the movie theater as "the spiritual saloon of the proletariat." "As long as the moviehouse will remain what it has been until today, we do well not to go there. For our own sake and that of others. For certain reasons we do not feel at home there and therefore do not belong there. Mainly out of a sense of responsibility toward all those seeking and unguided youngsters of these shallow times."[36] Not until after World War II would Calvinists come to take film seriously.

The Catholics, like the liberal bourgeoisie and the socialists, had early on accepted film as an important cultural medium. They contributed as much as the other two cultural blocs did to the early quest for a new critical language and a new aesthetics to apply to film as a novel art form. Whereas Ter Braak and Huizinga spoke for the elitist cultural views of a bourgeois intelligentsia, Jef Last and L. J. Jordaan mediated between the advocates of film as art and those fellow socialists whose concern was mostly with the moral integrity of a socialist culture. Similarly, among the Catholics people like Van Domburg or his younger colleague Bob J. Bertina tried to infuse the debate about film with their aesthetic and critical concerns. Clearly, however, they were a minority. More than any of the other sociocultural blocs, Catholics put up a strong moral offensive, not only to protect their flock from the pernicious influence of mass-produced entertainment films but also to produce Catholic films that would convey their views of a properly moral world. Much like the Dutch socialists whose debate formed part of a wider international discussion about socialism as a cultural movement, Catholics too could find inspiration abroad. There was the 1936 papal encyclical on film, "Vigilanti Cura," and there was the earlier American example of the Legion of Decency, which was inspired by the American bishops. Even in the absence of those examples, however, in the late 1920s the Dutch Catholics firmed up their moral defense against the commercial film market by gaining the right of an independent second review of films prior to their distribution in solidly Catholic regions of the country. Later on, in 1937, a group named Catholic Film Action founded the film magazine *Het Witte Doek,* in which Catholics provided moral guidance more explicit than that of any of the other sociocultural groups. Its tone of moral suasion is clear on every page: "Wee Willie Winkie as well can be seen by fourteen-year-old children. Only: in some theaters the opportunity is taken for showing advertisements on the screen for the Shirley Temple Club. Our Dutch fathers and mothers will on the whole be sensible enough to forbid their children to engage in such idolizing of film stars."[37] The regular column "About Youth and Film" yields this example: "There is much to be said for it, when the hunger for the image, the film hunger, be met sparingly and with pedagogical intent, under adult guidance and supervision, while at the same time proper respect should be taught for 'the word,' training the young particularly in understanding and using language. This is a demand of civilization."[38]

After one year *Het Witte Doek* merged with *Filmfront,* the journal of a small group of Catholic film aesthetes. Following the merger, under the new name of *Katholiek Filmfront,* the journal held the two groups together in creative tension, the film aesthetes and the guardians of morality.[39] Compared to the other sociocultural blocs in Dutch society, the Catholic view of America and of the American film production showed greater nuance. America was not as easily cast in the role of cultural villain, perhaps because of the inspiring role of the Catholic church's cultural offensive there.

■ ■ ■

These are no more than the broad outlines of the various fronts of cultural self-defense in the face of the challenge posed by film and the movie theater. To the extent that we can speak of a crusade against the forces of darkness, it was the darkness of the movie theater. And insofar as people tended to yield to those forces, surrendering to the dreamworld of Hollywood, it was once again America that became the focus of opposition. This time, however, it was an opposition not on aesthetic grounds, against an America corrupting film as art, but on moral grounds, against an America corrupting the film public. Without strong moral guidance people should not be led (or better, let) into the darkness of the movie house. As it happened, many of the negative views of American society and culture that had inspired many pure aesthetes of film to reject American films wholesale recurred among those whose main concern was with film as a moral challenge. Nonetheless, my exploration of the two separate discourses—of the aesthetes and of the moralists—does not point up only parallels.

To the extent that the aesthetes felt the need to define their ideals against a pervasive "Americanism," they tended to raise the banner of elite cultural standards, widening their view to embrace the European heritage. Whereas aesthetes tended toward a transcendence of the Dutch cultural landscape, the opposite happened in the case of the moral response to film. America may still have served as a point of negative reference—a facile metaphor for anonymous forces of social change—yet when it came to defining the standards of morality, critics tended to withdraw behind the lines that had segmented Dutch society. In their varied response emerge not the contours of an imperiled "European" culture but rather those of a Dutch cultural landscape that had hardened around militant core groups attempting to maintain their cultural specificity against the eroding onslaught of modernization.

Advertising

| THE WORLD OF DISJOINTED ATTRIBUTES |

It did not take long for this to happen: once chromolithography had made art accessible to a mass public, art became subject to the logic of commerce. Many tended to see this as a case of cultural decay, yet what escaped them was that commerce in its turn was touched by the spirit of art. "Commercial art" had long remained an oxymoron, a hybrid species that the established artistic discourse would never willingly acknowledge—or so it was argued. We know better now. Can we still, from our present vantage point, imagine the late nineteenth century without the colorful posters designed to bring the age's consumption goods to the attention of the larger public? They are as much part of the period as the great world's fairs or the award medals that were bestowed on industrial products and that are often displayed on their labels even today. They represent an early stage of our modern consumption culture. Their messages are now out of date; their incitement to action has lost its force. Where would one have to go to buy such bicycles, such automobiles? Which hairdo would wave so elegantly in the wind to form an art deco ornament? They still appeal to us, yet the message has changed. They now mostly sell themselves, purveying dreams of days long gone. We have taken them from their period and framed them in isolation.

The history of the modern era's consumption goods cannot be written without a history of their public presentation, exploring the "advertising space" that they have taken up in people's lives. There is no automobile museum without its collection of automobile posters. Not only do such museums show us old automobiles, like so many displaced mummies cruelly torn from their moment in time. Through posters they also display the automobile as an image, not only in the literal sense of a visual representation, introducing new cars to an earlier buying public, but more importantly in the sense of an imaginary phantom that properly belongs to the realm of our dreams. In that latter sense the image is a haunting presence, timeless, forever there, freely engaging in ever-changing unions with other phantasms. It gets woven into extended neural networks and becomes an inextricable part of our inner world. The Bugatti in the museum really does not need the sign "Don't touch, please!" In a strange way it already seems less tangible than its fictional version on the advertising poster. Only there does the Bugatti reappear in context; only there does it seem to move and to have meaning.

Consumption goods, doubling as phantom images of themselves, are living contradictions. They are meant to be consumed, yet at the same time they have reached consummation, a higher level of sense and meaning, of dreams and desires. The tangible goods have spawned an imaginary world that is entitled to its own cultural history. The automobile as an object of consumption has a finite life; its only future is the scrap heap. Nevertheless, as a dream object it keeps riding on.

The separation between object and image, between commerce and art, is not as neat as it may appear. Since the advent of the mass-consumption era, the consumption good itself has been touched by the human talent for creative design. Admittedly, a bag of potatoes has quite prosaically managed to hold its own, yet anyone who walks into a contemporary specialty bakery will feel tempted, in addition to buying the daily bread, to spend his or her dough on designer pastry. Similarly, the joys of tobacco may have engaged in artful connections with an imaginary world of dreams most convincingly in advertising. Yet at the same time the product in both its shape and packaging has been subject to the designer's touch as well, from Virginia Slims to the flip-top box. The ultimate rationale is always commercial: the consumption article in its design must already advertise itself. "Buy me, and ye shall find fulfillment of your dreams!" Of course, advertisements will further drive the point home, yet the object itself, in its very shape, must accommodate dreams and fantasies. Thus, American automobiles began to grow fins, gills, and a streamline of chromium in the 1950s; they held out a promise of freedom, of fish in the water, of spaceships on an intergalactic voyage. Radio sets in the 1920s, meant for little else than a fixed place on the mantelpiece, had a modernist streamline design, as if they too were ready to travel through time and space. Even when switched off, they continued whispering: "Buy me."

We hear that less clearly now. Radio sets and toasters are now on display in museums of industrial design, and every now and then individual designers will see their work honored by museums for modern art. Common objects like the Coca-Cola bottle or the Studebaker then suddenly reappear as the work of an individual maker, assuming the allure of a work of art. Once detached from commercial logic they lead a life of their own, ricocheting like pinballs in the imaginative space of modern American art. Coca-Cola bottles, Campbell's soup cans, and Ballantine beer cans all appear in the work of artists like Robert Rauschenberg, Andy Warhol, and Jasper Johns, changing face and meaning at every touch of the creative wand. Having returned as icons of Americanism in modern American art, these items previously had given expression to a different American modernism, shaping America's lunge into the culture of consumption, into a world of affluence and freedom of choice. "I shop, therefore I am," as one recent slogan puts it—a slogan that was itself recycled into art in a work by Barbara Kruger. The experience, or at least the promise, of freedom that U.S. citizens in their roles of consumer could share in became the central ingredient of America's modernity. Shopping became a reassertion of one's identity.

Strange things happened along the way. The aesthetics of the design of ordinary merchandise became a means to draw the average consumer's attention. The Ballantine beer can, which Jasper Johns reduced to its purely aesthetic form, with all the alienating effects this implied, had earlier in its life, in 1935, won a gold medal in the category "Metal Container." The advertisements that the famous marketing bureau of J. Walter Thompson had based on this event must have stuck in Johns's head. The advertisement shows a pair of cans on a pedestal, as if taking a bow on a stage, curtains raised, in front of a star-studded backdrop. Above, in capital letters, appear the words "Shelf Appeal." That, of course, was what it was all about: the ability of a particular product on densely packed store shelves to push aside the competition and to appeal to a picky public. Its design was one element of the product's "appeal," but other, more abstract associations could enhance the appeal in their own right. It was the task of advertising experts to produce such associations and to connect them to specific merchandise.

In a book appropriately entitled *Advertising the American Dream,*[1] Roland Marchand explores the intricate alchemy worked by the advertising wizards, transforming tangible products into abstract fantasies. His focus is on the 1920s and 1930s, when American advertising came of age. He refers to the advertising experts of that period as the "apostles of modernity," whom he portrays as being on a mission to introduce their confused contemporaries to the modern life-style of industrial America. They used their commercial messages on posters, in newspapers, in periodicals, and via the radio to bring order out of chaos and to project an image of progress. All those who wanted to partake of this brave, new world would have to follow their advice.

The America that emerges from the texts and images of advertising is highly one-sided; the "small town," the country, the small-scale America that had for so long defined the self-image of the American population, disappeared from view. The new America, with its skyscrapers, automobiles, and Hollywood-style entertainment, its flood of consumer knicknacks, its rapid changes of fads and fashions, now dominated the picture. Commercial messages became the new sacred texts for those who wanted to keep abreast of the times. The advertising wizards thus could pose as the high priests of modernity, as the true initiates who held the key to successful participation in the new America. They astutely played on the feelings of insecurity that many Americans experienced in their social contacts—indeed, not only astutely but also perfidiously. They made those feelings more acute for those who had them and even tried to instill a sense of insecurity in people who had never had it before. "Guilty!" one advertisement cries out; the accompanying photograph shows a man with his head down in embarrassment. He is surrounded by hands pointing fingers at him. He has dandruff. "End dandruff," the text goes on. "It offends all, this disgusting and common condition. Consequently, it affects your chances in love, society and business." Fortunately, help is at hand: a simple hair tonic will do the job.

Americans were bombarded with such messages. Their impact was double. Products were alleged to have qualities linked to the world of social success, in business and in love. At the same time, however, Americans were led to develop a sense of shame and embarrassment, an awareness of scrutinizing eyes and pointing fingers that truly made for a resocialization. They developed a social conscience, an awareness of constant scrutiny and judgment by others. They internalized the gaze of others as an inner radar device. More than ever before they were led to see themselves through the eyes of others. "The Eyes of Men . . . the Eyes of Women Judge your Loveliness every day," as an advertisement for Camay, "the soap of beautiful women," had it.

Only a hardened individualist could ignore such social control. Not only did such advertisements play on feelings of shame and inadequacy; they also conjured up a tempting world of luxury, elegance, and affluence that the proper mouthwash, hair tonic, razor blade, or what have you would open up to anyone. Like teenage boys daydreaming over girlie magazines, Americans could now vicariously partake of the joys of modern America simply by watching the imaginary world of the advertising pages. There they could behold women as they would never see them in real life, elongated, elegantly posing before stepping into a luxury vehicle, free and defiant. It was a world open to any woman that used Kotex, "The Safe Solution of Women's Greatest Hygienic Problem—Which 8 in 10 Better-Class Women Have Adopted." The new dreamwoman of the 1920s was epitomized in an advertisement in the *Strathmore Papers*: the imposing high-rise architecture on both sides of a busy avenue falls off sharply in perspective to render a dramatic V shape; emerging from that shape, against an empty sky, an elongated female figure strides forward, a rimless hat hugging her head snugly like a flyer's leather cap; she wears a long, elegant dress, the fur around her neck repeating the V shape. Quietly self-assured she emerges like a victorious heroine from the diminutive crowd behind her. The text exclaims, "Here SHE comes . . . your customer. Get her attention." The ad is meant as a call to advertise in the *Strathmore Papers,* but it does more than that. It provides a role model, an object of identification for a female public. It projects a view of the liberated woman in her role of "customer," of consumer. All those novices who break out in a claustrophobic cold sweat getting in and out of clothes in a changing room should follow her example. This woman is a commanding presence, the customer as king or queen. Above all the image conveys the sovereign joy of shopping, the exhilarating freedom offered by the department store and, later on, the shopping mall—the freedom to change identities, to be someone else, however briefly, simply by picking up some piece of merchandise and putting it back again. More recently authors such as John Fiske have playfully and inventively explored these aspects of freedom in the culture of consumption.[2] But in the 1920s this was all a novel experience. Advertisers still had to educate the public and introduce them to this brave, new world.

A much-used technique in this education was the social tableau, whose immediate purpose was always to provide a piece of merchandise with a social aura. The advertiser showed the public the particular situations in which a specific product was being used and the kind of people who used it. The advertisers thus attached the product to an imaginary world that consumers could enter by the simple act of purchase. In many of these tableaux women took center stage. This is not surprising; as early as the 1920s advertisers were aware that women accounted for around 80 percent of all consumer spending. To the extent that men play the central role in such tableaux, the setting is mostly related to their world of work. They appear sitting at their desks in their offices, and even when the setting has to do with leisure time, they always seem to radiate the social status of their work; even then they are recognizably businessmen or doctors. The scrutinizing eyes are those of colleagues or competitors. "Critical Eyes Are Sizing You Up Right Now," as one advertisement for shaving cream and aftershave lotion had it. "Let your face reflect confidence—not worry! It's the 'look' of you by which you are judged most often." An attractive male face—gleaming hair, a Clark Gable moustache, a muscular smile—projects the image of someone who, thanks to the recommended merchandise, has no fear confronting the jury of his peers. A different story is told in an advertisement by the associated American "Soap and Glycerine Producers." It shows a man engaged in a business interview, consumed by self-doubt. In anguish he looks over his shoulder to a ghostlike image of himself, his ruefully nail-biting conscience. "He had to fight himself so hard . . . he didn't put it over," the advertisement says. It goes on to say, "Oh why had he neglected the bath that morning, the shave, the change of linen? Under the other fellow's gaze it was hard to forget that cheap feeling." This man's cruel world is not without solace, however. The advertisement concludes on this pedagogical note: "There's self-respect in SOAP & WATER."

The strict separation between the worlds of work and the home that had occurred in the Victorian America of the late nineteenth century, mirroring the separation of the two sexes, still dominated the imagination of advertisers of the post–World War I era. Yet important shifts had occurred. The world of work and secular careers may still have been an exclusive male preserve, but no longer was the world of women entirely confined to the home, as had been the case in the late nineteenth century. In 1882, for instance, a color poster could still be produced offering the following social tableau: a party is going on in a large banquet hall. We see groups of formally attired people talking. It appears to be a reception, and the foreground reveals the occasion: dominating the scene is a newly wedded couple, turned toward the viewer. They take up more than the entire left half of the poster. The couple has briefly withdrawn from the festive crowd, for the groom wants to show the bride something. Arm in arm they stand, she in a long, white wedding dress, he in tails with the bridal bouquet in his right hand. In silent rapture she stands by his side, her head inclined devotedly toward him. Her gaze is focused on an object that he, with a gesture of his left hand, symbolically has unveiled: a Domestic-brand treadle sewing machine. Thus was her future unveiled to her.

In the 1920s marriage no longer tied women so strictly to the home. The advertisements of the period still show women in a sphere of life separate from that of men, yet the line of separation is no longer simply one between the private and the public, between the home and the larger world. The women represented in 1920s advertisements had begun to move outside the home. They are the defiant, demanding, and central characters on the new public stage that had emerged along with the culture of consumption and that had turned the world into one large shopping center. The walls surrounding the home had fallen away; a plethora of household appliances had made domestic chores less burdensome and time-consuming, thus creating a reservoir of free time to be spent outside the home. In the advertising version of this change household appliances had become the carriers of a promise of leisure and freedom.

The Domestic sewing machine did not yet hold out this promise. Of course, it was unmistakably a labor-saving device. It represented the mechanization of life that was affecting all of early modern America. Nonetheless, it offered no prospect of freedom outside the home. The white wedding dress would still have to give way to the apron and the head scarf. But early in our century things began to change. In 1908 General Electric's advertisements showed tableaux that presented electrical appliances as liberators from domestic servitude. They present two ladies engaged in relaxed conversation at a table, well-dressed, *bien soignées,* ready, so to speak, for an evening out, while an electric toaster is doing its work.

After World War I this trend continued. An advertisement for the American Laundry Machinery Company shows a young aproned housewife at the ironing board with a basketful of laundry on the floor. With a gesture of sadness she looks up from her work at a giant clock whose face displays three tableaux of leisure time. As these tableaux remind her, she could have been playing golf, reading her children a story, or seeing a play with her husband—all of them "might-have-been hours." The advertisement then asks, "how many of them are YOURS?" Women now had such options open to them, if only they chose to have their washing done for them and to make better use of "electricity and all the servants it puts at your command." The advertisement offers a view of freedom, yet it cannot entirely refrain from patronizing. At the bottom of the advertisement there are three little vignettes that, in a combination of words and visual images, show "how three women took the 'MIGHT' from their 'might-have-been hours.'" In one vignette a woman tells how, as the wife of a teacher, she now has more time for "social and civic obligations"; in the second a woman seated at a grand piano relates how she has more time to practice now and even has time to sing "in concerts, and at church." In the third vignette the woman has started a vegetable garden, informing us proudly about how much she is saving on the household budget.

The patronizing attempt at moral guidance is clearly there, but it is also an attempt to impose boundaries from the outside to the world of women. The advertising world was still a man's world and could not but reflect the dominant views regarding the separate spheres of life for men and women. It could not move too far ahead in its production of imaginary worlds that showed women liberated from the harness of social conventions. In its fantasy images of the new culture of consumption, however, advertising could not do without the iconography of freedom and liberation. Try as it might to give a conservative moral twist to its messages, its entire thrust worked mostly to undermine social conventions. To the extent that advertisers can be seen as high priests at all, it is as high priests of modernity, not of conservatism. They represented an America in its new guise of one large consumer market, capable not only of fulfilling any dream or desire through the goods it had to offer but also of creating those very dreams and desires. In fact, in the 1920s economic theory opened up to this new phenomenon of "induced demand." Through advertising consumers were led to act on cues and to experience needs that had never guided their purchasing behavior before.

Like a fertilized egg, America underwent a process of partition and duplication in the 1920s. It began to produce its virtual mirror image of a dreamworld, promising liberation from all the frustration, shame, restraint, and convention of everyday life. The automobile was arguably the central dream object in this mirror world. It took Americans out of the small-scale world that until then had been the setting for their individual lives. America became one large space in which they could freely move. Americans could once again, at least in their dreams, appropriate the larger space of their republic. In addition to the automobile, other instruments of the new world of consumption contributed to this expansion of imaginary space. From the late nineteenth century onward the big mail-order companies distributed their hefty catalogs to the far corners of the land. The most isolated homesteader in Nebraska on his or her meager farm could feel elated by the flood of merchandise that Sears and Montgomery Ward had ready for shipment in their Chicago warehouses. Entire settlements in the newly populated West had been created using prefab houses ordered from catalogs. Small town America had become hooked on the visual riches of America's dream mirror. The most trenchant contemporary study of this new addiction is undoubtedly the Lynds' classic book *Middletown*. The title is a well-chosen alias for Muncie, Indiana. The Lynds wanted to show how the modernization of America, which one normally tends to associate with its large urban centers, affected life in an average small town.

If we want to define the one central characteristic of American modernity at the time, it would be this dream of space and freedom. The dream had its antecedents, of course, as I have already shown; it is in a sense as old as the history of discovery, colonization, and the moving frontier. What was radically new, however, was the connection of this old dream to an America waking up to the consumption revolution. The high priests of American advertising were potent new agents in the transformation of this dream. Techniques of advertising that in the late nineteenth century had often relied on little more than densely printed information about the technical qualities of a product now developed into the illusionism of the trickster. From a simple assignment to bring commercial goods to the attention of the larger public, advertising had turned into a manipulation of human dreams and desires. In their creation of imaginary worlds advertisers forever changed the conventions by which people defined and experienced their identity and subjectivity. The boundaries of everyday life, with its set patterns of interaction and social roles, that had served for so long as a matrix for every individual's self-image gave way to the larger imaginary world of the culture of consumption. A totally new space was opened up for people's senses of identity, for their imaginary identification with other people and their worlds.

This particular appearance of America's modernity, with its linkage of dreams of freedom and space to a plethora of material goods, deeply affected the way that Europeans imagined America. When Wells, Duhamel, Huizinga, and the other critics whom I mentioned in the first chapter addressed the subject of American culture, seeing it—either with concern or enthusiasm—as Europe's future, what they had in mind was always an America as the citadel of modernity, in its blend of technological prowess, urban life, and commercially induced dreams. If we accept such views, we run the risk of being historically shortsighted, for well before its advent as an industrial giant, America had stood in the light of modernity, on precisely the grounds that I mentioned before. For much longer than our century "America" as a European dream had been the site of freedom and space. For much longer it had been the projection screen for a European hankering after a modernity offering escape from the straitjacket of Europe's social forms. After all, did not Alexis de Tocqueville, in the preface to his analysis of American democracy, make the point that what had drawn him toward America was his sense that in America he could see Europe's future? What had drawn him in particular was the modernity of America as a large-scale republican experiment in ordering space and freedom. What drew many millions of immigrants toward America after him was something similar. It may not have been as openly political as in Tocqueville's case, yet it was not unrelated. Many were moved by the dream of finding a new, independent identity in the open space of America. Moreover, had not an earlier French visitor and temporary resident, Crèvecoeur, argued that all immigrants coming to America's shores shed their European subservience, if not servitude? "Here they are become men."

America as empty space, the epic America of the frontier, America as a mythical West, had long before the consumption revolution been turned into a symbol of modernity. The West as a beckoning yonder had kept alive the dream, in faraway corners of Europe, of a life lived in freedom and independence. As the promise of a new world and a new era, it could vie with contemporary utopian views offered by Marxism or similar emancipation movements. Posters produced for shipping lines, emigration societies, and land-development agencies contributed their imagery to the continuing construction of America as the site of freedom and space. To many that particular image, rather than the feats of technology performed in the opening up of American space, must have represented the attractive modernity of America. Nevertheless, technology was not entirely absent from this image; after all, for the first time in history a huge migration took place with the aid of modern means of transportation such as steamships, railroads, and telegraph lines. Technology thus could add certain features of modernity to the great migration toward America, toward the West. Still, America itself, the West itself, took central stage in this mythical view of modernity.

If this constitutes the central appeal of "America" as an image, we need not be surprised at the craving for material that could manifest the image. Chromolithographs, photographs, and stereographs suggesting three-dimensionality all served to still this hunger. They allowed people to move beyond the limited horizons of their daily lives and to enter an imaginary space, a fantasy world. They offered reality and illusion at the same time.

Nor need we be surprised that such pictures soon were turned into advertising tools. If images of the West (or rather, of America as one huge space) could trigger fantasies of modernity and liberty, common merchandise might hope to benefit from an association with such images. Today everyone is familiar with the American West as "Marlboro Country," resulting from the successful wedding of a cigarette brand and the Marlboro Man. As early as a century ago, however, advertisements were trying to bring about such a union. A colorful 1860 poster advertises the Washoe brand of the Christian and Lee Tobacco Company from Richmond, Virginia. No tobacco leaf, cigar, or pipe is in sight. What does appear are images of the American West—western horsemen, far horizons—grouped around a medallion that pictures the goddess Columbia draped in the American flag, an eagle, a globe with the Western hemisphere turned forward, and a pot brimming with gold coins. The American West appears as a vision of plenty. Another poster from the same period advertises Westward Ho smoking tobacco. Its very name ties the tobacco to the beckoning call of the West, yet the producer, G. W. Langhorne and Company from Lynchburg, Virginia, did not leave it at that. The poster shows an allegorical female figure, a version of Columbia with stark Indian features, feathers in her hair, her extended hand holding forth a calumet, and her body, save her breasts, wrapped in the Stars and Stripes. This is not Europa abducted by Jupiter; this is America, impetuously galloping forth on elk-back: "Westward Ho!"

Apparently, well before the decade of the "roaring twenties," commerce had appropriated the allegorical repertoire of the American Dream. The images that through techniques of mechanical reproduction now flooded across the country were endlessly rearranged to render new symbolic messages. The West as a realm for the imagination could connect with the world of trite consumption goods such as tobacco or cigarettes. Advertising developed into an art of symbolic alchemy that has retained its potency ever since. The symbolic connection that advertisers sought to establish hinged on the concept of "freedom." This linking of evocative images of American freedom and space tended to work best with leisure-time articles, such as cigarettes, beer, an automobile or a motorbike, or a pair of blue jeans. Consumption, leisure time, and freedom thus became inextricably interwoven. Even today the concept of America can be counted on to trigger the latter association, the one with freedom. The iconography of America has become international. Italian jeans manufacturers now advertise their wares in Germany on posters depicting Arizona's Monument Valley. The German cigarette brand West mounted an international advertising campaign whose central metaphors revolve around the American West. The Dutch nonalcohol beer Stender used the imaginary West of American road movies for its television commercials, which portrayed brief encounters at gas stations in an empty western setting, an exchange of glances between the sexes, the half-inviting, half-ironic sizing up, the beginning of erotic tension. The release of tension occurs, surprisingly, when, irrespective of gender, the man or the woman, in gleaming black leather and in the true macho style of the West, flips the top of a bottle of Stender and takes off again on a shiny motorbike, into the empty distance.

America's national symbols and myths have been translated into an international iconographic language, a visual lingua franca. They have been turned into free-floating signifiers, internationally understood, free for everyone to use. Nevertheless, it is only a replay on an international scale of what previously occurred in the United States. Given the characteristic American bent for disassembling whatever presents itself as an organically coherent whole, only to reassemble it differently, this American leadership role need not surprise us. In the production of American commercial messages this same cultural bent has been at work, removing symbols from their historical context and rearranging them in novel configurations. The appropriate metaphor may be that of the Lego construction, which uses the individual pieces as "empty signifiers," combining them into ever-changing meaningful structures. Commerce and advertising—the topic of this chapter—are but one area where these rituals of cultural transformation are at work. Consumption goods as well can freely change their meaning, appearing in ever-changing configurations, furnishing a realm of virtual reality, turning into simulacra at the hands of the wizards of advertising. They become true phantasms set free by the human imagination. No bastion of conventional order is immune to this erosive freedom. In this area as well one can discern a moving American frontier affecting an ever-increasing number of social conventions with its "deconstructing" logic.

The last frontier in this connection may well be the area of conventional views of gender. As I already pointed out, by the 1920s the conventional view of the female world had already begun to shift. Recently the American imagination has moved to produce a much more radical disassemblage and rearrangement of the attributes that previously defined our views of what is typically male or female. Americans themselves have come up with an appropriate term for this: gender bending. Early examples of this process occurred in space fantasies, on television or in film, in productions like *Star Trek* or *Alien II*. These examples present characters with a confusing array of both female and male attributes; the enemy computer brain in *Alien II* is called "Mother," whereas the film's female lead copes in stereotypically male ways. More recently a "road movie" was released—*Thelma and Louise*—with all the usual characteristics of the genre save one: the two leading characters, both women, displayed forms of behavior previously common only to male characters. In many areas of contemporary mass culture one can see this rearranging of gender attributes at work: in the public image of pop idols, creating androgynous personae, or in the presentation of gender in television commercials and video clips. A telling recent example is a commercial for Levi's 501 shown on Dutch television. A young, dark-skinned woman, invitingly dressed with a bare midriff, is shown taking a New York cab. While the driver is ogling her in his rearview mirror, his lips suggestively moving a toothpick back and forth as if part of a mating ritual, she coolly adds a few final touches to her makeup. But then the tables are turned. What gives the driver a start and brings his cab to a full stop is the sound of an electric razor and the sight of his passenger shaving. The last shot is of the passenger walking away, the victor in another battle of the sexes, the jeans as snug and inviting as ever. As the text reminds us, in case we did not know already: "Cut for Men Since 1875." The pieces of Lego have fallen apart and are being rearranged in ever-changing combinations.

■ ■ ■

European observers have long been struck by the freedom that the American imagination allows itself with the conventional guises of reality. The world in which Americans live has a large admixture of fantasy images and has therefore struck Europeans as unreal, if not fake and inauthentic. In its ongoing rearrangement of attributes, meanings, and chains of association, America presented itself to them as one large display of unreality, like so many faces of the moon. For the most part Europeans tended to reject America on this ground; occasionally they let themselves get carried away, enraptured by America's free multiplication of simulacra. As in a Potemkin village, reality had gone into hiding behind the props of unreality. In its endless replicas America presents itself as a consumption article; it promises "excitement," the transient fulfillment of dreams of freedom and omnipotence. Exhilarated visiting consumers let themselves be hurled through a Disney World replica of the mining frontier, buckled up in what is purportedly a runaway ore train. The true history of misery and grandeur, of labor conflicts, of racial clashes at the real mining frontier, has been cut from the picture. It has all been turned into "good, clean fun" available at a price. It has become a consumption good.

In that sense the logic of commerce has given a potent impulse to a mental mode that is more generally characteristic of American culture. The ambivalence that many Europeans (as well as many American cultural critics) feel toward it is understandable. Indeed, the erosive, modularizing approach of Americans toward cultural forms in general does have its reinvigorating and liberating side. Americans are less respectful of established cultural forms and show less filial piety toward them. They tend more easily to take a fresh look at things. That freshness of approach does have its price, and many are the critics of American culture who deem the price too high. In the final analysis, however, this will always be a matter of individual appraisal and affinity. In the appraisal one shall always in the end have to come up with a balance of gains and losses. There will be those who will favor the Americans and what they, modularizing and recombining, have brought in terms of cultural innovation. But there will always be others who are left with a prevailing sense of loss, especially in those cases where America, on commercial grounds, has duplicated itself into simulacra while blotting out reality.

Let me offer one illustration of this. A few years ago I finally got around to making my pilgrimage to Holland, Michigan, an absolute must for a Dutch Americanist. I knew the history of its settlement, of its early struggles, disasters, and eventual success as a part of America's ethnic mosaic. I finally wanted to see for myself. I arrived in the center of town, finding myself in what looked like an attractive and rather typically American "Main Street." To my surprise I had no problem parking my car. Business on either side of the street seemed to be in a somewhat anemic state. There was an art gallery, a coffee shop, and other rather marginal enterprises. Many shops were vacant or boarded up. Main Street business was hanging on by the skin of its teeth. Where was everybody? I walked around for a while, but there was not much that could keep me long. I left the town by a road different from the one on which I had come, and all of a sudden, there it was: the replica that had eclipsed the real Holland, Michigan. A huge shopping mall came into view, its parking space filled to brim, a crowd of shoppers milling about in the open space between the buildings. There was a windmill, in one corner of the complex there were little brick houses along a diminutive canal, and there was a drawbridge; along the walkways, there was the mall, its walls green, its roofs red. Everything was done in plastic-age material. The colors were off: this was not the real green of Dutch sideboards or the real red of Dutch tiles. In a pancake house the waitresses wore mock folk attire. Thus, for purely commercial reasons, Holland, Michigan, had chosen to cut itself off from its history. It had replicated itself in a fake rearrangement of vaguely Dutch ingredients. It had turned itself into a mock ethnic spectacle, a piece of merchandise, a product of the commercial imagination. Behind this facade was the real Main Street, dying. What had historically grown had been shed like a cocoon, in exchange not for an imago but for a mere image.

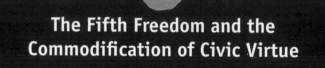

5

The Fifth Freedom and the
Commodification of Civic Virtue

In his State of the Union address to Congress in 1941, President Frank-
lin D. Roosevelt succinctly expressed four principles that he said should
guide America's action on the global stage. They have become known
as the Four Freedoms: the freedom of speech and expression, the freedom of worship, the freedom from want, and the freedom from fear.
America had not yet entered the war, but Roosevelt had long since seen
the gathering storm. Politically he was not yet able to declare war and
to join the battle against the Axis powers, yet his address had the force
of a rallying cry, a moral call to intervene in world politics in the great
Wilsonian tradition. Wilson, in World War I, had seen fit to cast his war
aims in terms of peace, explaining to his fellow Americans that America had joined the battle "to make the world safe for democracy." In a
similar vein Roosevelt called on his compatriots to fulfill such a moral
mission once again. His freedoms were redolent of the spirit of the classic democratic liberties, yet the wording had been adapted to fit contemporary needs. The last freedom in particular—the freedom from
fear—called forth a world that showed the ugly face of the wars in
Europe and Asia. Roosevelt envisioned a new world where people
would be made safe from fear by "a worldwide reduction of armaments
to such a point and in such a thorough fashion that no nation will be in
a position to commit an act of physical aggression against any neighbor—anywhere in the world." His words breathed an optimism that
was typical of Roosevelt, if not of America as a whole. In other respects,

however, they were typically American, for instance, in their sense of a moral mission as much as in their universalist, global reach. The words "anywhere in the world" gained in urgency through rhetorical reiteration. Each of the four freedoms that World War II threatened to curtail was in need of active protection. Three times Roosevelt referred to this need as existing "everywhere in the world"; the fourth and final time—as if he wanted to leave no doubt—he used the words "anywhere in the world." Anywhere, wherever it might be. The words preserved their inspirational potency until after the war, when in fact America would be a manifest force to be felt everywhere in the world.

Roosevelt's address is a beautiful specimen of America's political culture. The oratorical art as an instrument of political inspiration has a long tradition in America. One could write a political history of the United States purely on the basis of a series of famous public addresses. They tend to strike many Europeans as a trifle old-fashioned. In many contemporary political cultures in Europe there is a tendency to shun the classical tools of the public orator: the pounding reiteration, the striking metaphor, the rising vocal pitch, the forceful gesture. Many in Europe tend to lower their oratorical profile. As a consequence Europe's political history has no abundance of famous words comparable to America's. America in that respect still stands unabashedly in a long tradition of republicanism, in the literal sense of a res publica, with all that entails in the sense of a sphere of public debate, free discussion, and style of public discourse.

For all that, the rhetorical techniques of democratic politics are not necessarily loftier than the sales techniques of a market vendor. Quite appropriately the metaphor of the marketplace has long been applied to politics. Like vendors hawking wares, politicians too try to soar above the hue and cry of the public agora. At times they succeed without apparent effort; then one politician's single voice manages to subdue the roar of other voices. Abraham Lincoln was a master of this art. His language could bring the market to a hushed silence. It could inspire in his auditors a sense of transcending themselves in an experience of unity and atonement. His words have become a living part of the American political tradition, a usable past of inspired sayings.

In the very year that Roosevelt gave his rhetorical best to the proclamation of the Four Freedoms, the American composer Aaron Copland put Lincoln's words to music in his *Lincoln Portrait*. In much the same way that Roosevelt, with ever-more resounding echo, called his compatriots to the defense of freedoms everywhere in the world, Lincoln's urgent peroration to his Gettysburg Address soars above the music: "we here highly resolve that the dead shall not have died in vain, that this nation, under God, shall have a new birth of freedom; and that government of the people, by the people, and for the people shall not perish from the earth." There is an unforgettable television recording of a performance of the *Lincoln Portrait* with the composer as vocal soloist and his former student Leonard Bernstein conducting. Copland was no Abraham Lincoln: timid, small, unassuming, he does not look the part of an orator. Even so, he manages to rise above himself when, with his thin voice, he brings the text to its climax. He pays tribute to Lincoln, but above all he sings the praises of the high ideals of democracy. The market hearkens in silence.

Winged words are the most elevated form of the slogan. Previously, when I referred to Roosevelt's address, I used the phrase *rallying cry.* I purposely avoided the word *slogan.* It might have been too reminiscent there of the world of commerce and its sales pitches. Nonetheless, the two expressions are more closely linked than may appear at first sight. The word *slogan* goes back to an old Gaelic word that means "battle cry." But more than etymology links the words. Like market vendors, politicians must be able to sell their goods, to draw a crowd and get their votes. Politicians must, in other words, be able to sell themselves well. Like the commercial message, the politician's language will search for the catching phrase, the lasting slogan. The politician must find words that will go on to lead their own lives, as newspaper headlines, sound bites, or the name for an era. Thus Roosevelt was the man of the "New Deal" in the years of the Great Depression; he became the man of the "Four Freedoms" at the time when America had to reconsider its role in the world.

A slogan is successful only once it has become common coinage, when it has penetrated into everyday language and pops up in a great many different settings of mass communication. Generally, for this to happen the ideas caught in a slogan must already, in some indistinct form, be "in the air." In the case of Roosevelt's Four Freedoms we can still trace that connection. He did not invent them by himself, although the verbal form in which he cast his four freedoms was undeniably his. During a press conference of July 5, 1940, half a year prior to his State of the Union address, improvisation led Roosevelt to come up with a first recorded version of the four freedoms (of "information," "religion," and "expression" and from "fear"). He concluded his impromptu response by asking, "Does that cover it pretty well?" The interviewing journalist was not quite satisfied: "Well, I had a fifth in mind which you might describe as 'freedom from want'—free trade, opening up trade?" "Yes," replied Roosevelt, "that is true. I had that in mind but forgot it. . . . That is the fifth, very definitely."[1] For a moment it looked as if Roosevelt was stuck with five freedoms, but a little reshuffling eventually reduced the number again to four.

Why that magic number? A likely explanation is that the "Four Freedoms"—not unlike pop music groups in our day—had already acquired a relatively wide currency at the time of the New York World's Fair of 1939–40. There, alongside the main concourse that led up to an imposing statue of George Washington, stood four huge allegorical figures that together became known as "the Four Freedoms." The federal government had commissioned the work from the sculptor Leo Friedlander. The 1939 World's Fair motto was "The World of Tomorrow." The fair's purpose was to give its many visitors a view of the world that among other things highlighted the achievements of the New Deal. The focus then was still on the domestic achievements: the increased role for the government and the welfare state features of its legislative programs. By 1940, however, attention shifted to the outside world. The fair's motto then read, "For Peace and Freedom." The official poster showed the statue of Washington; behind him, like the wings of an angel of peace, a plethora of many nations' flags unfurled. Roosevelt paid an official visit to the fair and like the many millions of visitors must have become aware of the symbolic potency of the "Four Freedoms."[2]

The group of statues on the fairground was meant to express more than just freedom in a general sense. They were not simply the fourfold replica of the one Statue of Liberty in New York harbor. Friedlander's assignment was to give each of the four statues a distinct allegorical meaning and to make them the separate representations of the freedoms of the press, religion, expression, and assembly. Roosevelt, one might say, picked up his ideas in the public domain; he then gave his own individual twist to them, producing a version that again entered the public domain.[3]

This was due not only to Roosevelt's mastery of public communication. In popularizing Roosevelt's Four Freedoms once again an artist played a leading role—not a sculptor this time but a painter and master draftsman: Norman Rockwell. He was already widely popular among the general public for his covers for the *Saturday Evening Post*, where he had put his artistry in the service of the nostalgic representation of an America as many were wont to remember it, an America of small-town life, of secure and happy families with their little dramas, tragedies, and joys. He was the right man to render Roosevelt's rallying call in a toned-down, slightly more reassuring version.

Roosevelt's own advisers had already balked at the global implications of Roosevelt's call. When, in his White House office, he had dictated a version of the Four Freedoms that differed only in detail from the final version, his adviser Harry Hopkins had this immediate reaction: "That covers an awful lot of territory, Mr. President. I don't know how interested Americans are going to be in the people of Java." In this particular version, however, Roosevelt referred to "freedom everywhere in the world" only in the case of the first two freedoms. It is typical of his willfulness that in his final version he decided to have this universalist ring voiced four times.[4]

Rockwell, however, chose to ignore these wider echoes. In four oil paintings based on carefully arranged group photographs—a technique that he developed in the 1930s—he reduced the four freedoms to the familiar scale of small-town America, with its civic and democratic virtues. His work captured the same unbending America of the "common man" that was caught in the documentary photography of the depression, that was celebrated in Aaron Copland's "Fanfare for the Common Man," and that had given its populist inspiration to Frank Capra movies such as *Mr. Deeds Goes to Town, You Can't Take It with You,* and *Mr. Smith Goes to Washington.* A similar populist sentiment pervades Rockwell's rendering of the four freedoms.

■ ■ ■

With the first painting, *Freedom of Speech,* the viewer looks down from an oblique angle on a small group of people. They are clearly only a segment of a larger gathering. Row on row of citizens have assembled on simple wooden benches for a political meeting. Their faces are raised attentively, not, as one might expect, toward "tonight's invited speaker" but toward one of their own. Some have half turned on their bench to have a better look. From their midst a man has stood up, his hands firmly planted on the back of the bench in front of him. He wears simple worker's clothes. He has the rugged "good looks" of the populist heroes in Frank Capra's films, of Gary Cooper, Gregory Peck, or Jimmy Stewart. He has stood up to vent his opinion, to exercise his freedom of speech.

For the second painting, *Freedom of Worship,* Rockwell used the photographic technique of the close-up, once again looking down, "zooming in" from a position above his subjects. The painting shows the faces and hands of people immersed in prayer, "each according to the dictates of his own conscience," as the headline to the painting reminds us. The picture gives poignant expression to America's traditional freedom of religion. No American will have trouble reading this message.

The third painting illustrates freedom from want. According to Roosevelt, this meant, "translated into world terms, . . . economic understandings which will secure to every nation a healthy peacetime life for its inhabitants—everywhere in the world." Rockwell translates this back into the more familiar terms of a traditional Thanksgiving dinner enjoyed at home in one's domestic circle. The painting shows several generations gathered around the table, whose rectangular shape is projected across the canvas starting from the lower left- and right-hand corners. To the left and right are people caught in the course of jocular exchange. At the head of the table stands an elderly, rotund man, merrily watching his aproned and equally rotund wife bend forward to set on the table the meal's pièce de résistance, a beautiful, shiny turkey. That was the way in which Americans may have wished to picture Roosevelt's world, free from want to be sure, but first of all familiar, homely, cozy, and secure.

Even in his fourth painting Rockwell manages to keep Roosevelt's evil outside world of war and wanton destruction at arm's length—almost literally so. Along the entire central axis of the painting a father stands erect in shirtsleeves and suspenders. His left side is turned toward the viewer. To his right his wife lovingly bends forward to tuck in their two children, who are already asleep. Their day's play is done; a doll lies face up on the floor, as if orphaned. That, one might say, is freedom from fear: having your parents watch over you when you are asleep. There is only one faint echo of the threatening outside world. In his left hand, "at arm's length," the father holds a newspaper. Partial headlines are visible: "Bombings ki . . ." and "Horror Hit . . ." Rockwell has translated Roosevelt's concern about the wider world into the concern of parents about the future of their children.

Rockwell's representations of Roosevelt's ideas gained wide currency. Millions of reproductions of the four paintings were made and, under government and private auspices, distributed across the world. The U.S. Treasury Department sent the four original oil paintings on a tour of sixteen cities in the United States, where they drew 1,222,000 visitors and contributed to the sale of $132,999,537 of bonds to sustain the war effort. With the help of Rockwell's images Americans could picture America's interests in an Allied victory in World War II.

Rockwell himself had found his mission in life. For the duration of the war he put his pictorial talents in the service of the war effort; he produced narrative illustrations of troop transports, food rationing, and the homecoming of soldiers. "G.I. Joe"—the common soldier, the simple American boy who had a job to do—assumed under Rockwell's hands a face in which people could recognize the familiar features of their beloved, their sons, their relatives, or boys from the neighborhood. Seven different covers of the *Saturday Evening Post* showed Rockwell's impressions of G.I. Joe's return to the family fold. On calendars, on posters, and in advertisements Rockwell continued to show the world in its impact on the homefront. Before the war he had been mostly a commercial artist, drawing advertisements and magazine covers; during the war he used his popular appeal to promote the common interest, the res publica, in a time of distress. His particular talent was to render such abstract issues as the point and purpose of a world war in pictures that could appeal to the many. He translated America's abstract and ideal battle cries into the picture language of a mass culture. He pasted his posters over America's political marketplace as if it were a commercial market to be addressed via billboards. His art, during the war or for that matter before or after the war, was never high art. A talented craftsman, he produced middlebrow art at best, and he probably did not aim any higher. At the same time, however, what he did during the war and shortly after, in his feverish documentary production, certainly ranks high along that other scale of distinction in the United States: it was a true specimen of democratic art in the great Whitmanesque vein.

■ ■ ■

For Rockwell, it was only a small step from commercial art to art that was politically committed. His iconography remained the same even though the portent of his messages changed. As I pointed out before, this was not unusual: the cultures of the political and the economic markets smoothly shade into one another. This tendency appears most clearly in an advertisement by the Hoover Vacuum Cleaner Company in a 1944 issue of the *Saturday Evening Post*. It is an illustrated ad in the style of Norman Rockwell. Both the setting and the faces are familiar: an old woman, a middle-aged man, and a young girl—"people from the neighborhood." They look upward toward a beam of light; providence, if not the good provider, is smiling on them. In their arms they hold an abundance of packages, all of them gift-wrapped. This is Norman Rockwell country, but with a difference: Rockwell's mythical small-town people, carriers of democratic virtue, now appear in the guise of Americans as consumers. Three years after Roosevelt decided that there were four freedoms, not five, the Hoover advertisement reminded Americans that "the Fifth Freedom is Freedom of Choice." If America had joined the struggle to safeguard democratic values, then this implied safeguarding the freedom of choice. By a simple semantic sleight of hand the (con)text—or should I say the "con"text?—of the advertisement shifted the meaning of freedom of choice: the signified was no longer the realm of politics but the citizen as consumer. Again spheres of freedom smoothly shaded into one another. The commercial art that Rockwell had put in the service of politics now reclaimed its rights. Political freedom and economic freedom were indissolubly linked.

Many European theorists of democracy, from John Stuart Mill to Karl Schumpeter, had argued this all along. According to Schumpeter, one can analytically distinguish the spheres of politics and economics, but he could think of no historical case where freedom in the political realm had coexisted with a centrally controlled economy. The conservative thinker Friedrich van Hayek turned this insight into his central polemical proposition. Every attempt at centrally coordinating and planning a national economy cannot but usher in political serfdom. American followers such as Milton Friedman eagerly adopted this conclusion.

But average Americans did not really need such theoretical underpinning. They had always lived by the practical tenet that freedom evidently implied the freedom of enterprise, production, advertising, and consumption. The dream eventually to be able "to set up shop on your own" had always turned them away from socialism and class consciousness. The German "academic socialist" Werner Sombart, in his famous 1904 treatise "Why Is There No Socialism in the United States," had already argued this. Admittedly, the scale in which the culture of consumption penetrated the United States during the 1920s was unprecedented. Never before in the Puritanism of a production-oriented society had America condoned the principle of installment buying.

From the 1920s on, however, a consumptive urge captured American culture, spurred on by advertising; from then on the country blithely ran up its consumptive debts. It was a clear break with a cultural tradition emphasizing austerity and thrift, but it was no break with established cultural norms regarding freedom of choice as applying equally to the political and the economic market.

■ ■ ■

If both markets do indeed follow a similar logic, then it need not surprise us when marketing techniques move freely from one market to the other. As I have shown, the freedom of choice, hailed as the fifth freedom, changed from a political to an economic pitch in 1944. That change is only one example of a sales technique that had come into its own in the 1920s. At that time advertisers had already begun to use a variety of narrative ploys to sell their products. One of those was the parable of the "Democracy of Goods." Pleasures of consumption that until recently had been the sole privilege of the moneyed classes were now within everybody's reach, if people simply bought product X or Y. Even if the service of a maid was beyond people's means, young housewives could still keep their hands soft by using Ivory soap.

This democratizing logic applied to more than just pleasures; ailments fell equally within its sway. One 1920s advertisement shows a gentleman aboard his yacht, in relaxed conversation with a beautiful young lady. The text reminds us, "You'd like to be in this man's shoes . . . yet he has 'ATHLETE'S FOOT.'" Rich and poor alike were visited by the same ailments, by athlete's foot, body odors, and bad breath, but both could avail themselves equally of the same cheap remedies. The average American had access to a life of luxury and ease of which not even the kings of old had dreamed. The best things in life may not have been entirely free, yet they had come within everyone's reach for a slight fee. Thus, the same promise of equality that had reigned supreme in America's political creed had taken hold within the realm of consumption.

Ideas could also move the other way, from the world of advertising and commercial promotion toward the realm of politics. For American consumers, a new world had already opened up in which tangible goods, ranging from soft soap to automobiles, engaged in ever-changing relationships with free-floating signifiers, in a round robin of dream and reality directed by the wizards of advertising. Every single piece of commerce could be turned into a dream, and every dream could be commodified and merchandised. There was no compelling reason why this commercial logic would stop at the borderline separating the economic and the political markets. Whether it was a matter of persons or programs, of candidates for public office or political parties, they were no different than merchandise in that they too had to be sold to a larger public. Like passive merchandise, they could be connected at the whim of marketing wizards with any range of signifiers; like wax, they could be molded into any public image. The era of blithe amateurism in which the market vendor sold marvel concoctions to a gullible crowd and the politician engaged in whistle-stop campaigns to address the electorate was long gone. With the advent of modern mass-communication media the techniques of public representation, of either commercial or political merchandise, had changed drastically. Selling had become a science—or rather, the world of advertising had arrogated the aura of the doctor's white coat and the status of a professional guild that went with it. Nevertheless, the wary observer could not help feeling that behind the pompous display of depth psychology and research techniques lurked the cynical features of W. C. Fields as the quintessential traveling quack, the impersonation of the great American confidence man.

Ever since the 1920s the professionalization of advertising had proceeded apace. The trend culminated with the advent of television and its potential of deep market penetration. Only then could a modern, if not postmodern, America fully come into its own, as the veritable hall of mirrors in which it could endlessly duplicate into virtual images of itself, spawning the manifold simulacra that so fascinate contemporary (mostly European) semioticians. Only then could a rule of cultural transformation that may have always been at the heart of the American way with culture, but that now was given free rein, fully assert itself. It is a transformation that ruthlessly eats away all established cultural boundaries between high and low, between genres, cutting up narrative flow and organic cohesion and leaving a mere array of disjointed elements reduced to the homogeneity of blocks of broadcasting time for sale to any bidder and any purpose. News flash and commercial message, reporting and entertainment, information and propaganda—all were equally modules of broadcasting time, reassembled at will into a wild jumble.

The commercial rationale was only one factor of this development. It turned broadcasting time into a commodity; it transformed the television audience into consumers. The ratings became the single quantitative measure of a television program's success. Instead of choosing the role of cultural guardian that many European governments assumed in granting broadcasting licenses, the American government opted for passive restraint. Commerce was given free range. We cannot begin to understand this unless we consider that in this area, too, there was an underlying belief in a freedom of choice, a belief in the abundance that the free market could deliver only if left to itself. As a consequence television mushroomed in the United States, while in Europe, with its regulated broadcasting systems, people had to make do with only one or two programs that aired from seven to eleven in the evening.

In yet other ways America's cultural habits tended to facilitate the modularizing effect of American television. Americans had already developed forms of team sports, such as baseball and football, that are characterized by fragmentation rather than flow. They are an assemblage of self-contained "plays" that easily can be interspersed with different elements, such as commercial breaks. Similarly, the narrative structure of television drama, soap operas, and situation comedies reflects this reduction to self-contained scenes, toward the fragmentation into an intrinsic serial installment logic. It is meant to leave the viewers sufficiently spellbound so as not to lose them during the commercial breaks. The use of such narrative techniques predates the television era and goes back to the cliffhanger effects of prewar, moviegoing days.[5]

Whatever the specific instance, these techniques are all equally illustrative of an underlying modularization, of a freedom of reassembling disjunct elements. This modularizing logic appears not only in the splicing of simultaneous acts of communication, such as newscasting, entertainment, and advertising. It is also at work within each of the constituent elements. Thus, for instance, commercial messages often incorporate techniques that go back to the days of the printed poster. Imaginary worlds are conjured up in which tangible consumption goods engage in intricate connections with a world of dreams, desires, and fantasies. The conceptual realm created by the commercial message consists of the imaginative rearrangement of associative elements. No matter how illusory the result, its suggestion of reality is enhanced by a medium like television because of that medium's claim to be a merely objective window on the world. It is one of the many ironies of this medium. On the one hand it is the modern version of the spyglass, extending our view while we remain unseen; it holds the promise of an unprecedented visual quantum leap. In fact, it resembles more closely the mirror in *Alice in Wonderland*: slouched in front of our television set, we in fact go through the looking glass, entering a world that no longer listens to the conventions and logic of our familiar, everyday world. Whether it is news flashes from the Gulf War that look more like Star Wars fabrications or the presentation of the "new and improved" Chevrolet, what we see are images cut and arranged according to the logic of television presentation. It is a logic far removed from any full and complex reality. Our heads thus are filled with mere morsels of the world, leaving an illusion that we have been witnessing reality.

This potential of television was apparent early on to those masters of illusion, the advertising experts. They could move effortlessly beyond the confines of the strictly commercial message and offer their services to the actors on the stage of American politics. Again, television might seem to be the ideal new medium, in the age of mass democracy, for reviving a democratic process as small-town America had known it. Rather than shaking your hand on the sidewalk, candidates could now come right into your living room. Once again candidates could hope, through television, to address the individual citizens in a contemporary version of face-to-face contact. The vast, anonymous, democratic public—once ominously represented by Washington Irving as a "headless ghost"—could now be approached by an army of "talking heads" on television, alternating with video clips and commercials, inviting the audience to join them in a new symbiosis. Yet many sobering lessons were to be learned. Under the relentless scrutiny of the television camera's cold eye, politicians became painfully aware of their many unguarded moments, of facial tics and nervous perspiration that, more than anything they actually said, determined the way in which the public perceived them. Thus, Richard Nixon, looking wan and unshaven, came across as a shady character in his famous television confrontation with his opponent, John F. Kennedy. The impression was merely visual, mediated through television; radio listeners were left with an entirely different view of how the debate had gone.

Shortly before, during the 1950s, a widespread concern had become manifest in the United States regarding the reduction of democratic politics to a matter of mere presentation and manipulation. In learned symposia on mass culture and the mass media, intellectuals expressed alarm at such corruption of democratic politics. In one of the classic books from this era, *The Lonely Crowd*, sociologist David Riesman discussed the problems of a viable public opinion in a society that, like America's, found itself under a constant barrage of messages and calls to action. No longer could a single individual make sense of all this. People anxiously took their cues from others, in endless games of bluff and one-upmanship. In yet another book historian Daniel Boorstin gave a name to what many had come to see as the central problem of their age: he entitled his book *The Image,* thus introducing a catchword for contemporary problems that was instantly taken up by other languages in other national cultures. As he put it, "Now the language of images is everywhere. Everywhere it has displaced the language of ideals. If the right 'image' will elect a President or sell an automobile, a religion, a cigarette, or a suit of clothes, why can it not make America herself—or the American Way of Life—a saleable commodity all over the earth?"[6]

Boorstin's book came out in 1962. A few years earlier, in 1957, another author had reached a mass audience with a less intellectual book that, if anything, was even more alarmist in tone; Vance Packard's *Hidden Persuaders* became an instant bestseller both in America and abroad. In the grand manner of bestsellers the book offers everything that the author claims to denounce. It promises sensation and disclosure; the tone is one of urgent alarm, yet at the same time it promises to answer the pressing concerns of the day. The front cover of my paperback edition reads like a veritable sales pitch: "What makes us buy, believe—and even vote—the way we do?" "Do you know **WHY** automobiles get longer and longer? **WHY** men think of a mistress when they see a convertible in a show window?" It goes on thus, in hammering boldface WHYs. "This book gives the startling answers to these and hundreds of other eye-opening questions and facts that show how today's advertising men are using our hidden urges and frustrations to sell everything from gasoline to politicians." Slick as the book may be, it is still a must for all those interested in problems of politics and mass-marketing techniques.

To a certain extent the success of Packard's book contradicts his central argument that citizens, in their roles of either voters or consumers, had been reduced to mere puppets on a string. Clearly the puppets took a vital interest in a diagnosis of their common condition. They cast off their strings and chose to read a book of their own free will. They forgot about television for a while and pondered their own situation. Their behavior was the precise opposite of all those bleak and caricatured views of the state of the union and its doubtful democratic stature.

Such somber self-reflection by Americans on their own collective condition was not unprecedented. Their critique of mass culture and the mass media in the 1950s was one episode in a longer line of critical observation. From the early days of the republic there had been a lurking fear of the unsophisticated mass—of Irving's "headless ghost"—seen as forever incapable of full democratic citizenship in the classical terms of free discussion and the exchange of mature views. Even before the advent of the modern mass-communication media such as radio and television, Walter Lippmann, in his classic observations entitled *Public Opinion*, had reflected on the lack of information among the larger public. People tend to gear their political action toward rough-and-ready stereotypes, toward the kind of secondhand, fragmented "pictures in their heads" of the world around them. In keeping with the spirit of the age Lippmann vested his hope in an educated elite who alone would be able to transcend such limited vision and to assume the role of natural leaders in a modern mass democracy. Lippmann thus conjures up a deus ex machina to help him escape from an impasse of his own making. Nevertheless, reality is never cast in as starkly black-and-white terms as he or others like him would have us believe.

All those who found their critique on a caricatured view of passive couch potatoes blithely swallowing their television fare along with chips and beer neglect all those aspects of America as a democratic marketplace of ideas in the classical sense. Once we open our eyes to the flood of opinions, commentary, information, and reportage in any area of public debate that is disgorged daily, weekly, and monthly in print and, yes, on television, we need not be unduly worried about the viability of a public opinion in the contemporary American republic. Public opinion has always been a many-headed thing, a Hydra rather than a headless ghost. It has always been a matter more of plurality, of many publics and many opinions, free and open to all. Anyone who, at one time or another, takes an interest in the res publica can join the debate. Regarding those who would rather wash their cars while dreaming of their mistresses, more power to them.

The American Dream and the Five Freedoms

"The American Dream" is one of those potent slogans that for many Americans concisely render a wide range of ideals and expectations. It catches the repertoire of promises that have always defined America—and not only for Americans, I should add. The American Dream has appealed to people anywhere in the world (to paraphrase Roosevelt).

Immigrants, adventurers, refugees, and exiles alike have come in their millions to America as the land of promise. And they still come. The main immigration streams may have different wellsprings today, originating in parts of the world other than Europe, yet immigration numbers have far from decreased. The dream is still very much alive.

Like any successful slogan, the "American Dream" ranges across a wide array of associations, from freedom, autonomy, and self-fulfillment to material abundance and social success. In that sense the American Dream effortlessly encompasses the realm of political ideals—such as Roosevelt's Four Freedoms—and that of the more earthly desires of a cornucopia as envisioned by the Hoover Company's advertisement of the fifth freedom, the freedom of choice. America has long lent itself to the projection of such dreams. Surprisingly, however, the tonic slogan of the "American Dream" is of relatively recent coinage.

The earliest version that I have been able to find is in a piece of rhapsodic writing by Katharine L. Bates, her hymn "America the Beautiful," which was published on the Fourth of July 1895. The tone of rapture and praise that characterizes the piece was not uncommon for the genre of Fourth of July rhetoric. The American Dream as the author evokes it in her hymn is "a patriot dream that sees beyond the years," a lasting inspiration that flows from the political ideals of the American republic. This clearly political version of the American Dream has never lost its appeal. In the Kennedy years—an era that was not averse to large rhetorical gestures—the poet Archibald MacLeish put it thus: "There are those who think that liberty and human rights is but a dream. They are right. It is the American dream."[7]

It was not long, however, before the alternative, more earthly version showed up. In 1931, in his book *The Epic of America,* the American historian James T. Adams identified the American Dream as "that dream of a land in which life should be better and richer and fuller for every man, with opportunity for each according to his ability or achievement." In this version the American Dream appears as the classic story of individual success, from rags to riches.[8] Adams's timing may have seemed a little off, though. His version of the American Dream as a promise of success and abundance was rudely shattered in the decade of the Great Depression, when most references to the American Dream were uttered in a tone of disabusement, if not cynicism. A poignant illustration of this is a product from the one industry that was relatively unaffected by the depression, the entertainment industry, the one remaining factory of dreams. The product in question was a theater production, with all its attendant glitter, dance, music, and girls; its title was *The Great American Dream*. One of the show's posters presents a group of show girls—the Great American Dream Dancers—dressed mostly in plumes. They are gracefully arranged atop a huge roulette wheel.[9] The message could hardly have been more cynical: the American Dream in the 1930s had become a mere game of chance. The commonweal had turned into a wheel of fortune. Quite tellingly the 1930s saw the rise to popularity of a great many games of chance, both lotteries and board games. On their bare kitchen tables families could play Monopoly and imitate the mad dash for profit that had turned many into real losers at the end of the preceding decade.

The Great Crash brought to an end a decade in which, ironically, the American Dream had assumed its guise of a democracy of goods, promising affluence for all. Roosevelt may have been a master at preserving the American Dream in its political version, as a rhetorical tool that helped him to keep political hopes and idealism alive, yet the dream of a cornucopia seemed broken forever.

Did this mean that the American Dream, in its sense of an imaginary dreamworld that one could enter at will through acts of consumption, was gone as well? The answer must be no. During the 1920s, in addition to dreams of affluence, dreams of freedom had become associated with consumption. It was one of the feats of magic performed by the advertising masterminds of the culture of consumption. As they had discovered, any in a range of free-floating signifiers could be associatively connected to the most pedestrian of consumer goods. As they had intimated all along, the freedom of choice always implied a seductive choice of freedom, a promise of freedom in any form, of freedom from constraints, of liberation, of leisure and cultural rebellion. This latter conjunction in particular—of freedom and consumption—survived the 1930s. For a token fee almost anyone could gain entry into the imaginary world of the silver screen and find at least a couple of hours' escape from the pressing concerns of everyday life. In this highly symbolic and imaginary way the American Dream survived the depression.

Nonetheless, it was not until the return of prosperity, during and after World War II, that the American Dream was restored in its full range, as a dream of freedom *and* affluence. In these contours the postwar world came to conceive of America in its imaginary guise of a dreamland, a realm of freedom and abundance.

Even today these are still the two aspects that centrally define the appeal of America as a cultural symbol. Perhaps even more strongly than before, "America" now stands as a concise, symbolic code that sets the semiotic reading of forms of behavior, of products and messages, in terms of such abstract values as freedom and affluence. The intrinsic appeal of many forms of American mass culture, from soap operas to blue jeans and Coca-Cola, always derives from their imaginary connection to these two dimensions of the American Dream. Rarely can we speak meaningfully of Americanization; the term is usually much too imprecise and lends itself to any kind of sweeping statement concerning the dismal impact of America on other national cultures. At this point in my discussion, however, I am indeed able to characterize Americanization in a rather more precise sense. It is unmistakably the case that "America," in the sense of an American Dream as described here, has been added to the symbolic repertoire of many non-Americans. Not only do they vicariously enjoy the beguiling force of the American Dream in their consumption of American products; in addition, when advertising their own domestic consumption goods, they have begun to draw on the repertoire of "America" as a symbolic code. The code has become international.

There are many examples of European advertising drawing on this repertoire. We "get the message" in television spots, on posters, and in newspaper ads when all we see are images of the American West, a Harley-Davidson, or the Statue of Liberty. In addition to this, however, there are the more interesting cases where the message is not as visually explicit yet equally defined by the use of "America" as an internationally recognized semantic code. A beautiful example is the first of a series of television commercials for the soft drink Seven-Up that shows a cartoon character named Fido Dido. Although the character is an American creation, most viewers abroad will not be aware of his national origin. His first appearance is a gem of concise storytelling. Fido Dido, unkempt, free-and-easy, early adolescent little brat that he is, enters the picture, his yo-yo in one hand, a can of Seven-Up in the other. Then he meets the hand of his maker. Briefly it may seem like a lighter cartoon version of the scene in the Sistine Chapel where a drowsy Adam, touching fingers with God, is brought to life. But Fido Dido's meeting is of a different kind. His confrontation is with parental authority, with the commanding hand of social propriety. The hand of the maker, "in living color," holds a pencil and gets ready to retouch Fido Dido. First his unkempt hair gets neatly combed and partitioned. Fido Dido indignantly shakes his hair back into its previous state. The pencil continues the attack and dresses Fido Dido in jacket and tie. It moves on to the object in Fido Dido's right hand, also in full color, as real as the hand and pencil: the can of Seven-Up. The pencil tries to erase it, yet the can is beyond such manipulation. Fido Dido meanwhile has moved toward full rebellion. Jacket and tie already have been thrown off; a well-aimed kick hits the pencil. Its tip breaks and hangs limply— a fitting symbol of parental impotence. Victoriously Fido Dido walks off the screen. In final retaliation his yo-yo now hits the pencil, and the broken point falls off. His victory prize is a taste of the elixir of freedom: cool, sparkling Seven-Up. The semiotics all merge into one message: a simple soft drink has been turned into a symbol of freedom. The product, the commercial, and the cartoon character may be American, but the message is understood internationally.

This technique of semiotic merging is as old as the sales wizardry of American advertising. Abstract entities like freedom are wedded to material consumption goods. Political ideals like freedom and equality are commercialized and commodified. Ideals are turned into illusions, and illusions are turned into merchandise. Such was the critical gist of an earlier critique of the culture of consumption, from old-fashioned liberals as much as from neo-Marxians in a Marcusian vein. Nonetheless, the fifth freedom does not solely stand in the world of commerce and consumption. In keeping with more recent writings in cultural studies and cultural history, I argue that it is precisely the political echoes of both "freedom of choice" and the "choice of freedom" that have bestowed on many American products their semiotic load of subversiveness and cultural rebellion. Those same echoes have made the American Dream reverberate worldwide.

■ ■ ■

Many things have happened along the way since American mass culture started traveling abroad. American icons may have become the staple of a visual lingua franca that is understood anywhere in the world, yet their use can no longer be dictated solely from America.

For one thing, as I already showed, it is clear that European commercials made for European products may draw on semiotic repertoires initially developed in and transmitted from America. In a creolizing freedom not unlike America's modularizing cast of mind, however, Europeans in their turn now freely rearrange and recombine the bits and pieces of American culture. They care little about authenticity. T-shirts produced in Europe are as likely to say "New York Lions" as they are "New York Giants."[10] What is more, American brand names, as free-floating signifiers, may even be decommodified and turned into carriers of a message that is no longer commercial at all. Admittedly, the T-shirts, leather jackets, and baseball caps sporting the hallowed names of Harley-Davidson, Nike, or Coca-Cola still have to be bought. What one pays, however, is the price of admission into a world of symbols shared by an international youth culture. Boys or girls with the name *Coca-Cola* on their T-shirts are not the unpaid peddlers of American merchandise. Quite the contrary; they have transcended such trite connotations and restored American icons to their pure semiotic state of messages of pleasure and freedom. Within this global youth culture the icons that youngsters carry are like the symbol of the fish that early Christians drew in the sand as a code of recognition. They are the members of a new International, geared to a postmodern world of consumerism rather than an early modern one centered on values of production.

There are many ironies here. What is often held against the emerging international mass, or pop, culture is precisely its international, if not cosmopolitan, character. Clearly this a case of double standards. At the level of high culture, most clearly in its modernist phase, there has always been the dream of transcending the local, the provincial, and the national, or in social terms, to transgress the narrow bounds of the bourgeois world and to enter a realm that is nothing if not international: the transcendence lay in being truly "European" or "cosmopolitan." What is good at the level of high culture, however, is seen as a threat when a similar process of internationalization occurs at the level of mass culture. Then, all of a sudden, the defense is not in terms of high versus low, as one might have expected, but in terms of national cultures and national identities imperiled by an emerging international mass culture. There is a further irony in this construction of the conflict, which contrasts an emerging global culture seen as homogenizing with national cultures seen as havens of cultural diversity. In the real world, of course, things are different. There may be a hierarchy of taste cultures, yet it is not a matter of higher taste cultures being the more national in orientation. It seems to be the case that this hierarchy of taste cultures is itself transnational, that there are international audiences who at the high end all appreciate Beethoven and Bartok or at the low end all fancy Madonna or Prince. In a replay of much older elitist tirades against low culture, however, advocates of high art see only endless diversity where their own taste is concerned and sheer vulgar homogeneity at the level of mass culture. They have no sense of the variety of tastes and styles, of endless change and renewal in mass culture, simply because it all occurs far beyond their ken.

Allow me a final observation. When American mass culture travels abroad, in many cases the exploration of cultural frontiers is taken to more radical lengths than anything one might see in America. Whereas sexual joy and freedom are merely hinted at in American commercials, where Coca-Cola at best holds the promise of more intimate intercourse in its vignettes of rapturous boys and girls on the beach or floating down rivers in boats, European posters and television commercials often are more explicit. There is a brooding, erotic Italian wall poster of a macho, bare chested young man standing astride a scantily clad, sexually aroused young woman crouched between his legs. She wears a crown reminiscent of the Statue of Liberty. There is an American flag. The commercial is for the one piece of clothing on the man's body, his pair of blue jeans. Similarly, in the Netherlands a government-sponsored poster and television campaign inviting (in small print) people to become organ donors and to carry a donor certificate shows a young couple making love, both naked, the woman sitting on his lap and curving backward in rapture. The text, in large print, reads, "Give your heart a new lease on life." Pasted across the country on railway platforms and on bus stops, the poster must have made visiting Americans bashfully turn away their heads. To them the campaign would not appear as the outcome of a process of Americanization taken a few daring steps further. Nor for that matter would another poster campaign, again sponsored by the Dutch government, on behalf of safe sex. These posters show couples taking showers or engaged in similar forms of foreplay. Shocking stuff indeed, but there is more. Yet another frontier is being explored, if not crossed: both heterosexual and gay couples are shown.

Admittedly these poster campaigns no longer convey commercial messages, although the Dutch government has adopted advertising techniques to get its messages across and uses advertising billboards, rented, one assumes, at the going market rate. In a sense we have come full circle. Where the Hoover Company advertisement drew on republican language to claim the freedom of the advertiser, we now see advertising space being reclaimed for statements *pro bono publico*. If democracy is a marketplace, it has become inseparable from the economic market. It is in fact one indivisible and noisy place with cries and calls vying for the public's attention, echoing back and forth. The perfect illustration of this is being pasted all across the Netherlands as I write this. A huge poster—produced by a Dutch advertising agency only for the Dutch market—advertises Levi's 508 jeans yet playfully draws on American political language for its commercial message. What the viewer sees is the lower part of a half-nude male torso, covered from the waist down by a pair of jeans. Playing on the classic version of the Four Freedoms, the poster rephrases them as follows: the freedom of expression, the freedom of thought, the freedom of choice, and the freedom of movement. The third freedom, as I have shown, already makes the transition from the political to the commercial; the fourth, political though it may sound, is meant to convey the greater room of movement provided by the baggier cut of the 508. The picture illustrates the point by showing the unmistakable bulge of a male member in full erection, casually touched by the hand of its owner. Clearly the semiotics of American commercial strategies have been taken to lengths, so to speak, that are inconceivable in America. Whereas America may have been less embarrassed in exploring the continuities between the political and the commercial, Europe later on may have been more daring in its pursuit of happiness, graphically advertising it all across Europe's public space.

Indeed, as European examples from the political and the economic marketplace serve to illustrate, the logic of a choice of freedom knows no bounds once set free from controlling American standards of taste and decency. As is a lingua franca's wont, it moves in a realm of free creolization, where the controlling authority of a parent culture no longer holds. Americanization then should be the story of an American cultural language traveling and of other people acquiring that language. What they actually say in it is a different story altogether.

Mediated History

| THE VIETNAM WAR AS A MEDIA EVENT |

Our knowledge of the world rarely derives from direct observation. More often than not we have to rely on stories told by others who in turn are simply passing on what they have heard. Normally we manage quite nicely to reach a workable consensus on how the world is put together. Such loose ends as remain dangling can always be tied together over a drink or two. If at one point or another in our lives we had not badly burned our fingers, our knowledge of a real fire would not be unlike that of the characters in Plato's cave. Chained to one another, they sit in a circle, their backs turned toward a fire; from their experience they cannot tell us more than that it scorches their backs and looks like flickering shadows on the walls around them. Our common knowledge of the world is often not much different; it is like a shadow of ourselves cast by something outside us. Our images of reality are always at the same time shadow images of ourselves. We always obtrusively block our own view; it is never unmediated and direct. There are always intervening obstacles, like so many filters and grids that affect our perceptions and the way we neatly order them into conceptions.

Walter Lippmann, who was among the first to put the quandary of Plato's cave dwellers into the novel language of stereotypes, of "pictures in our heads," did not really explore much beyond the insights of the Platonic parable. Nevertheless, he was a major influence in drawing attention once again to a problem that should concern everyone who takes an interest in the functioning of democracy and public opinion. The classical *Homo politicus*—the fully informed citizen, whose image of reality resembles the original like a contact print—is a mere ideal type, a construct, like *Homo economicus* in classical economic theory. Both had to give way to a more sober and disenchanted view that sees human beings as caught in prejudice, prone to irrational impulses, and equipped with no more than mere morsels of knowledge. Generally— and this applies to Lippmann as well—this kind of gloomy diagnosis has an elitist ring; instead of reflecting back on the author, it diagnoses the plight of others. There is always the implied assumption that a tiny band of well-informed citizens still resembles the classical image of the *Homo politicus;* it is always others—the lower classes, the uncouth new immigrants—who are seen as the threat to democracy in America. At the same time, however, Americans endearingly never despair, in spite of such disparaging views of their compatriots. There is never a problem too big to be solved by a good, spirited crusade. At the time that Lippmann vested his last hope in a well-educated and well-informed elite, others actively engaged in a campaign aimed at the moral and political uplift of those fellow citizens who were lagging behind. Quite appropriately the period is known as the Progressive Era, the age of reform. The idea of egalitarianism in America has always gone hand in hand with the idea of human perfectibility; it has always been averse to a philosophical pessimism that conceives of the large majority of mankind as hopelessly prone to the instincts of the herd.

Nonetheless, one need not be a pessimist to share Lippmann's concerns about the unhinged state of the American republic at the turn of the century. Indeed, the large mass of the population bore little resemblance to the ideal image of a democratic citizenry as the repository of a well-reflected public opinion. In fact it looked more like a herd, if not a horde, that in its orientation to the world was guided mostly by sensationalism and a quest for diversion and entertainment. In the late nineteenth century the mass-circulation papers—the so-called yellow press—had burst on the scene, shamelessly catering to this popular demand. The press, the fourth branch in the ideal view of liberal democracy, had lowered itself, like a cheap whore, to the gratification of prurient interests and vulgar instincts. Every swing of popular emotion was grist to its mill. On the eve of the war with Spain, in the late 1890s, it played on popular jingoism, stirring up a groundswell of bellicosity.

Readers of the quality press could not but watch this in frustration. Demagoguery had taken the place of a journalistic code that insisted on the separation of factual reportage and editorial opinion. The yellow press blithely repeated current stereotypes rather than expose them or at least weigh them against other stereotypes.

The press, the traditional domain of the printed word, seemed to confirm Lippmann's dim view of mass communication and public opinion. In addition to relying on the printed word, however, the nineteenth century had witnessed the rise of other carriers of world news that may have seemed to offer a more objective, unmediated view of current events. The new techniques of mass reproduction now brought pictures of the contemporary world to a mass audience, first through lithographs and later through photographs. Reality appeared to offer itself immediately—without any mediator—to the eyes of the beholder. Were pictures not the natural antidote to the demagoguery of the printed word? Had not photographs provided people with the sobering view of the American Civil War that no amount of verbal warmongering could hope to undo? Had not the time come where everyone could see for him- or herself events happening elsewhere in the world and see through the fabrications of the printed press?

After all the manipulation of mass-distributed images in our own century, we should know better. Even Mathew Brady's famous photographs of lifeless bodies on the battlefields of the Civil War had offered a carefully arranged view of reality. For one thing, the long exposure times that were required then made it impossible to photograph war actions. Even when photographing bodies that would never again move of themselves, however, Brady had often intervened choreographically. Of course Brady reached a wider audience through his photographs than he would have as a painter, yet the wider impact of his war images is unrelated to any inherent quality of his chosen medium of photography; Brady's representation of the horrors of war is not necessarily more real or truthful than Francisco Goya's rendering of those horrors in *Desastros de la Guerra* a few decades before. Irrespective of whether one looks at photographs or paintings, the hand of the maker is always present. Even photographs, although they may seem to be objective and the mechanical contraption that produces them may be emotionally neutral, always interpose a maker between the viewer and the world viewed. What photographs show are always mere fragments of reality taken out of their context.

Nevertheless, some photographs undeniably have the power to leave an indelible imprint on the viewer's memory as if on an etcher's plate. They turn into the icons of events beyond our individual horizons. They come to represent the density of emotion that such events called forth. Often in such cases we are left feeling manipulated when we see such iconic images in the context of a larger repertoire, as just one shot from a larger series. There is the example of a Vietnam photograph of children running toward us, crying for help in utter dismay, their clothes torn off, wounded by napalm. Apart from a few soldiers in the background—part of the setting of war—we seem alone with them. We feel directly confronted with the horrors of war. Why then the sense of having been manipulated, of having been "had" even, once we see this photograph alongside others that the photographer decided to leave unpublished? One of those other photographs shows the same children, yet this time we see behind them a group of press photographers and television camera operators, all equally engaged in getting a good shot. This particular photograph shows us the conditions of its own making. The impression of direct confrontation vanishes. We become aware of mediating agents. We are in their hands. As if by a postmodern sleight of hand, we are being distanced, if not put in our place. We are made aware of the fact that this is a case of photographers doing their work, as in so many other places of distress and human suffering. By publishing only the one photograph that we all remember, by keeping the other photographs stored and removing his colleagues from the scene, the photographer in a sense vanishes from the picture, creating the illusion that we were present on the spot ourselves. He was absolutely right. Only in this way could he show us the horrible face of the Vietnam War. The picture could turn into an icon of reality only because the photographer chose to arrange reality for us.

In our century this problem of a reality encroaching on us through a variety of visual material, through a variety of intermediaries, has increased. Before and during World War II film had already made us aware of its use as a medium of propaganda. Incontrovertibly the new medium was capable of vividly representing events elsewhere in the world, yet its appearance as an objective informant could leave its audience unaware that not only reality but the audience itself was being framed. Again, as in Plato's parable, the audience could be mistaking mere shadows for the real thing. With the advent of television the realm of shadows has increased its sway. To many it has become the main source of news; television delivers the world right to our living rooms.

The prominence of these new visual media has deeply affected our view of contemporary history. World news has acquired a visual directness that may bring it closer to home without necessarily making it any easier to grasp. The Vietnam War is a clear case in point. It was the first war that people anywhere in the world could watch on television day in and day out. Both the press and the visual media had a degree of access to the war greater than ever before (or after, for that matter: witness Operation Desert Storm). Never before had the home front been as bombarded with images—from the war front as well as from the home front, in endless feedback—as during the Vietnam War. Without a doubt this contributed to the war's traumatic effect on American society. With the exception of the Civil War, no other war divided Americans against themselves to such an extent. The tragic result of this was that after the war the only true eyewitnesses, the half-million or so soldiers who had served in Vietnam, were no longer welcome to tell their story. People no longer wanted to hear about the war—that is, until Hollywood decided to step in.

From the late 1970s on America produced a steady stream of Vietnam movies that all, in one way or another, show how Americans were grappling with their collective war trauma. Of course these were not the first war movies to come from American studios. War movies had been a genre for decades; borrowing from the narrative traditions of the Western, they told stories of individual heroism and of the showdown between the "good guys" and the "bad guys." The dividing lines were unambiguous, irrespective of whether the stories were set in the Pacific theater or in Europe. The war in Korea as well was made to fit into this pattern. This is not the case with Vietnam movies. Even if at first glance they resembled the familiar genre of the war movie, telling stories of heroism, self-effacement, and camaraderie, as in a number of *Missing in Action* movies, the effect more often than not was therapeutic. The message of such movies appeared to be that, yes, after all, the Vietnam War was indeed like any of the just wars that America had fought before. An early example of this subgenre, the film *Green Berets* (1968), with good old John Wayne, developed this message as its central theme. The story of a rescue mission in Vietnam that Wayne, a battle-hardened old hand, is called on to carry out is linked to the parallel story of how the reluctant home front, whose war weariness is constantly fed by a bleeding-heart liberal press, can be made to see the real issues of the war. The conversion experience of the home front is exemplified in the character played by David Janssen, the typical representative of a skeptical press corps that pretends to know better. At the behest of John Wayne's character the journalist joins the rescue mission; at the end of the movie he returns a wiser man.

■ ■ ■

The Vietnam War may have been the most directly visible war so far, but the world could not have watched without a plethora of visual aids, including television and film. As it is, no technical contraption can play its supporting role without affecting our perception. Even a simple pair of glasses will tend to bend, refract, and color what we see. How much stronger then will be the effect of carriers of visual information like photography, television, or film?

As regards this effect in the case of the Vietnam War, there are two rival hypotheses, each of them a clear overstatement yet not necessarily untrue. It is argued in certain circles that America lost the war because of television's impact on the home front. As for film, the French writer Jean Baudrillard in particular has suggested the provocative hypothesis that America is still busy winning the war in movie theaters all over the world.[1] Let me consider both views more at length. Particularly in those circles in America that are still reluctant to face up to America's defeat, a modern variant of the stab-in-the-back, or *Dolchstoss,* legend has gained currency. The true culprit behind America's loss of nerve and its eventual withdrawal from the war was not the enemy in Vietnam but Americans at home. The antiwar front at home, these critics contend, would never have been sufficiently strong had not the media—the press, but more importantly television—for all practical intents sided with the enemy. Day after day the media presented a view of the war that demoralized the home front, a view that depicted the war as endless and unwinnable and in the end worked to undermine the credibility of the war effort. Moreover, according to this hypothesis, a direct view of the horrors of war caused a moral revulsion among the American public and left it with a sense that Americans in Vietnam were squandering their moral capital by the sheer excessiveness of their use of force.

Without a doubt television played a crucial role affecting public opinion in the United States concerning the Vietnam War. Still, it is questionable whether its effect has been so unambiguous and one-directional. In fact, the impact of television has been much more diverse and complex.

Media experts on the whole tend to relativize the role of television as a source of systematic and coherent information. According to the *Dolch-stoss* reading, television would have worked gradually to convey to the general public one coherent view of the war in Vietnam, but, the experts argue, that is not how television works or how people use television. What television offers, particularly in prime-time news, is a brief, spasmodic burst of imagery, fragments of events not uncommonly—at least at the time of the Vietnam War—one or two days old and devoid of meaning but for the admixture of spoken commentary. Analyses of television news about Vietnam, which was always only a mere part amid snippets of other news, make clear that the visual images as a rule had only a distant and tenuous relation to the spoken news.[2] Moreover, the need for a drastic fragmentation of messages that results from the competition for valuable airtime among messengers carrying totally different information ("The painkiller that doctors recommend most!") prevents any continuity and cohesion in the presentation of news as contemporary history. The American television audience has become adapted to this. Americans do not really sit down to concentrate on the news. With the television set switched on, people move about, get a beer from the fridge, have conversations among themselves, and thus manage to pick up no more than the mere fragments of fragments.

The relationship between television and the domestic antiwar movement was also far from simple. Television did not merely record and broadcast protest activities, thus simply reinforcing them, although this multiplier effect may have been intended by the organizers of many antiwar demonstrations. In fact many of the expressive means of protest were designed to be highly "mediagenic." An angry speaker on a soapbox in a city park will never make the evening news. On the other hand, youngsters in outlandish garb engaged in collective happenings that in their anti-Americanism could hold a candle to anything of the sort occurring in Europe could count on television coverage. They burned their draft cards or even the American flag, they set ROTC training centers on university campuses ablaze, they let themselves be gunned down on campus by a taunted and nervous National Guard, and they engaged in pitched battles with the Chicago police, making themselves as newsworthy as the Democratic party convention that took place at the same time. The radical wing of the protest movement had promised "to bring the war home"—a radical echo of the more moderate demand "to bring the boys home"—and they stuck to their guns. On balance, what they achieved was to contribute to the mishmash of television images, leaving the average viewer in bewilderment, if not actual revulsion. These latter feelings, more than any considered and widely shared views of the political and strategic significance of the war in Vietnam, were behind the war weariness of many Americans.

Much as this widespread attitude may have objectively run parallel to the aims of the antiwar movement, it was clearly not a case of shared views and motives. Quite the contrary; as opinion poll data show,[3] wide sections of the American people—summarily described as the "silent majority" by Republican party strategists at the time—found themselves in total disagreement with the antiwar protest as they saw it presented on television. The strategists were proved right: the majority vote that brought a series of Republican presidents to the White House, from Nixon to Bush, cannot be meaningfully understood without the rightward lurch effected by the commotion of the late 1960s. Other opinion poll data,[4] concerning the support for a continued war effort in Vietnam, confirm this view. Americans do not like protracted wars. This applied to the war in Korea as much as to the one in Vietnam. In both cases broad initial support began to collapse once it became clear that no rapid, decisive victory could be won. The waning political support for the incumbent administration translated into a transfer of allegiance to those candidates who promised to bring the war to a rapid end or, as in the case of Nixon, more cautiously if somewhat vaguely announced that they "had a plan." Vietnam of course differed from the Korean war to the extent that it acquired the added historical dimension of a "media event"—of a war that penetrated into every living room in the United States. On balance, however, television did no more than contribute to the general state of uncertainty and bewilderment. The structural attributes of the medium, at least in the way in which it functions in American culture, contributed to further fragmenting the audience's view of contemporary world events. The resulting fragments certainly did not make for a view of the Vietnam War that was any more comprehensive and coherent than the popular view of earlier wars. Americans got to see more of it, yet in fact they were once again watching their own flickering shadows.

The proposition then that America lost the Vietnam War because of television's impact on the home front is not as simple and clear-cut as it may seem. What about the second proposition, that America continues to win the war on film screens across the world? Much depends on how we interpret this simple statement. Jean Baudrillard, in his *Amérique,* gave the following, rather convincing, reading. He does not mean to argue, as one might think, that Vietnam films are one prolonged fantasy on how a few more Rambos would have sufficed to do the job. What concerns him is America's commanding control of our collective imagination of the Vietnam War. In the movie theater or at home watching a video cassette, we look at the war through American eyes. Our view of the war is constantly being shaped by the creative imagination of Americans. They present the war in the context of their own recollections, their experience, their preoccupations. They have free rein in transforming a historical episode into an imaginary world that listens to their narrative conventions, their style, their cultural conventions. We let ourselves be taken in by this world of our own volition, in record-length queues if need be, like the French on the Champs-Elysées when *Rambo* opened in Paris. Europeans may have demonstrated in larger numbers against the Vietnam War, yet when will we see our collective memories of our protests turned into film?

In that sense Baudrillard is right. America has won when it comes to the imaginative representation of the Vietnam War. That is partly a matter of money, power, and cultural hegemony. Vietnam simply has neither the economic wherewithal nor the control of the international film market to present us with a Vietnamese film image of the war. Yet it is also a matter of American culture's capacity to appeal to an international mass audience. American Vietnam films may be for or against the war, they may show the war only in its impact on the lives of their protagonists, yet whatever their precise thrust, they manage to appeal to a wide, international audience. They are not unlike other Hollywood box office successes in their use of star actors, their narrative pace, and their emphasis on action. They have the same frankness in their deliberate mixture of cultural standards, of high and low, the sublime and the trivial, kitsch and camp, in an endless recycling of the elements of American culture that are the common possession of Americans and that in any pattern of rearrangement will set responsive chords vibrating. Between the American film audience and the American filmmaker there exists a complex rapport, a form of eye contact as one finds only among true initiates. Non-Americans always find themselves in the role of relative outsiders to such semiotic transactions. They will miss a clue here and there. They do not have the right repertoire of shared memories. At those moments when Americans will feel stirred, outsiders may remain untouched. This is not to say, of course, that Vietnam films, or for that matter other forms of American mass culture, will have no impact whatsoever beyond this enclosed sphere of cultural familiarity. In all likelihood the outsiders in their turn will have their own moments of recognition and response. Mutinous soldiers in Manila who spent the eve of their umpteenth coup attempt watching a *Rambo* video will have seen the movie in a different light than will have Dutch cultural custodians to whom films like *Rambo* tended to confirm their anti-Reagan or even anti-American feelings. All recipients of American mass culture tend to conceive of the package in their own terms. In the final analysis, however, non-Americans will always find themselves in the position of people looking in from the outside, attending rituals of cultural consumption where Americans are the only true connoisseurs. It is something like eating out in a faraway country: we may not have been able to make sense of the menu, yet we like what we get on our plate.

■ ■ ■

I cannot do justice in mere written language to what Vietnam movies offer in a mixture of sounds and images. In truly American fashion I would have to cut up my argument, interspersing it with video clips and film fragments. Only thus could I make the point that every Vietnam film from America shows more about America than about Vietnam. More specifically the point would be that Vietnam films as a separate genre of American mass culture draw on the general repertoire, endlessly recycled, of a cultural environment that has come to define the daily living conditions of Americans—and increasingly, of non-Americans as well.

Yet I fear that I will have to rely on language only. With a view to getting my argument more precisely in focus, let me first illustrate what I do not have in mind. Those who have seen Oliver Stone's film *Platoon* will remember how Stone does the war once more, with feeling. We see before us in a thrilling war movie everything that at the time of the war drove the people into the streets in protest (such as villages being destroyed "in order to save them"), the very irrationality of a war in which every clear line of demarcation between friend and foe among the Vietnamese had vanished. Lest there be a misunderstanding—the audience might be tempted to believe it is watching just another Hollywood action movie—Stone uses a classic recipe for setting the proper interpretive mode: the sound track adds Samuel Barber's elegiac Adagio for Strings to the images on the screen. Audiences anywhere will recognize the manipulative ploy; they know it from their own national radio: funeral music when a king has died or a plane has crashed. It is a device for setting a national mood that leaves no one in doubt as to the required facial expression. Nonetheless, it is not what I explore here.

Things are entirely different with a film like *Apocalypse Now,* Francis Ford Coppola's masterpiece. It is a film whose very production had the epic quality of a challenge, if not to the gods then certainly to the moguls of Hollywood. The production itself was worthy of a movie and has in fact been turned into one: *Hearts of Darkness* presents the mad, mad world of Coppola's production methods, which in the end resulted in *Apocalypse Now.* The entire enterprise, in its scale and ambition, not to mention its absurdity and megalomania, comes a close second to the Vietnam War itself. The result does breathe the spirit of its production—of chaos, improvisation, and absurdity—yet at the same time manages magisterially to transcend it. The Vietnam War is transformed into a symbolic stage, displaying a world that has cast off all sense and cohesion, all rationality and order. Viewers find themselves in a world of nihilism beyond the reach of an ordering civilization, much as in *Heart of Darkness,* the Joseph Conrad novel that Coppola used as inspiration. All that is recognizable in terms of our own culture and technical civilization has broken into fragments. As if in a *danse macabre* the pieces get up and join together in novel patterns.

I will try to summarize one characteristic sequence. The scene takes place on board a boat that in the course of the story will take the viewers on its odyssey, up a river into the interior, toward the "heart of darkness." The atmosphere is still one of a somewhat grim outing. One soldier is sunbathing on deck, with a reflecting piece of aluminum fastened, like a drip pan, under his chin. A black soldier fiddles with a portable radio. Suddenly, at full blast, we hear the *Rolling Stones* doing "I Can't Get No Satisfaction." The black soldier, briefly dominating the screen, makes accompanying dance movements. Then, in the same improvisational vein that characterized the production of the film itself, the handful of men on board the boat decide to go waterskiing at the mouth of the river that later on they will have to follow inland. The spot offers wonderful possibilities but lies awkwardly within firing range of a small coastal village. No sweat. Helicopters are summoned for protection. What follows is an absurdist caricature of the images that Americans must have remembered from Vietnam footage on television. Like a threatening swarm of locusts the helicopters approach, equipped with lethal arms and audio equipment. Wagner's "Ride of the Valkyries" blares from their loudspeakers, evoking a carnavalesque apocalypse. After strafing the village from the air, with Germanic mythology and modern means of war, the helicopters land and hunched soldiers rush across the screen. A loud voice is heard admonishing the soldiers to run on and not look into the camera. The next shot shows the soldiers with a camera crew in the background. The man shouting directions appears to be Francis Ford Coppola himself in a cameo appearance. What are we to make of this? Is this a form of ironic realism? After all, the real Vietnam War was filmed on the spot as well. Or is it rather intended as a Brechtian alienation effect, an illusion-shattering look behind the stage reminding us of the conditions of the film's making? We may be reminded as well of the photographs of the napalmed children in Vietnam, one with and the other without press photographers. Releasing only the latter photograph for publication, the photographer opted for the illusion of unmediated contact and the imaginary merger of his vantage point and that of his distant public. Coppola did the opposite. He enters the picture to shatter the illusory nature of this merger, reminding us that this is film, this is Coppola's world, and nothing is as we know it. Fantasy takes over from history and changes the Vietnam War.

The sequence as described continues with Robert Duvall in the role of commanding officer, strutting like a hero straight out of the macho pantheon of American Westerns. We finally witness the consummation of this episode: an exhilarated water-skier cutting grooves through the coastal water that has been "liberated" for the purpose. The entire sequence is a self-contained vignette and offers a synopsis of what the entire film shows us at length: an allegory of the war seen as an apocalyptic madhouse. In a sense that had been done before. Films about the war in Korea such as *M.A.S.H.* or about World War II such as *Catch-22* had already introduced the genre. What is particularly striking in Coppola's approach, however, is the way in which his construction of the madhouse illustrates the more general rules of transformation that underlie the American way with culture. Here again is the more general inclination toward fragmentation and clipping, toward the cutting up and rearranging of cultural repertoires, ignoring their traditional context and inner cohesion. Freely reassembling cultural quotations the film offers a mélange of *Rolling Stones* and Wagner; of Western heroes, warfare, and waterskiing; and of traditional narrative techniques and postmodern tricks that foreground the narrator. Such rules of transformation as have structured Coppola's imagination are reinforced by the structural rules of every film narrative, the rules of montage. Montage as a technique that literally "cuts up" a sequence of images ideally lends itself to the visual representation of a reality seen as irredeemably fragmented. There is a happy congruence between the technique of film montage and the peculiar characteristics of the American imagination that Coppola beautifully illustrates in his movie.

In this more precise sense as well one can argue that non-American audiences watching American Vietnam movies expose themselves not only to American views of the war but more generally to American cultural habits and conventions. And this is not all. In yet other ways foreign audiences watch American Vietnam movies almost vicariously, as if through American eyes, letting themselves be drawn into an American imaginative realm. Films like *The Deerhunter* by Michael Cimino and *Birdie* by Alan Parker show the war's disruptive impact on the lives of ordinary Americans. In the case of Cimino's film the impact is on the life of ethnic America, as typified in an imaginary small town in the steel belt of Pennsylvania and Ohio. Cimino takes his time affectionately evoking the ethnic community in which his main characters have grown up. The viewer sees the somewhat shabby blue-collar America that in a great many forms of dense communal life has found its place and sense of itself in a blend of ethnic tradition and adaptation to the wider environment. The Vietnam War is presented as a crude force rupturing the many ties of family, friendship, and marriage that have woven the community into one dense texture. Non-American audiences see the disruption taking effect yet will not feel more than vicarious emotions. They will never have a sense of recognition, of an experience that they lived through and remember.

The case of *Birdie* is somewhat similar. Once again the setting is ethnic America, a working-class neighborhood in Philadelphia. The film shows two boys becoming friends, unlikely though their affection may seem. One is a dreamer, an introvert with an affinity to birds bordering on identification; the other is streetwise, the assertive working-class boy who has a way with girls. Both go to Vietnam and come back physically and mentally dislocated. The latter has been badly wounded; his head is bandaged. The dreamer has withdrawn into a deluded identification with a bird. He no longer speaks and has become inaccessible even to the approaches of his friend. The viewer has not witnessed their experiences in Vietnam. Only gradually, through the persistent attempts of the bandaged veteran at reestablishing contact with his "bird-man" friend, does the war surface occasionally as a flash of memory. The home front is shown as emotionally cold, incapable of empathy, a matter of filling out forms and going through the routines of standard therapy. The two friends have been thrown back on their own little private worlds. They have only each other. No other Vietnam film, to my knowledge, renders the experience of the loneliness of Vietnam veterans quite so movingly. It is all the more remarkable, then, that its maker is not only not a Vietnam veteran but not even an American. Coming from Britain, director Alan Parker had the outsider's keen eye, which enabled him to give such striking allegorical form to the divide separating the Vietnam veterans from their home environment. His feat may also remind us that we should not exaggerate the problems that non-Americans may have understanding American Vietnam movies. The very success of many of these movies outside the United States proves that there is no hermetic screen shutting out non-Americans. Foreign audiences have acquired the codes needed to decipher the complex messages of American movies. They may miss a clue here and there, and they may even on occasion give a reading to the message that differs from the American reading. In general, however, American movies have always managed to speak a language that is understood across the globe. A likely explanation may be that the United States as a nation of immigrants has always had to cope with the problem of finding a vernacular that could be understood across the many ethnic dividing lines in its society. By its very nature, therefore, the vernacular is international; by the same logic the outsiders are all immigrants. America speaks to all of them at the same time that it addresses its domestic audiences.

Thus, the raging Rambo who in *First Blood—Part Two* single-handedly tries to undo the cowardly treason of the American government could count on instant international recognition. He was only the latest in a long line of lonesome American heroes, a man who is as good as his word, driven by populist resentment, anti-intellectual, anti-establishment, the unbending loner who takes the law into his own hand. He has a populist appeal that could find resonance not only in America but far beyond its borders as well. He is the imaginary agent of all our fantasies of omnipotence and freedom.

■ ■ ■

There is a three-minute sequence in Barry Levinson's *Good Morning, Vietnam* that brings together everything I have said so far about television and film. The lead character (superbly played by Robin Williams) is a disc jockey in Saigon who produces a radio show for the troops in Vietnam. The show is an endless stream of one-liners, silly stories, and imitations, all in an upbeat, improvisational mood and interspersed with music. The deejay and his program are a transplanted America, an illustration of that more general American habit, whenever Americans mount large-scale missions abroad, of packing up their country and taking it with them. As if it were a matter of an assembly kit, they set up their own cultural biosphere abroad, with the food, sounds, and images that they know from back home. Thus, in the heads of Americans, their recollections of the Vietnam War could coincide with a remembered American mass culture, with its top hits, rock stars, pop idols, and other such ephemera. When Coppola, for instance, has the opening shot of his *Apocalypse Now* accompanied by the Doors on the movie's soundtrack, the combination works to call forth those tangled memories that among outsiders will never quite find the same collective echo.

Good Morning, Vietnam moves this mass-cultural context of the war toward center stage. The context has been turned into the text. It is a striking reversal that at one particular point produces a moment of magnificent transcendence. Suddenly viewers find themselves soaring far above the noisy and fake world of a man who makes a living playing records. They see him announce just another record and then hear the song from beginning to end. On the screen they see scenes from Vietnam in odd, jumbled order. First they see Vietnamese women with pointed straw hats working in a rice field. Behind them, suddenly, the forest seems to explode. They see urban scenes, people running, a café where a bomb explodes, and helicopters in the air. The accompanying sounds have been cut out. All they hear is the music, the voice of Louis Armstrong, the words of "It's a Wonderful World." For three minutes America's fragmenting way with the world coalesces into a wry and poignant message. The visual snippets, in no way different from what Americans were offered as news every evening, and a song by a popular entertainer merge into a novel assemblage, a recycling of everyday culture that suddenly produces a sense of transcendence, of repentance and catharsis. Non-Americans should be humbled by the experience. After all, in their condescending repertoire of cultural anti-Americanism they had repeatedly argued that American mass culture, centering on consumption, could never lead to consummation, could never produce moments of transcendence.

The same would hold for those American critics of their own culture who, slavishly applying European cultural hierarchies, tended to look for high forms of American art while ignoring its lower forms.

■ ■ ■

A few words in conclusion. I have argued so far that American Vietnam films show us the war as seen, experienced, and remembered by Americans. We are always looking vicariously, as it were, through American eyes. But is it quite as simple as that? Recently there has been a debate among those who study the dissemination of American mass culture abroad. One party to this debate tends to conceive of the recipients of American mass culture as passive puppets on a string subject to an Americanization of their thinking, feeling, and volition. It is the party that refers to Euro-Disney near Paris as a cultural Chernobyl. The other side does not take such a dim view of things. It tends rather to emphasize the freedom of the recipient of mass culture, a freedom of selection and interpretation that can work to subvert the implied semiotics of messages and exhortations circulating in our contemporary mass culture. Vietnam films are a good case in point. Rambo, for instance, may have become a cultural icon, an icon of America, of resistance and indomitability, of a muscular masculinity, or of whatever one may wish to read in his bared chest, yet as a symbol he has become a free-floating signifier whose use America can no longer dictate. For instance, when protests erupted in the Netherlands during the 1980s against the deployment of American cruise missiles on Dutch soil, the Dutch developed their own polemical picture language. The cartoon character of an angry little woman, done in the style of children's drawings, toppling a missile with a well-aimed kick became the central icon of Dutch anti-arms-race sentiment. The Dutch also made Rambo their own, however, holding him up like a distorting mirror to reflect back on American foreign policy. President Reagan saw his first name distorted to Ronbo, a cipher that summarized the more general rejection of America's muscular bellicosity. Rambo had been appropriated by the Dutch and gave muscle to Dutch pacifism.

Breathless

THE FRENCH *NOUVELLE VAGUE* AND HOLLYWOOD

For outsiders there is much facetious pleasure in observing the French ambivalence toward American culture. Up to the highest governmental levels the French exercised themselves to attract Euro-Disney to France rather than to other European countries, yet before it had even opened its gates they already spoke of it as a cultural Chernobyl. Jack Lang, minister of culture in a number of recent Socialist governments, is not averse to denigrating American mass culture occasionally, yet he also designated the comic strip as an artistic genre worthy of preservation and bestowed the French Order of Arts and Letters on Sylvester Stallone, of *Rambo* fame. When France rallied to defend its cultural identity in late 1993, the minister of culture, in a lame symbolic gesture, proposed to ban *Jurassic Park,* presenting it as a threat to the national identity.[1] I have made the point before: the French have their own special relationship with American culture. In fierceness of rejection they are second to none, yet it is never long before they openly reappraise what they previously rejected. Time and time again the French were first to adopt bits from an American throwaway culture, as if picking up cigarette butts from the sidewalk, proclaiming their status as art. This happened to jazz music, the hard-boiled detective novel, comic strips, and Hollywood B-movies. I examine the last category in this chapter.

France initially was only one voice in a larger European chorus rejecting Hollywood's standardized production, although with its own characteristic cultural twist. One quotation may exemplify this. In his book *Les Etats-Unis d'aujourd'hui*, first published in 1927, André Siegfried makes the following observation in his concluding remarks: "'Fordization,' the essence of American industry, . . . results in the standardization of the worker-as-such. Craftsmanship, an outmoded form of production, has no place in the New World, but with it have gone certain conceptions of man that we in Europe consider as the veritable basis of civilization. To create with personality is still the ideal of every Frenchman: it is not compatible with mass production."[2] Here again is the same familiar theme that many other Europeans belabored: the resistance to the standardization of both labor and labor product, to the dismantling of the production process into empty repetitive manipulations, and more generally, to the fragmenting logic of the "American Way." Here also is the typically French concern about the demise of individuality. And Hollywood was only one among many examples of what was found so objectionable in American culture.

As I said before, however, France never takes long to develop an addiction to the taste of the forbidden fruit. In the 1920s, the era of the silent movies, France was still "in line." There, as much as in other European countries, early advocates of film as a form of art had given up on Hollywood. To them, the American mass production of film for mass audiences meant the corruption of everything they valued as film's artistic promise. The coming of sound did not improve matters. Many of the early enthusiasts lost interest in film at precisely the time that dialogue and music were wedded to the visual imagery of film. For highbrow advocates of the cinema, it lost its autonomy as a form of art right there and then. As they saw it, the medium traded its vital pulse, set by camera movement and montage, for the borrowed rhythms of spoken dialogue and acting parts. Instead of transcending reality in a compelling rearrangement of image and time, film retreated—or so its disappointed advocates argued—into a documentary realism aspiring at nothing more than spinning a good yarn and making it look real. Film as a narrative instrument had passively succumbed to the logic of the story it was made to tell.

One French film critic refused to see things quite in this light: André Bazin. To him, the power of film, silent or not, was precisely in its creation of an illusion of reality. The alleged realism of film stories, according to him, was based on a misunderstanding. Film was always a matter of imagined worlds, of imagination at work, in spite of its semblance of reality. In fact, anything that would work to undercut this semblance, such as an obtrusive use of montage, cutting up reality and presenting it as a collage to the audience, was not in his book. Such manipulation of images as Bazin had seen in, for example, Soviet film reduced images to the mere carriers of a message. Even human beings were cut up into individual shots that derived their meaning from the context that the filmmaker gave them in the cutting room. Actors no longer were given the time and space, under the intruding eye of the camera, to produce a fully rounded individual character. When used in this way, film worked to dehumanize, to deindividualize. Its makers obtrusively took center stage, rearranging reality in the service of such ideological messages as they sought to convey.

Bazin's critique of the modernist use of film may seem a little out of character. One might have expected a Frenchman to have a special affinity with a style of filmmaking that so clearly showed the imprint of its individual maker. Instead, the characteristically French preoccupation with artistic creation as an individual act gave a different twist to Bazin's argument. To the extent that he brought individuality to bear, it was with a different emphasis. For one thing, as an individual member of the audience he felt manipulated by modernist film techniques. There was more than that, however: those same techniques deprived actors of the opportunity to create individual characters. As Bazin argued, film can allow its audience to identify with imaginary fellow human beings, yet for this illusion to take effect filmmakers must avoid making their presence felt. Bazin therefore advocated the unobtrusive use of film technique. He favored using long shots, allowing a scene to develop according to its own inner logic. Montage must come as naturally as an observer's need to single out a particular detail while never losing sight of the whole. Visual continuity should be organized in such a way as never to disturb the public's illusion of being an unseen participant in the film's narrative. Precisely that illusion was the central power of film for Bazin. Those whom he saw as truly great filmmakers were those able to direct the public's gaze while remaining in the dark, unseen. Only in this way could the individuality of all parties involved—the director, the actors, the public—be duly respected.

These and similar views of Bazin concerning direction, narrative technique, camera use, and montage have had a long-lasting influence in France. After World War II a younger generation of film critics adopted his polemical position and developed it further, particularly in the pages of *Cahiers du cinéma*. Known as the *cinéphiles*, this group took Bazin's ideas to build their radical case in defense of the *cinéma d'auteur*, of films that characteristically show the hand of their individual maker and that together constitute an oeuvre.

Once again, as in the case of earlier generations of youthful, cultural rebels, the *cinéphiles* turned toward America, not to reject it but to reappraise it. The *cinéphiles* recognized in the mass products from Hollywood's dream factories the illustration of what they had been arguing. Their more general infatuation during the late 1940s and early 1950s with the vitality of American mass culture had made them aware of aspects of individual creativity where others could see only the uniformity of the cliché. They were better observers, better listeners, and better readers. They had keen eyes and sharp ears for the hidden meanings that gave American culture its worldwide resonance. They were able to recognize the force and power of the American mythological repertoire with its lonely, existential heroes, irrespective of narrative genre, whether in Westerns, gangster movies, or American film noir. Above all they recognized and acknowledged the hand of the individual maker, the genius of the auteur, in items of mass culture. Thus they elevated Hollywood movies far beyond their assigned status of low culture, casting them in the light of their own highbrow sense of existential alienation.

Years ago British film historian Thomas Elsaesser convincingly argued that this reevaluation of Hollywood by the French *cinéphiles* totally ignored the actual conditions of production of Hollywood movies.[3] In their quest for a *cinéma d'auteur* they tended to exaggerate the freedom of the individual film director in Hollywood. They left unmentioned the endless compromises, the many interventions by others, that every director had to accept. The studio system was based on teamwork, with its attendant division of labor. Only rarely was the director also the scriptwriter; only rarely therefore, as in the case of Orson Welles, could directors be considered as auteurs. Surely Elsaesser had a point. As he went on to argue, however, although the French *Cahiers* critics may not have correctly sized up the real Hollywood, they created a "Hollywood" all their own, allowing them to conceive of American movies in a new light.

America in Paris: Godard's *A bout de souffle*

By the end of the 1950s a number of writers in *Cahiers du cinéma* had traded in their pens for film cameras. The films that they made became known as the *nouvelle vague* (new wave) in French film history. Their breakthrough had a clear generational character. They wanted a renewal of French filmmaking, a farewell to the *cinéma de papa;* they sought to apply in practice what they had been advocating on paper in *Cahiers.* They now appeared as auteurs themselves, after the image of the masters that they had discovered in American cinema. Their films clearly carried their own stamp; one could recognize the hand of the maker. But what else had they chosen to adopt from their American models? How much "America" was there in their films? The general answer must be, not much—not much, in the sense of American examples shimmering through in *nouvelle vague* films. To the extent that America occurs at all, it does so in a game of ironic unmasking, of disturbing the illusions that films—particularly in their seductive Hollywood version—conjure up before us. A telling case in point is François Truffaut's *La Nuit américaine,* a film about filmmaking, with Truffaut in the role of director and Jacqueline Bisset playing an American film star in a French production, with all the attendant friction between national styles of film production. The film star as a capricious public idol and film itself as an illusion are Truffaut's true subject. His title gives it all away. The "American night" is not a real night but a film trick brought about by the use of filters that on celluloid turn day into night.

Probably the best example of film games played by Europeans trying to unmask and demystify the imaginary America that haunts their inner worlds is *A bout de souffle* by Jean-Luc Godard. It is one of the first *nouvelle vague* movies, an homage to the America that these filmmakers had internalized as much as an attempt at breaking free from it. Modeled after the Hollywood film noir genre, the film in fact leads to the genre's utter deconstruction. Unlike in the pages of *Cahiers du cinéma,* here the meeting of a highbrow Frenchman and a lowbrow form of American culture did not lead to the upward revaluation of the lowbrow but rather to its unagonized dissection. To the extent that Godard recycles American cultural bits and pieces, he offers a cultural critique in the form of a cinematic rehash of much that Europeans had been saying about America all along.

Godard managed to do this using the cinematic means that he, as auteur, had at his disposal. The way in which he used them, however, was a far cry from what Bazin argued. Godard's use of montage and the camera always is meant to shake up every illusion of reality his images might threaten to create. He always catches his audience on the wrong foot, distancing it from the film's story. Thus, a continuing dialogue on the sound track can be accompanied by jump cuts, creating discontinuities in the visual registration, as if to emphasize the point that the continuity of a conversation is a mere illusion, a conversation being no more than a series of single statements lacking logical coherence. The protagonists appear as if ruled by random impulses, erratic, incapable of the larger continuity of action that one traditionally expects. If there is any continuity at all, it is in the sovereign control of the maker imposing his view of a deranged world on his story.

For the story as such Godard makes use of the ingredients of the American gangster movie and the American film noir. Godard dedicated his film to Monogram Pictures, the Hollywood studio that had produced many low-budget B-movies in the 1930s and 1940s. The film's main character, Michel (played by Jean-Paul Belmondo), lives on the seamy side of French society. He steals American cars when he needs transportation or cash. On his way to Paris to see a shady friend about money, he kills a motorcycle gendarme. The film story is in essence that of a fugitive getting ensnared. Michel's picture appears in the press, forcing him into hiding. The story line is typical of the gangster movie genre. A second story that Godard interweaves with the first one more closely resembles the genre of the melodramatic film noir. It is the story of the relationship between Michel and Patricia, an American student in Paris peddling the *Herald Tribune* while dreaming of an opening into the world of art journalism. She is the ingenue, the typical American innocent in Europe; at the same time she personifies the femme fatale. She calls down misfortune on the male protagonist like so many women before her in American crime melodramas. Toward the end of the movie, as if on a whim, she reports Michel to the police. A long, final shot shows Michel, hit by a police bullet, running down a Paris side street, staggering, losing control, collapsing. His face mimics a few expressions that the viewer has seen him rehearse before in front of a mirror; he says something that his girlfriend does not understand. "*Dégueulasse* [disgusting], what does that mean?" she asks. The audience does not quite know the answer either. Was Michel referring to himself, to his girlfriend, or to life in general?

The audience is able to arrange the narrative components into a coherent story, with beginning and end, yet nowhere does the order of narration follow any psychological cues. Godard has willfully withheld any ingredients that an audience would normally need for identification and empathy with a story's plot and characters. Reality as he shows it follows a different logic. He places his characters in a second-order

world, more a set than a setting, composed of references to worlds elsewhere, a semiotic patchwork that constantly changes the color and
meaning of the story's protagonists. Michel models himself after Humphrey Bogart, the hero of the American film noir. We see him pause
before a Bogart film poster, mimicking—in a ritual of identification—a
mannerism of his hero: his thumb slowly, almost pensively, moves along
his lower lip. He is busy borrowing an identity that is already imaginary, that of the existential loner, of the man who prefers a life of action to one of passive self-reflection. Michel steals American cars as
much for their cultural aura of freedom and lack of constraint as for
their utility value. He falls in love with an American girl, but she remains strangely unaffected, out of reach. She moves through the film
like an "empty signifier," a 3-D poster for America, acting on impulse,
playing a record of the Mozart clarinet concerto, attending an art ex-
hibit, and quoting Faulkner ("between grief and nothing, I'll take
grief"), but none of this provides a clue to her character. It is as if a repertoire of floating cultural meanings enters into ever-changing configurations, briefly connecting to a person only to vanish again into thin air.

Equally fleeting are the flashes of insight Godard's protagonists have
into their own condition. Godard holds up before our gaze a world of
alienation and disrupted social contacts to which Michel at one point
gives expression: "We are talking to each other all the time, but not with
each other." He justifies his repeated attempts at making love with Patricia by pointing out that in the modern world sex and love have become the same thing. Nonetheless, it is never long before these flashes
of insight, disillusioned if not cynical, literally fade into platitudes, recycled truisms, and catchpenny philosophies: "I don't know whether
I'm unhappy because I'm not free, or whether I'm not free because I'm
unhappy."

If reality has come to consist of the images and sounds, the symbols
and meanings, with which the mass media have been surrounding us,
the only way left in which persons can establish their identities is to
penetrate into that surrounding world. Patricia makes an attempt but
remains on the outside. A press conference by some cultural hero or
other makes her aware of more elevated forms of life; she comes up with
a question, trying to catch the guest of honor's attention. Her question
remains up in the air, however. There is no more than an indeterminate
exchange of glances. Michel is more successful. At one point he avows
his ambition first to become immortal and then to die. In an Andy
Warhol kind of way he succeeds. According to a well-known Warhol

quip, it is everyone's democratic right to be world-famous for fifteen minutes. Immortality in the modern vein is a matter of the moment. People are briefly at the center of attention, in the public eye, until the cameras move on to the next topical interest. In that pointless sense Michel has become immortal. His photograph has been on the front page. He has become a news item. He has penetrated into reality as a replica of himself. Now he is ready to die.

■ ■ ■

In *A bout de souffle* Godard has constructed a world, using cinematic tools like montage, camera movement, and mise-en-scène, that shows reality as being no more than a random assemblage of unconnected parts, a semiotic collage. It is a world of alienation and lost identity, a world we know so well from modernist literature by both European and American authors. In that sense we can call Godard a literary cinematographer. He shares the intellectual preoccupations of the masters of literary modernism. He uses the cinematic equivalent of their literary techniques of cutting and collage with a view to evoking the alienating sense of a reality that has lost all inner logic and cohesion.

I must emphasize a further and crucial point, that the notion of America features prominently in Godard's recycling of elements from our everyday cultural setting. This is not pure happenstance. The common European environment has become saturated with Americana, ranging from objects of material culture to the symbols and icons representing an imagined America. Europeans have come to live in a cultural setting that increasingly draws on American repertoires. Godard's film amply illustrates this. Rock-and-roll music on a transistor radio; Lucky Strike cigarettes; Patricia's *New York Herald Tribune* T-shirt; Michel's alias of Laszlo Kovacs (a reference to the American camera man and director of photography); American dreamcars such as Thunderbirds, Cadillacs, and Oldsmobiles; posters of Humphrey Bogart— all are examples of an America, replicating itself in simulacra and icons, that now fills the imagination of non-Americans.

But Godard's film does more than merely illustrate this globalization of American culture. His film in a sense follows the logic of American culture while at the same time turning the mimicry into critique. On the one hand Godard recycles American culture. He improvises on themes provided by Hollywood film genres, using narrative routines that non-

Americans, in the dark of the movie theater, have mastered as well as Americans have. Nonetheless, in his improvisations he is more the exorcist than the sorcerer's apprentice. His film noir is like a deconstruction of the genre, an alienating analysis of a world subject to Americanization. Godard's film is a form of cultural critique; he caricatures an American film genre to show us a cultural wasteland, an America in Paris that is the spitting image of the America that so many Europeans before the war were wont to reject. He uses the same repertoire of metaphors employed by earlier critics of American mass culture. Thus, using cinematic means, the leading characters in the film remain on the surface; they lack the depth and coherence of a well-rounded personality. Their mutual relations are literally superficial. They further lack a sense of history or a proper perspective on time. They act impulsively; their dreams are infantile and narcissistic. Above all they move in a world devoid of inner consistency and meaning, a world of borrowed props arranged in no apparent order, without any hierarchical sense of high versus low, of kitsch versus art, of authentic versus fake.

If Godard had done no more than visualize these stereotypes on the screen, his film most likely would have been duly forgotten. The complex and lastingly fascinating thing about *A bout de souffle*, however, is that for his critical deconstruction of American mass culture Godard uses the very tools that he critiques. The order of his critical discourse derives from precisely those maligned rules of transformation that make American culture so "empty," so "superficial," so utterly devoid of meaning and coherence. In his deconstruction of Hollywood movies Godard may in fact have made the most radically "American" film to date. Bazin may have located the appeal of American film in its mise-en-scène, in action within the picture frame rather than in the manipulation of the order of frames and shots through montage, but Godard found his freedom as auteur precisely in montage. In his use of montage he shows an affinity with the clipping, or rather disassembling, logic of the American way with culture. He modulates his argument through modularization, through a ruthless willfulness of montage that strikes the observer as quintessentially American yet that was way ahead of the use of montage in American film at the time.

Rap

In my reflections on American culture so far I have rather loosely used a number of terms, such as *mass culture* and *popular culture,* without attempting to define them. Entire wars of words have been fought trying to do precisely that, separating the terms, as well as the worldviews that people think the terms represent. I have watched colleagues get worked up engaging in these battles, frothing at the mouth. I must not let things go quite that far, yet it may be good, before entering my discussion of rap music, to be a little more precise in my language. For a start, it should be clear that terms like *mass culture* and *popular culture* refer to forms of culture that have found wide distribution. In a literal sense, as forms of culture, they are widely popular. But the similarity between the two may end there.

When using the term *mass culture* people mostly think of those cultural products whose very emergence, if not character, is critically linked to the invention and introduction of the techniques for their reproduction and distribution. The production of mass culture cannot be conceived as separate from the culture industry. The printing press is the classic case of a reproduction technique that turned books into a mass-consumption product. Photography, phonography, film, radio, and television are all later inventions allowing us to record, reproduce, and circulate sights and sounds, in addition to words on paper. Markets for the consumption of such forms of mass culture have opened up, often through the use of techniques of advertising that, in the way they styled their messages, became themselves elements of mass culture.

As regards the term *mass culture,* this could well be a sufficient definition, yet there are those who refuse to leave it at that. As they see it, the word *mass* cannot be used solely and simply to mean "a large public." To them, the word has a negative ring, and so has the term *mass culture.* The term then comes to mean a culture of the lowest common denominator, catering to commercial motives of market share and profit rather than to standards of quality. A critique of mass culture along these lines often goes hand in hand with a wider critique of capitalism. According to one view current among many neo-Marxists, mass culture helps to perpetuate the capitalist system. Through false dreams of freedom and riches the consumer is brought passively to accept the entire system. Mass culture, in this view, is the new opiate of the masses.

Against that negative view of mass culture the term *popular culture* is often proposed as the positive counterconcept. The term still refers to cultural forms that are widespread and "popular," but it is restricted to those forms that seem to have come from the "populus," the common folk, rather than from the factories of the culture industry. Popular culture in that sense is seen to connect to traditions of folk art, of folk stories, folk music, and craftsmanship, and more generally is felt to breathe the authenticity of a collective past. Much of the resistance to the rise of a consumption culture under capitalist auspices, which was manifest in many countries in the immediate post World War I period, incorporated attempts at modernizing and revitalizing traditions of folk culture as an answer to the temptations offered by the movie theater and the dance hall.

More often than not such attempts produced little more than artificial results, yet the old fighting spirit is still there. Many countries still try to erect barriers with a view to stemming the flood of American mass culture. In many cases, however, the battle is already lost, and the enemy already inside the gates. Especially in the area of television programming, the logic of market shares and ratings have begun to have their effect, leading to complaints of television stooping to the lowest tastes of the masses.

There is a patronizing element in such cultural concerns. On the basis essentially of their own cultural conventions and preferences, cultural gatekeepers aim at regulating the cultural consumption of their captive audience inside the gate. Only rarely do such cultural guardians allow themselves a taste of what they are proscribing; only rarely do they try to fathom the range and depth of the pleasures and enjoyments of those who are at the receiving end of mass-cultural production. Fortunately, though, things have begun to change. In the last decade or two students of mass culture have begun to take the subject seriously, exploring such questions as how the individual consumers of mass culture handle the mass-cultural fare they are being offered and what degrees of freedom the individual recipients have in creatively manipulating, reinterpreting, and recontextualizing the messages they receive.

It will be clear that I feel greater affinity with this latter approach. Accordingly I use the term *mass culture* in a neutral sense, as applying to all those forms of culture that reach a large audience and that, for their production and distribution, depend on techniques of mechanical reproduction and on modern means of mass communication, from the printing press to the electronic media. If there is a need for the term *popular culture* as distinct from *mass culture,* it could be as a sensitizing concept, reminding us that mass culture, as produced by the culture industry, continually draws on and recycles repertoires of culture that have a folk character, in the sense of having emerged or having been carried by groups within society that have a common sense of history, of shared experience, or common locale.

A third term that is sometimes offered as an alternative to *mass culture* is *vernacular culture*. Again, as with *popular culture,* I propose to use it as a sensitizing concept, something to help me refine the notion of mass culture rather than to replace it. The term *vernacular culture* may in fact help us to become aware of sources feeding into mass-cultural production other than the repertoire of the folk and all it suggests in terms of tradition and local roots. Vernacular culture may speak for the common people as much as popular culture, yet its emphasis, as a sensitizing concept, is more on aspects of invention and vitality, on the spontaneous regeneration of the idioms of everyday culture. It is not unlike the study of language and its idioms: there are dialects, folksy and traditional, and there is the everyday spoken language, always changing, beyond the standardizing reach of the written language— language as spoken in the street. In discussing rap music I cannot really do without a term like *vernacular culture*, or more appropriately perhaps, *street culture*.

People who have watched, in amazement and admiration, groups of children in American cities tormenting their skateboards in dogged pursuit of weightlessness and levitation know what I am talking about. They have witnessed an American ritual of challenges sought and met, of daredevil acts performed just for their own sake. If you are a skateboarder, the challenge can be the steps in front of a public building or the stone rim of a water basin in a city park. The battle against gravity is unending. There is much stumbling in what seems like an endless rehearsal, but every now and then, suddenly, briefly, we witness perfection—a flawless performance. One of the boys gracefully, victoriously, as if in slow motion, beats gravity and lands on the high rim, circling the water. Victory is brief, and the rehearsal resumes. This is street ballet, done purely for its own sake and pleasure, for those brief moments of aesthetic rapture when people are able to fly. There is no paying audience and no producer. Nevertheless, the forms of mass culture are not altogether absent. Their T-shirts make the boys the unpaid advertisers for iconic brand names like Coca-Cola or Levi's. Their basketball shoes have coveted and hallowed names such as Adidas, Reebok, or Nike. Their skateboards are commercial emblems of masculinity. Even though the boys may be following the dictates of mass culture in such respects, however, they mix them in rituals of freedom that follow only their own dictates.

Much of the vernacular culture (or perhaps I should say, much of the street culture) of America's black population has been picked up by the mass-culture industry; it has been packaged, transformed, duplicated, and marketed for mass publics. Jazz musicians and blues singers have been taken to the recording studios; their music, with all the freedom of oral traditions and improvisational techniques, was not only recorded but codified. It was produced initially for the separate market of black consumers. Black music—or as it was called at the time, "race music"—found its way to a black clientele; "race movies" were shown in theaters for blacks (then called "colored people") only. To the extent that borders were crossed, as in the case of cultural crossovers, the black product was adapted to white tastes and performed by white musicians. Nonetheless, even in its most watered-down versions jazz retained clear echoes of a raw vitality that, as far away as Europe, inspired avant-garde composers such as Igor Stravinsky, Darius Milhaud, and Maurice Ravel. Most likely what they recognized in the music was not so much an exotic America as the primitivism of an imaginary and mediated Africa. In that sense the African masks in Picasso's paintings are on a par with the jazz ingredients in, for instance, Milhaud's *La Création du monde*. A similar romantic sense of the exotic and non-Western can perhaps explain the attraction, during that brief period of Harlem nightlife in the 1920s, of blacks playing black music in clubs accessible only to a white clientele.

■ ■ ■

At the same time, however, there were others, such as George Gershwin, who recognized in jazz an authentic American idiom, a truly vernacular culture, that could allow American composers finally to shake off the hegemonic European model and to make an authentic American music. This view of the music of America's blacks rapidly won out against rival views of its alleged Africanism. The dance crazes of the 1920s, the radio shows of the 1930s with their (white) swing bands, the avant-garde appeal of the masters of bebop, the breakthrough of rock music in the 1950s—all these exciting and vital forms of American mass culture derived their quintessential "Americanness" from the pulse of black music. Throughout it all black music fed into the production of mass culture as almost an aquifer, a substrate of black vernacular culture constantly renewing itself.

For many recent crazes in mass culture it is still possible to retrace these back-and-forth exchanges. Breakdancing, with its daring feats performed to music blaring from ghetto blasters, developed in the streets in displays of inventiveness and physical one-upmanship not unlike that of skateboarders. Any old rag or piece of cardboard would do to set the stage for breathtaking, if not neckbreaking, antics that later were transformed into a dance style transmitted across the world by the mass media. In the case of rap music, with its staccato antiphony and virtuoso, rapid-fire versifying, there was a similar development. In its call-and-response, its qualities of a playful singing contest, of a battle of wits and words, it stands in a long tradition that goes back to African and Caribbean roots, yet in its present vernacular form it is definitely a product of the streets of America's black ghettos. As with other forms of vernacular black culture, it was picked up by the mass-culture industry, recorded, and distributed worldwide.

The Dutch broadcasting network VPRO produced a beautiful documentary a few years ago about rap music on the eve of its recycling by the mass-culture industry. Black street children from the Bronx displayed their mastery in dance and song before the documentary camera. With their mouths as their only instruments they produced a popping staccato rhythm as an accompaniment to the rap singing. In their improvisational texts anything could be picked up and recycled: advertising slogans, brand names, ghetto slang, news flashes, bits of autobiography. "We take it apart and put it together again," as one of the boys put it. It is as if we hear an echo of Gertrude Stein, a desire "to make things new." The semiotic overload, the veritable deluge of messages to which Americans are exposed, is transformed, in an almost Dada-like rearrangement, into the text of rap songs. Mass culture in a sense is being reassembled and reappropriated as street culture. The VPRO documentary caught rap music in precisely that stage of a vibrant street culture. But the boys who were interviewed already had their dreams of recording studios and market success. The documentary shows them knocking on a studio door for an audition. Others had already gone there before them. The documentary also shows a rap group—RUN-D.M.C.—that had already "made it." The signs of their success were unmistakable: they drove around in a Cadillac. They had already become the carriers of rap music as an ingredient of mass culture. The circle had been closed. Their music had returned to the level of mass culture that it had initially drawn on to develop its brand of vernacular culture.

Not all the elements of what radio and television clips now deliver into our homes as rap music have such a direct relation to street culture. Certain stylistic elements originated precisely at the interface between the production and consumption of mass-cultural items. Thus, disc jockeys at one point abandoned their supporting role of compulsively talkative conveyors of the ready-mades from the music industry; they developed into the active coproducers of the records they played. They began to intervene in the process of mechanical reproduction of sound, through the traditional needle in the traditional groove, and invented scratching. By rhythmically moving one record back and forth on the turntable, they add new rhythmic sounds to the music on a recording. With the tools of the computer era they can disassemble music into single fragments, store the fragments as samples, and rearrange them into new patterns. The primal scream that was James Brown's trademark has become the most sampled sound in recent pop history. Consumers have given up their roles of passive receivers and now give their own creative twist to mass culture.

Rap music can be seen as the happy symbiosis of a number of stylistic elements that all have one characteristic in common. Everything that I have mentioned so far, rap as street culture, scratching, and sampling, is an example of that one rule of transformation underlying American culture in general, taking things apart, cutting up context and cohesion, and then rearranging them freely into new patterns. Consequently, anything that is subject to this modularizing logic can enter into this realm of endless recombining. It need not surprise us, then, that rap, with its staccato reordering of loose components, forms natural material for the modularizing logic of American television. A television channel like MTV finds its raison d'être precisely in the endless stringing together of videos, mixing music and pictures. But the fragmenting logic does not stop at the individual video as the smallest constituent element. The video itself is subject to clipping. Initially a documentary form, showing the musicians performing a particular number, on a narrative plane parallel to the performance, the music video has evolved into an art of free visual association that often is only remotely connected to the music. The documentary form's unity of place, time, and action has given way to a wild jumble of images, produced using montage, computer technology, and stroboscopic effects, that all work to fragment further the internal order of the video. Often the only connection linking images and music is the music's rhythm; the rhythmic element of the music determines the pacing of the visual images. In its later form the video appears to be the ultimate visual rendering of the meaningless deluge of images and sounds that now constitutes our everyday world.

There are cases, however, of videos that offer more than a mere replica of the hectic setting of contemporary life and that, in noisy introspection, briefly transcend reality. There is the beautiful example of the video for "Walk This Way." The song was recorded earlier by a white hard-rock band named Aerosmith. No matter how deeply indebted white rock may be to the music of black America, there are still separate publics and divided tastes even today, not unlike the days of "race music" before the war. Apparently whites were doing things to music, regardless of its black roots, with which blacks could no longer affiliate. I remember a television interview a number of years ago with a black student in America, of clearly middle-class background, who had spent several years at a white college but had then decided to pursue her studies at a black school. She said that changing colleges felt like a "homecoming." She recalled parties at her previous school, with students dancing to the music of white rock groups, where she felt like a stranger. Now she was home again, among her own kind. All the subtle codes of interaction and behavior, of taste and pleasure, fell back into their familiar order. There was a mutual rapport that had been lacking at the white school. The previously mentioned video illustrates these cultural distances.

"Walk This Way" was rereleased in a cover version by RUN-D.M.C., the rap group that I mentioned before. The video shows Aerosmith and RUN-D.M.C. in two adjacent rooms separated by a wall. The white band, clad in the paraphernalia of rock stars and with all the appeal of their established public image, starts playing the number as they had recorded it years before. The camera then moves to the other room, where a ragtag group of blacks—straight from the Bronx, it seems—are rendering the same song in their own rap style. A musical battle royal takes off, each group shouting to the other to stop. The blacks start banging on the wall, breaking through it literally and metaphorically. In the final shots both groups perform together before a rapturous audience.

The video shows a cultural crossover in more than one sense. Black street musicians are seen to break through into the world of mass culture and of the culture industry. Their music is being recorded and turns out to be a success. They are doing more than that, however: by taking up music that had previously been done by white colleagues and giving it their own twist, they produce a cultural fusion that appeals to publics on both sides of a cultural divide. "Race music" has left its ghetto; it no longer needs the mediating, and expropriating, translation by whites for whites. For altogether too long blacks have had to put up with whites capitalizing on adapted versions of what blacks had developed in the first place.

The video of "Walk This Way" gives a glimpse of the way things might develop further: this way, so to speak. But I am afraid things are not that simple. Instead of seeking fusions and crossovers, black artists, fearing a renewed expropriation of what they consider to be their cultural property, have time and again resorted to a strategy of defiant protectionism. Thus, for example, bebop was meant to take jazz music to such dizzying heights of complexity that white musicians could no longer hope to steal and adapt it. More recently, similar trends seem to have occurred in rap music. In their lyrics some of the more notorious rap groups express a vicious sexism and racism, an utter obscenity and nihilism, whose sole aim may seem to be to erect barriers beyond which white groups will fear to tread.

Americanization

WHAT ARE WE TALKING ABOUT?

A paradigm shift has been underway in cultural anthropology during the last several years. The Swedish cultural anthropologist Ulf Hannerz has been foremost among those who hold that the dominant perspectives in their field of endeavor have increasingly lost touch with the contemporary world.[1] Hannerz makes the point that colleagues in the various social sciences—historians, anthropologists, sociologists, economists, and political scientists—have been developing theories that have kept abreast with the increased interdependence among human societies in this world. Those theories tend to focus on the lines of economic and political interwovenness that stretch across the globe and that have produced worldwide patterns of societal subordination. According to the various ideological perspectives of the observer, this subordination may be conceived of in terms of interdependence and inequality or, more radically, in terms of exploitation and subjection. Whatever the precise ideological view, the world is seen as divided between centers of economic and political power that have subordinated the rest of the world as a mere periphery.

Such a globalization has taken place culturally as well. One can distinguish centers for the production of meaning that have subjected the rest of the world to their semiotic auspices. According to Hannerz, cultural anthropologists have so far failed to account for the effects of this cultural globalization on the recipient periphery. Like true cultural archivists, they have hurried to chart the cultural diversity of the world before it becomes too late, before the last indigenous cultures fall prey to the Coca-colonization of the world. Hannerz makes two accusations against his colleagues: either they tend to ignore processes of cultural globalization, pretending that the local communities that are the object of their study are still untouched in a time and space entirely their own, or they see globalization as a process of cultural homogenization, eroding all cultural diversity and therefore unworthy of their expert attention. Hannerz begs to differ. As he sees it, cultural anthropologists have the special responsibility of bringing their talents of cultural empathy to bear on the situation of people and societies that find themselves at the margins of the world system. Thus, anthropologists can hope to gain an insight into the ways in which people at the so-called periphery undergo cultural bombardment from a distant and alien world.

In this context Hannerz uses the term *creolization*. It is a felicitous metaphor inspired by the changes that languages undergo when, far from their cultural home base, they have to serve as the means of communication among groups of diverse geographical and cultural origins. In a process attendant on the increased economic and political interlinking of human societies across the globe, many cultural meeting grounds have come into existence where the cultural heritage of each of the parties involved has undergone a transformation. Creolization as a linguistic phenomenon is a case in point. Thus, languages from "center" cultures, such as Spanish, French, Portuguese, and English, have served as the mold for the creole languages of the Caribbean; thus also, at the southern end of the African continent, Dutch has been creolized into Afrikaans. The languages of the center countries in creolized versions allowed meaningful exchange among people from the world's "periphery." The center countries were instrumental in uprooting these people in the first place and in bringing them together, through colonization, the slave trade, and migration.

The metaphor of creolization is a felicitous one because it takes the structural transformations of languages in the melting pot of the world's periphery as an illustrative case of the more general processes of cultural change that take place there. Linguistically, creolization refers to the reduction of the structural complexity of a language in the sense that strict rules of grammar, syntax, and semantics prevailing in the parent country lose their controlling force. Words no longer obey the structural discipline of spelling, inflection, conjugation, gender, syntactic order, connotation, and denotation; they align themselves more freely and more simply. Away from the parent country, at the meeting ground of alien cultures, no authority figure is in place to rap a person over the knuckles for saying "I is" and "we be" or, even more to the point, "I is, therefore we be."

What could the notion of creolization mean when transferred to cultural forms other than language? It must have to do with the simplification of their structural principles, with their "grammar," "syntax," and "semantics." Every parent country always has an arsenal of means of cultural reproduction and preservation, in institutions of education and in the social control of everyday life, but beyond its span of control these means have no effect. Such areas are free from the cultural syntax that orders cultural matters hierarchically in the parent country, as high or low, "done" or "not done," or as Nancy Mitford would have it, "U or non-U."[2] There the grammar that defines the proper form of cultural conventions and rituals of social intercourse collapses. There, finally, the cultural semantics of the parent country can be cut adrift, allowing cultural forms and meanings to interact freely, beyond any meddling of the parent country's semantic authority.

In all these respects the parent country's structural mold collapses, with the consequent liberation of cultural forms and meanings from their prescribed patterns of interlinkage. In the wake of the worldwide political and economic expansion first of Europe and then of America, their cultures have also spread across the globe. In many ways these cultures have been cut adrift from the authoritative sway of the parent countries. The inhabitants of the world's periphery, not unlike beachcombers, are scavenging along the tide line of Western expansion, appropriating its flotsam and jetsam. They feel free to rearrange the order and meanings of what they collect. They turn things upside down, beads turn into coinage, mirrors into ornaments. Syntax, semantics, and grammar become jumbled. At the same time, however, in their selective appropriation people at the periphery create their own environment, doing so under their own auspices. They are their own free agents. In roughly this way one could make sense of the metaphor of cultural creolization.

■ ■ ■

This line of argument suggests a somewhat malicious reading of what we might call the rules of transformation of the American culture. Many European observers have been struck, if not dumbfounded, by the American tendency to disassemble cultural forms into their component parts and to rearrange them freely into new patterns. Americans do not follow European rules of syntax in dealing with the culturally high and low, in their undaunted recycling of the low and their unacademic achievement of the sublime through reassemblage. They take liberties with accepted European cultural grammar; in their cultural "aphasia" they show a freedom from rules of cultural spelling that can render surprisingly new formations. Whereas cultural forms always appear in a particular hue to Europeans, the Americans do not shrink from taking hue-turns, subverting the established order of hue and nonhue. If Europeans are spelling-bound—so to speak—by rules of grammar, Americans tend to question the rules. Their mental mold is inclined to conceive of cultural structures as open-ended. If their state is a federation, it is never in solid state; new states can always be added. When they build, their skyscrapers are not self-contained forms. They could have been higher, and they might as well have been lower. A unity of style, rules of scale and proportion, has given way to the freedom of selective appropriation from European cultural repertoires. One single building in America can look like a veritable catalog of European building conventions, in a mad mélange of era and locus. When writing music composer Charles Ives could play with the idea that "if you can have two 3ds, major or minor, in a chord, why can't you have another one or two on top of it?" To him it was as natural as thinking, "If three bases in baseball, why not four or five?"[3]

This cast of mind, which struck Johan Huizinga as being antimetaphysical and which others such as John Blair have described in terms of the logic of replaceable parts,[4] could perhaps best be compared to a catalytic converter. In their selective appropriation of the European cultural heritage, Americans have tended to dissect patterns of traditional and organic cohesion while feeling free to rearrange the component parts into new wholes. They enjoy a freedom from academicism, from cultural orthodoxy, that has struck many European observers. Whereas Huizinga called it an antimetaphysical bent of mind, Tocqueville and others saw it in connection with the egalitarian ethos in America. The two views are not necessarily compatible. The democratic impulse may have led Americans to dissolve the membranes that in Europe separated the high from the low, the trivial from the sublime, but what remains is never solely a desecrated Europe, robbed of its metaphysical grandeur. In America, in the great Whitmanesque tradition, there is always some celebration of democratic equality, of the recognition of the sublime in the trivial, which is far from being antimetaphysical. The American cultural tradition has its moments of transcendence, its moments of rapture toward its own creative potential, and the object could be the great experiment of their republican order, technical marvels like the Brooklyn Bridge, the illumination of Niagara Falls, or the creation of a nocturnal cityscape through commercial neon signs—they are all equally moments of a confrontation with the sublime.[5] Not only have Americans broken the European cultural syntax and grammar, they have also changed Europe's cultural semantics. Whenever Europeans made fun of American enthusiasms for the low and vulgar, their reaction was born of ignorance. They weighed an American aesthetics against European standards, as if these would apply equally to America.

Perhaps at this point an alternative view suggests itself. As I pointed out before, there is the somewhat facetious possibility of conceiving of the rules of transformation that characterize the American cultural mold as the outcome of creolization. It is more than a little facetious because it implies a view of America as a country at the periphery of a Eurocentric world. This hardly characterizes the present century—the "American century"—in which the United States has come to constitute a potent center of political, economic, and above all, cultural radiance. The case might well be argued for earlier periods of America's national existence, however. For a long time America did find itself at the tide line of the European expansion. Then the flotsam and jetsam of foreign cultures that had been cut adrift through the agency of the European expansion washed ashore in random order. Settlers from Europe, slaves from Africa, and poor immigrants from peripheries elsewhere in the world came together to fill the empty space of America. The setting was one of a cultural deracination and contact, which naturally made for creolization.

Umberto Eco once referred to America as "the last beach of European culture." His point was made tongue-in-cheek. Although the authentic version of European culture was crumbling in Europe, prey to the erosive forces of time, acid rain, and exhaust fumes, America was serving as the repository of the European heritage, which was reproduced in a thousand replicas, enlarged or reduced, in plastic or plaster, juxtaposing King Lear and King Kong, Rimbaud and Rambo, Plato and Puzo. These echoes from Eco render a caricature more than a real-life portrait of America, yet his tirade does have its points. In a sense Eco, too, is referring to creolization, and more than only European cultures have been involved in the process.

There has always been a clear dividing line among the people who washed ashore at Eco's "last beach." There were those who resembled Robinson Crusoe, representing as they did the culture of the Anglo-Saxon parent country. Large numbers were more like "good man Friday," however, cut adrift from their own cultural moorings and taken in tow by their new masters. Whereas they were like Friday's child, working hard for a living, the Crusoes were like Sunday's child. They enjoyed positions of social, economic, and cultural authority. They were the branch directors in America on behalf of the parent culture of England. They constituted the replica of the center at the periphery. They were the true guardians of a cultural continuity that would keep them oriented toward England.

But Friday's children, no matter how subservient and lowly, have never been passively and exclusively subjected to the cultural hegemony of their masters. As the cultural history of American subservience has taught us (e.g., in the work of Herbert Gutman or Eugene Genovese), slaves and immigrants alike have managed against all odds to create their own cultural environments, freely drawing on cultural repertoires that could be traced either back to their homelands or to their new social setting in America. It always meant that cultural elements, regardless of origin, underwent creolization. They were divested of the control systems that prevailed in the parent country; they were rearranged into new patterns, and they assumed new meanings. Thus, under conditions of slavery or of life at the frontier, varieties of Christianity sprang forth that emphasized emotionalism rather than dogmatic nuance. In a context of commercial mass media Christianity appeared in the guise of a televangelism, calling on its audience "to come to Jesus" as if it were a matter of buying the latest model Chevrolet. European forms of music, such as marching music, European musical instruments, and European standards on how to play them underwent drastic creolization in that American musical idiom par excellence, jazz. In the case of the parent country's language—English—things were no different. Among the slave population, in black urban ghettos, in ethnic neighborhoods, on the shop floor, and on the street, vernacular forms of English developed that differed in pronunciation and vocabulary, in syntax and semantics. In all those speechmaking settings English gained a freedom from outside control, as well as a vernacular vitality, that later on, in the endless recycling of American culture, gave its flavor to ethnic literature, ethnic movies, and American popular music. The international appeal of American English, as of so many other forms of American popular culture, must be tied to these ingredients of freedom and looseness. Although America may have moved all the way from the periphery to the center of our present-day world system, it has never lost its early habits of creolization.

As I already pointed out, however, in every country at the periphery there are always replicas of the distant center country, local branch offices staffed by the center's representatives. I called them collectively the Sunday's children of America. They are the local managers of the interests of the home country, politically and economically but also culturally. Lawrence Levine's book *Highbrow/Lowbrow: On the Emergence of Cultural Hierarchy in America* assumes its full meaning against this background. What he describes as the gradual assertion of elitist cultural standards in nineteenth-century America can be seen as a movement of resistance against the creolization of culture. When earlier in the century Shakespeare, Verdi, and Beethoven in a great many forms of blithe bastardization had been appropriated by the general populace, a social elite of Sunday's children rallied to turn the tide. Under such elite auspices theater, opera, and music were once again restored to their holy status of high art and drawn within the exclusive domain of elitist tastes. In this forcible assertion of standards that were quintessentially European, the elite reaffirmed the cultural dominion of the home country, turning America into a mere province of England, if not Europe. This trend most strongly exerted itself in the heyday of a cultural Victorianism that held sway in America as strongly as it did in England. Against this genteel hegemony of an established bourgeoisie a younger generation of cultural rebels, such as Van Wyck Brooks, Waldo Frank, and Randolph Bourne, rose up in anger and protest. Brooks challenged the genteel highbrows to face up to America's vibrant vernacular cultures. Bourne called on his compatriots to cut the umbilical cord that tied the country to England and that would forever doom it to remain a mere provincial echo of Europe. Ironically, in much of their feverish search for an authentic and truly American culture, they tended to overlook much cultural creativity in the America of their time.[6] In their views of an American equivalent of high art, they unconsciously still toed the line of European conceptions concerning a hierarchy of cultural forms. Time and time again this pattern would repeat itself among later American critics of American culture. But that is a different story.

If the authenticity of American culture consists in its picaresque tradition of creolization, its freedom from genteel control, its freedom to borrow, to cut up and hybridize, we are back once again at what I called the rules of transformation of American culture. European observers have always had an intimation of these rules, even if their response was one of disgust and rejection. Their opprobrium mostly went toward what they found lacking in America: there was no soul, depth, warmth, or authenticity. Underlying their reaction was an unwillingness or inability to conceive of American culture in terms of its "Otherness," of its difference from the structural logic of European cultures. They weighed America against European standards and found America wanting. To the extent that their diagnosis went beyond this litany of estrangement, they still cast their discourse in terms of absences, of things missing in America. As they saw it, America lacked the European sense of the historical and organic cohesion of cultures. Up to a point that observation was relatively astute. The European critics of American culture noticed the effects of a modularizing, fragmenting cast of mind in every cultural domain. Education, for instance, was no longer the continued, time-consuming appropriation of a "body of knowledge"; the transfer of knowledge in America had been disassembled into a range of disconnected modules. Europeans noticed the same characteristics in American sports and games; American football in particular was a prime illustration of this fragmenting attitude. In architecture, literature, constitutional thought and institutions, industrial production, the semiotics of advertising and political messages, the use of radio and television time—everywhere the European observer could recognize the transforming logic of disassemblage and reassemblage, the logic of a catalytic converter.

So far I have chosen to relate this molding force to a history of cultural creolization in America. In this view America's historical position at the tide line of the European expansion, at the periphery of a Eurocentric world, would have trained its inhabitants in their particular ways with culture. That may well be the case, yet it seems to be less than the whole truth. Other readings begin to suggest themselves when, for instance, one enters the Library of Congress. There, on opposite sides of the entrance hall, are two bibles on display. One is the result of monastic endeavor, a product from the age of individual craftsmanship. The other is a Gutenberg bible, an early product of the printing age, the age of mechanical reproduction. An explanatory note gives the following information:

The Gutenberg Bible is the first great book printed in Europe from movable metal type. It is therefore a moment which marks the turning point in the art of bookmaking, and consequently in the transition from the Middle Ages to the modern world. Through the invention of printing it became possible for the accumulated knowledge of the human race to become the common property of every man who knew how to read—an immense forward step in the emancipation of the human mind.

The printing of this Bible was probably completed late 1455 at Mainz, Germany. To Johann Gutenberg, who lived from about 1400 to 1468, the credit is usually given for inventing the process of making uniform and interchangeable metal types and for solving the many other problems of finding the right materials and methods of printing.

The text continues, but what is of relevance to my story here is in the quoted passage. Confronted with these two bibles, which the accompanying note puts into historical context, the visitor has a brief moment of delusion. He or she may feel briefly like a latter-day Menno Ter Braak, Johan Huizinga, or André Siegfried and like them may feel tempted to look at these two bibles in terms of the contrast between Europe and America. Huizinga's longing for what is "old and silent," Siegfried's elevation of the individualism and the creative spirit of the artisan, and Ter Braak's evocation of Europeanism seem to be embodied in the first of the two bibles. Next to it, the Gutenberg bible appears as almost American, an impression that is reinforced by the accompanying note. Its choice of words breathes an American spirit of optimism and a belief in progress, in the ongoing democratization of humanity. More specifically, however, its use of phrases like "movable metal type" or "the process of making uniform and interchangeable metal types" seems to place the invention of printing in a characteristically American framework. Are not uniformity and interchangeability precisely the attributes of an American cast of mind against which so many European critics have cried out in protest?

Such a view is soon rejected. Incontrovertibly both bibles have their origins in Europe; they are both products of European culture. Nor can it be denied that with the advent of modernity, a spirit of catalytic conversion captured people's minds in Europe, ruthlessly factoring a metaphysical world into its physical components. Newton dissected meta-physical concepts like motion and stasis in terms of measurable physical forces. John Locke reduced the mystery of social order to the level of the rational calculation of individual interest. Adam Smith robbed social production of its hallowed luster of individual craftsmanship by taking the organic process of production apart into its separate constituent activities. Karl Marx stripped his teacher Hegel's worldview of its metaphysical features by "turning it upside down" and conceiving of world history as the result of clashing class interests.

Such considerations should caution us against opposing "America" to "Europe." Everything that strikes European observers of America as the expression of a modularizing cast of mind is really not more than a radical version of trends that are indigenous to Europe. America thus shows us, in "pure culture," so to speak, only what Europe has never quite managed to bring to full fruition. In Europe there have always been powerful, entrenched forces of opposition to the demystification of the world.

This reading of America as the country where cultural trends that in Europe will be forever stunted could fully come into their own is not without precedent. In the 1950s consensus historians in America further developed an essentially Tocquevillean idea. As they saw it, a liberalism that can be traced back to John Locke had sunk roots in America more deeply than anywhere in Europe, unopposed as it had been by rival ideologies, in a setting that was free from the European dialectics of class. Also, more recently, Baudrillard in his style of apodeictic aphorism maintained that America is the one truly modern nation. Unencumbered by the debris of the European past, a spirit of modernity established itself in America. Europe has never been able fully to replicate itself in America. From the selective transplants of parts of Europe's many societies and cultures a new organism developed that has its own rules of growth and development. Creolization, then, is only one metaphor that can help us to grasp America's rules of culture.

America at the Center

In our century the tables have been turned. America has irresistibly moved toward center stage, while Europe finds itself on the receiving end of a wave of American culture that washes across the globe. That leads me to questions that have harrowed many cultural observers in Europe for many years: the questions of Europe's exposure to a pernicious Americanism and of the attendant Americanization of Europe's cultures. In alarm or exhilaration Europeans have been pointing to an influx of American cultural products, tangible or abstract, goods or ideas. "America" is a presence in our lives, a part of our imagination, to a greater extent than ever before. In that sense our lives unmistakably have undergone an Americanization. We have acquired a set of cultural codes that allow us to understand American cultural products, to appreciate them, and to consume them as if we were Americans. We have no more trouble deciphering American messages—be they commercials, television programs, or Hollywood movies—than does the average American. That is not naturally so. We have had to get the hang of it. Time and time again generations in Europe have parted ways in their appreciation of American culture. Time and time again younger generations in Europe have had to explain to their elders what was so appealing about jazz music, about Laurel and Hardy, about blue jeans and sneakers, about Western movies. Principles of form and of narrative technique, contexts of association—we all have had to make them our own.

Of course, we were never complete outsiders, fully uninitiated. To the extent that America holds up a phantasm, a dreamworld, to the extent that it conjures up a world of freedom, without inhibitions and constraints, we are reading a leaf from our own book. The European imagination had already invented a mythical West before America was discovered. To a certain extent America has merely kept our collective dreams alive. Even today it still holds up before our eyes a gigantic screen for the projection of fantasies that are European as much as they are American. It provides a repertoire for identification with epic worlds that derive their attraction from the fact that America is conceived as a non-Europe, that it provides a counterpoint to our culture, a utopian realm for our dreams of escape. That is precisely why America has never been a consensual matter in Europe. What to some may appear as a repertoire for identification and creative escapism appears to others as the repertoire for their indictment. Anyone who truly cares about the European store of cultural conventions will tend to look on America as the distorting mirror of our culture. Conventions have been torn asunder, hierarchies turned upside down, and connections broken. On the rear balcony of Amsterdam streetcars we no longer find Ter Braak's newspaper boy, immersed in the reading of a musical score, deciphering the code of Europe's cultural heritage. Now there stands a boy with his Walkman turned on, removed from Europe, in total surrender to the raptures of American mass culture. Those around him are reduced to the status of strangers on their own turf, beset by an American culture that as a rhythmic hiss prevents them from reading their newspaper. Newspaper boy, where have you gone?

America's culture has become an unavoidable presence. Its reception knows many varieties. There is the form of an unreflected aping, as almost a miniplayback show on television. Little girls of seven mimic their idols, up to the minutest details of pronunciation and expression, yet they have no inkling of what the words are about. Does that make their aping mindless? I say it does not. What is happening is an act of cultural appropriation, an experiment in creative identification with their admired examples. Creative identification is the key word. Whether it is little girls of seven or European jazz musicians, the French *cinéphiles* of *Cahiers du cinéma,* or someone like the Dutch columnist J. L. Heldring (who once confessed his admiration for the American soap opera *Dallas*), the admiration and identification always involve the contrapuntal aspects of the American culture compared to Europe's, its freedom from academic constraint, its professionalism in the production of a vernacular culture.

Often there is an element of nostalgia in our admiration, of a return to adolescent dreams when the world was still one of endless potential. America as a realm of dreams has preserved that quality. It still holds out the option of an escape from what we have become. America in that sense is a country that in its cultural production has refused to grow up and to assume a fixed form and shape. It is a Disneyland where suddenly we are again as young as our children. Every enjoyment of American culture now always takes us back to a remembered America, to the early rapture that we felt while discovering jazz, when we were Elvis Presley fans, or when we stopped in our street in silent admiration of one of America's dream cars. There is a paradox here: our imaginary return to a remembered adolescence always makes us more keenly aware that we have grown older. But American culture could not be bothered; it rushes on, forever young.

There are those who argue the opposite case. They call America's contemporary culture postmodern, because as they see it, the country has lost its innocence and sense of invention. It has become aware of its own underlying rules of transformation, of its modularizing penchant, its freedom to fragment and rearrange. In this view America has grown old in the weary awareness that everything has already been done, that every experiment has already been tried. America has seen through the secret of its own vitality, losing its élan in the process. Nothing much remains to American culture other than endlessly to quote itself, as merely an ironic gesture, in a conscious recycling of cultural clichés. A European cultural critique that always has tended to see little more than the cliché in American culture now seems to have gained a foothold in America.

■ ■ ■

Nonetheless, this is nothing more than a repetition of what has previously happened in America. There have always been cultural elites who in the critique of their own culture have let themselves be guided by European standards while remaining blind to what went on before their very eyes in terms of cultural vitality and innovation. Today things seem to be no different. Those who, within the walls of academia in America, keep chattering about postmodernism, poststructuralism, and deconstructionism have set out to subject the entire range of America's cultural forms to deconstruction. Theirs is a quest for the tacit premises, if not the conventional stereotypes, that have turned American culture into a potent means for the oppression of cultural Others, such as women, blacks, American Indians, and other ethnic minorities. To the extent that they examine the repertoire of American culture, it is with a view to deconstructing the cliché.

There is an irony in all this. In their busy deconstruction of American cultural forms, the postmodernists are in fact pursuing a more radical version of the rules of transformation underlying American culture. To the extent that American culture has moved in the direction of canonization, with lists of great books and great authors, of the Great White Whale and the Dead White Males, the deconstructionists have ruthlessly broken the reigning consensus, bringing a renewed and further splintering to the American cultural tradition. Under their hands American literature has splintered into manifold American literatures from which emerges a whole host of voices and stories that had been ignored in the established academic canon. This modularization and fragmentation of America's cultural past seems to be a worthy latter-day illustration of the American way with culture. If one chooses to call it postmodernism, then most likely America has been postmodern from the beginning.

Nevertheless, we should not forget that all this commotion is limited mostly to the ivied domain of American universities. Outside the walls, unhampered by any weary sense of postmodernism or by the existential quest of the deconstructionists, there is still an innocence and a freshness of cultural creation that show no signs of a midlife crisis. There the endless recycling of street culture, of popular culture, of mass culture, of cliché and collage, of high and low, of kitsch and art, is still proceeding apace in an unreflective forward surge. There are moments of transcendence, as there always have been. The film *Pretty Woman*, for instance, is a prime example of the sort of romance, if not fairy tale, that Hollywood's dream factories churn out endlessly. At the behest of the directors of the Disney studio the story has a happy ending. The male protagonist, played by Richard Gere, appears as the knight in shining white armor about whom his love, a cheap street hooker, has been dreaming. The story is over and the audience gets ready, contentedly, to leave the theater. In a final scene, on a Hollywood sidewalk, a roving black character that we remember from the opening shots reappears. Once again we hear his voice, and with the camera wandering off to the capital letters HOLLYWOOD high above Beverly Hills—a classic icon of America—he repeats what he keeps hollering all day: "This is Hollywood. This is the city of dreams. This is the place where dreams come true." The film ironically deconstructs itself. A cliché regains its cutting edge. If this is postmodernism, so be it.

■ ■ ■

America has replicated itself into icons, clichés of itself that leave their imprint everywhere, on T-shirts, in commercial images, and in our heads. They have lost their lifelines to America and circulate as a free-floating visual lingua franca. Several years ago the English historian Reyner Banham published an interesting piece entitled "Mediated Environments."[7] The piece appeared in a volume that set out to explore the impact of American culture on Europe for a range of cultural domains. Banham asked whether America's architecture had exerted a noticeable influence on Europe. He arrived at a rather surprising conclusion. With a few notable exceptions European architectural environments show little imitation of American examples. To the extent that America has left any traces at all, it is in our collective imagination. Through a host of mediating agencies—among which are the modern mass media—our heads have soaked up a range of images of the America that Americans have built, the skylines of Manhattan, Chicago, and Houston and street scenes from San Francisco and Los Angeles. We have seen them in newspaper photographs, in films, and on television. When we go to America for the first time, we have moments of recognition, of déja vu. We remember the places in America not only as places in our heads but also as fragments of television news and movies that we have seen in Europe. We remember how old we were then, in whose company we were. America has become a part of our individual life histories. It calls forth recollections that are solely ours and that Americans can never share. Their culture has become other people's property.

The word *mediation,* which Banham uses and which occurs in many other studies of America's cultural radiance, should be central to any treatise on Americanization. America reaches us through a great many media of transmission. Every single one of them affects the context of our perception. American pop music, when interspersed by the inane babble that Dutch disc jockeys have borrowed from their American confreres, assumes a different guise. The deejay may have modeled his role after American examples, but he remains hilariously Dutch: "Veronica is er voor JOU!" American news flashes are accompanied by Dutch voices. While watching footage of the recent Los Angeles riots, viewers hear a Dutch schoolmaster's voice pontificate, "Los Angeles is burning. America is burning." It is the voice of the moral censor. It is Dutch preaching rather than information and analysis. There is the undertone of "what happens there can never happen to us."

We are always the last link in these chains of mediation, the final recipients of messages from America. In that position we are never purely and only passive, gradually losing our Dutchness while becoming ever more American. We make room for "America" in a context of meaning and significance that is ours. If, along with so many Americans, we opposed the war in Vietnam, we could join them in protest against that war; at the same time, however, the suppressed recollection of war atrocities that the Dutch themselves had perpetrated at the time of Indonesian decolonization could resurface and for the first time provoke a public debate in the Netherlands. If in England and the Netherlands groups of young people began to make music in idioms that drew on American blues and rock music, they were not simply the agents of an American cultural imperialism. They wrote their own lyrics, they made their own music, and they gave vent to sentiments that were their own. They, as well as their fans, recognized themselves in the music. They created a cultural space of their own to which they gave sense and meaning. Dutch-language classics in the genre, such as "Kom van dat dak af" or "Oerend hard," gave an added twist to the borrowed musical idiom that further illustrated the processes of mediation that were at work.

Even in the early years of Dutch television, when the medium could still function as a social bonder, assembling family members, friends, and neighbors in front of the television screen, a number of Dutch television productions were modeled after American examples. Television quiz shows became popular, and the word *quiz* itself entered into the Dutch language, along with the word *quizmaster*. Some quizmasters acquired a fame and popularity that made them the first Dutch examples of the American phenomenon of the "television personality," enjoying the transient fame promised by Andy Warhol. I recently asked my students whether they remembered the name of Theo Eerdmans. There was an embarrassed silence. They had never heard of the man. As others will remember, however, he was one of Holland's first television personalities, the highly popular quizmaster of a show on the socialist broadcasting station, VARA. My point here is that, in spite of all the echoes of the American example, no viewer at the time would have been aware of the American origin of the program. Eerdmans was the epitome of Dutchness. Instead of Dutch television becoming Americanized, American models had been Dutchified.

We are at the tide line of the waves of American culture that wash across the globe. Their impact will become stronger with the impending revolution in mass-communication techniques. Satellites will be revolving around the earth oblivious to the alarmist and highly paternalist attempts at patrolling our cultural borders, at preserving our national cultures as members of parliament and ministers of culture see them. As inhabitants of a cultural world periphery, it is our turn now to devise a daring creolization of what reaches us from faraway centers of the global culture industry. Old chimeras of a leveling, eroding, homogenizing American mass culture reappear. The Netherlands has already coined a new term for the process: *vertrossing*. It does not translate easily into English, and doing so would require a full exposé on the peculiarities of the Dutch mass-media setting.[8] That is precisely as it should be. The concept of Americanization has through mediation turned into *vertrossing;* it has been given a Dutch twist, even though the word, given its critical edge, seems to deny this. Paradoxically, it is a highly appropriate metaphor not for a process of Americanization but for the reverse process of Dutchification. Only Netherlanders can grasp the full reverberation of what the term implies. We may call it mediation; we may also call it creolization. Whatever we call it, there is a resilience to the old European cultures that refuses to be washed away easily.

Notes

INTRODUCTION

1. E. Said, *Orientalism* (New York: Random House, 1978).
2. A. Camus, *American Journals* (London: Sphere, 1990), 41.
3. C. Vann Woodward, *The Old World's New World* (Oxford: Oxford University Press, 1993).
4. I refer the reader to Edward Said or Jean-Philippe Mathy. They also argue on behalf of what we might call "fuzzy methodology" when it comes to drawing on an unwieldy corpus of texts with a view to finding the discursive formation that underlies them. See Said, *Orientalism*, 4, and the more recent study by Jean-Philippe Mathy, *Extrême-Occident: French Intellectuals and America* (Chicago: University of Chicago Press, 1993), 10, 11.

CHAPTER 1: AMERICAN CULTURE IN EUROPEAN METAPHORS

1. Seneca, *Medea*, ll. 375–80 ("Venient annis secula seris, / Quibus Oceanus vincula rerum / Laxet, et ingens pateat tellus. / Tethysque novos detegat orbes, / Nec sit terris ultima Thule"). My translation.
2. Dante Alighieri, *Divina Commedia: Inferno*, canto 26, ll. 117–42. My translation.
3. Most of Columbus's writings that I refer to here have been available in a number of languages for a long time. A good edition in English is J. M. Cohen, ed., *The Four Voyages of Christopher Columbus* (London: Cresset, 1988). The *Libro de las Profecias* did not come out in English until the recent Columbus year of 1992; a Latin version came out earlier (ed. F. M. Padron and F. A. Seisdedos [Millwood, N.Y.: Kraus, 1984]).

As regards Columbus's views of the newly found land as the terrestrial paradise, see S. E. Morison, *Admiral of the Ocean Sea: A Life of Christopher Columbus* (Boston, 1942), 2:282–85. There are a number of more general studies on this theme of the terrestrial paradise. See, for example, H. Baudet, *Paradise on Earth: Some Thoughts on European Images of Non-European Man* (New Haven, Conn.: Yale University Press, 1965); H. Hofmann, "Adveniat tandem Typhis qui detegat orbes: Columbus in Neo-Latin Epic Poetry," in *European Images of the Americas and the Classical Tradition*, part 1, 420–656, vol. 1 of *The Classical Tradition and the*

Americas, ed. W. Haase and M. Reinhold (Berlin: de Gruyter, 1994); E. O'Gorman, *The Invention of America: An Inquiry into the Historical Nature of the New World and the Meaning of Its History* (Bloomington: Indiana University Press, 1961); C. L. Sandford, *The Quest for Paradise: Europe and the American Moral Imagination* (Urbana: University of Illinois Press, 1961).

4. See B. Keen, ed., *The Life of the Admiral Christopher Columbus by His Son Ferdinand* (New Brunswick, N.J.: Rutgers University Press, 1959), 18.

5. On this point, see, for example, R. F. Berkhofer Jr., *The White Man's Indian: Images of the American Indian from Columbus to the Present* (New York: Knopf, 1978); U. Bitterli, *Die "Wilden" und die "Zivilisierten": Grundzüge einer Geistes- und Kulturgeschichte der europäisch-überseeischen Begegnung* (The "wild" and the "civilized": basic traits of a spiritual and cultural history of the meeting of European and non-European) (Munich: Beck, 1976); D. Echeverria, *Mirage in the West: A History of the French Image of American Society to 1815* (Princeton: Princeton University Press, 1957); L. Fiedler, *The Return of the Vanishing American* (New York: Stein & Day, 1968); A. Gerbi, *The Dispute of the New World: The History of a Polemic, 1750–1900* (Pittsburgh: University of Pittsburgh Press, 1973); H. Honour, *The New Golden Land: European Images of America from the Discoveries to the Present Time* (London: Allen Lane, 1975); T. Todorov, *La Conquête de l'Amérique: la question de l'autre* (The conquest of America: the question of the other) (Paris: Editions de Seuil, 1982).

6. M. de Montaigne, "Des Cannibales" (On cannibals), chap. 31 of *Oeuvres complètes de Montaigne, essais* (Paris: Editions Fernand Roches), livre premier, 2:92.

7. W. Shakespeare, *The Tempest,* act 4, scene 1.

8. Ibid., act 2, scene 2.

9. Ibid., act 5, scene 1.

10. For a more elaborate reading of Cotton Mather's book along these lines, see S. Bercovitch, *The Puritan Origins of the American Self* (New Haven, Conn.: Yale University Press, 1975).

11. G. Berkeley, quoted in W. H. Truettner, ed., *The West as America: Reinterpreting Images of the Frontier, 1820–1920* (Washington, D.C.: Smithsonian Institution Press, 1991).

12. M.-G. de Crèvecoeur, *Letters from an American Farmer* (London: Dent, 1912), 39.

13. Ibid., 42.

14. Ibid., 40

15. J. W. von Goethe, *Goethes Werke,* ed. E. Trunz. Vol. 1, *Gedichte und Epen* (Hamburg: Christian Wegner Verlag, 1948), 333. In English it would read thus: "America, you have it better / than our continent, the old, / You have no ruined castles / No basalt. / Your inner self is not perturbed / in the present time / by useless remembrance / and futile fights" (my translation).

16. H. G. Wells, *The Future in America: A Search after Realities* (Leipzig: Bernhard Tauchnitz, 1907), 82.

17. H. Melville, *Clarel: A Poem and Pilgrimage in the Holy Land,* part 4, canto 21, ll. 158–59, vol. 12 of *The Writings of Herman Melville,* ed. H. Hayford, A. A. MacDougal, H. Parker, and G. T. Tanselle, 25 vols. (Evanston, Ill.: Northwestern University Press and the Newberry Library, 1991).

18. See Echeverria, *Mirage in the West,* 32–33.

19. T. Dreiser, "Life, Art and America," *The Seven Arts* 1 (Feb. 1917): 363.

20. G. Steiner, "The Archives of Eden," *Salmagundi* 50/51 (Fall 1980/Winter 1981): 57–89.

21. Joel Barlow, in *Poetry,* bk. 2, ll. 705–10, vol. 2 of *The Works of Joel Barlow,* intro. W. K. Bottoroff and A. L. Ford, 2 vols. (Gainsville, Fla.: Scholars' Facsimiles and Reprints, 1970).

22. Truettner, *The West as America,* 135

23. "Le désir de l'égalité devient toujours plus insatiable à mesure que l'égalité est plus grande" (A. de Tocqueville, *De la Démocratie en Amérique* [On democracy in America], 4 vols. [Paris: Librairie de Charles Gosselin, 1839–40], 3:278).

24. "Lorsque les hommes sont à peu près semblables et suivent une même route, il est bien difficile qu'aucun d'entre eux marche vite et perce à travers la foule uniforme qui l'environne et le presse" (ibid.).

25. "Quelques démocratiques que soient l'état social et la constitution politique d'un peuple, on peut donc compter que chacun de ses citoyens apercevra toujours près de soi plusieurs points qui le dominent, et l'on peut prévoir qu'il tournera obstinément ses regards de ce seul coté" (ibid).

26. M. ter Braak, "Waarom ik 'Amerika' afwijs" (Why I reject "America"), *De vrije bladen* 3 (1928); reprinted in Ter Braak, *Verzameld Werk* (Collected works), 7 vols. (Amsterdam: Van Oorschot, 1950) 1:255–65.

27. J. H. Huizinga, *Amerika levend en denkend: Losse opmerkingen* (America living and thinking: loose observations) (Haarlem: Tjeenk Willink, 1927), 126. The translation is from the English-language edition, published, together with other material, under the title *America: A Dutch Historian's Vision, from Afar and Near,* trans. Herbert H. Rowen (New York: Harper and Row, 1972), 312.

28. J. H. Huizinga, *In de schaduwen van morgen* (In the shadows of tomorrow) (1935); reprinted in *Verzameld Werk* (Collected works), 9 vols. (Haarlem: H.D. Tjeenk Willink, 1950), 7:313–424.

29. J. Oppenheim, *The Seven Arts* 2 (June 1917): 199.

30. V. W. Brooks, "Toward a National Culture," *The Seven Arts* 1 (Mar. 1917): 540.

31. "Das Leben [in Amerika] ist ausschliesslich wirtschaftlich gestaltet und entbehrt der Tiefe, um so mehr als ihm das Element der echten geschichtlichen Tragik, das grosse Schicksal fehlt, das die Seele der abendländischen Völker durch Jahrhunderte vertieft und erzogen hat" (O. Spengler, *Jahre der Entscheidung. Erster Teil:*

Deutschland und die weltgeschichtliche Entwicklung [Years of decision. Part 1: Germany and world-historical development] [Munich: Beck, 1933], 48).

32. J. H. Huizinga, "Over vormverandering der geschiedenis" (About the changing form of history), *Mededeelingen der Nederlandsche Akademie van Wetenschappen,* afdeeling Letterkunde, nieuwe Reeks (Amsterdam: Noord-Hollandsche Uitg. Mij., 1941), 4:3.

33. A. Camus, *American Journals* (London: Sphere, 1990), 42.

34. In his early postwar study of European views of America, André Visson, an expatriate Frenchman, commented on the ironies of this peculiar complaint by European intellectuals. There is indeed a strange psychological mechanism at work among European intellectuals who tend to pride themselves on their tragic sense of life rather than admit to feelings of collective guilt about Europe's suicidal orgies in two world wars. They turned feelings of envy and inferiority toward America, the country that had twice saved Europe from its worst excesses, into a sense of intellectual superiority. The contrast indeed between the splendor of life in a victorious America and the miseries of war-torn Europe may have been too much to confront directly. Only rarely do we come across an unmediated expression of this contrast. Camus comes close to putting it into words: "I am literally stupefied by the circus of lights. I am just coming out of five years of night, and this orgy of violent lights gives me for the first time the impression of a new continent. An enormous, 50–foot-high Camel billboard: a G.I. with his mouth wide open blows enormous puffs of *real* smoke" (Camus, *American Journals,* 32). According to Visson, Sartre, like many other European intellectuals, seemed convinced that Americans are fundamentally unhappy. Sartre—and Visson quotes him—met Americans who, "though conventionally happy, suffer from an obscure *malaise* to which no name can be given, who are tragic through fear of being so, through that local absence of the tragic in them and around them" (in A. Visson, *As Others See Us* [Garden City, N.Y.: Doubleday, 1948], 149). But clearly, the perception of Americans as a people essentially unhappy because they are unable to rise above their collective mad dash for happiness is as old as Tocqueville's observations on "the sentiments of Americans" (Tocqueville, *De la Démocratie,* 3:272 ff.). Equally clearly, it is an ineradicable habit among observers of cultural difference to translate their experience of outsidership—after all, they are the outsiders trying to look in—into the language of quasi-inside reports. Small wonder, then, that never having been on the inside, they tend to report on voids and absences. Never having probed much beyond the surface, all they find worth mentioning is that the "other" culture has nothing but surface to offer. In all such cases, observations from the outside are not more than observations of the outside.

35. Listen to Camus: "New York rains. Incessant, sweeping everything. And the skyscrapers in the grey haze rise up whitened like the immense sepulchers of this city inhabited by the dead" (*American Journals,* 52).

36. L. Jeffries, quoted in A. M. Schlesinger Jr., *The Disuniting of America* (New York: W. W. Norton, 1992), 67–68.

37. G. Duhamel, *Scènes de la vie future* (Scenes from future life) (Paris: Mercure de France, 1931), 61.

38. Camus, *American Journals,* 34.

39. M. Gijzen, *Ontdek Amerika* (Discover America) (Brussel: N.V. Standaard Boekhandel, 1927), 8, 9.

40. J. B. Priestley and J. Hawkes, *Journey down a Rainbow* (London: Readers Union, 1957), 43–45.

41. "Dans cette profusion de robes, de blouses, de jupes, de manteaux une Française aurait peine à faire un choix qui ne choquât pas son goût. Et puis on s'aperçoit bientôt que sous les papiers multicolores qui les enrobent, tous les chocolats ont le même goût de cacahuète, tous les *best-sellers* racontent la même histoire. Et pourquoi choisir un dentifrice plutôt qu'un autre? Il y a dans cette profusion inutile un arrière-goût de mystification. Voici mille possibilités ouvertes: mais c'est la même. Mille choix permis: mais tous équivalents. Ainsi le citoyen américain pourra consommer sa liberté à l'intérieur de la vie qui lui est imposée sans s'apercevoir que cette vie même n'est pas libre" (S. de Beauvoir, *L'Amérique au jour le jour* [America day by day] [Paris: Gallimard, 1954]; 27).

42. J. Huizinga, *Amerika Dagboek, 14 april–19 juni 1926,* ed. A. van der Lem (Amsterdam: Uitgevery Contact, 1993), 44.

43. D. W. Noble, *Historians against History* (Minneapolis: University of Minnesota Press, 1965).

44. Huizinga, *Amerika levend en denkend,* 31.

45. Ibid., 175.

46. J. Baudrillard, *Amérique* (Paris: Bernard Grasset, 1986), 58.

47. J. Kirkpatrick, ed., *Charles E. Ives Memos* (New York: Norton, 1972), 120.

48. Henry James, letter to Thomas S. Perry, Sept. 20, 1867, in *Henry James Letters,* ed. L. Edel, 4 vols. (Cambridge, Mass.: Belknap/Harvard University Press, 1974–84), 1:75. As T. S. Eliot, writing about Henry James, put it, "It is the final perfection, the consummation of an American to become, not an Englishman, but a European—something which no born European, no person of any European nationality can become" (quoted in M. J. Laski, "America and Europe: Transatlantic Images," in A. M. Schlesinger Jr. and M. White, eds., *Paths of American Thought,* 465–92 [London: Chatto and Windus, 1964], 483).

49. Wells, *The Future in America,* 42 ff.

50. As quoted in the *Guardian,* Monday, Oct. 14, 1991.

51. C. Dickens, quoted in P. Gay, *Freud: A Life for Our Time* (New York: Norton, 1988), 563 ff. Much later Sigmund's daughter, Anna Freud, wrote in a letter to Ernest Jones, "I quite agree that one should avoid publishing adverse remarks of my father about America" (Archive of the British Psycho-analytical Institute, London—with thanks to Dr. Han Israels for bringing this to my attention). See also H. L. Kaye, "Why Freud Hated America," *Wilson Quarterly* (Spring 1992): 118–26.

52. Wells, *The Future in America,* 80.

53. Guglielmo Ferrero, *Fra i due mondi* (Between the two worlds) (Milan: Treves, 1913), vii. Quoted by Roberto Michels in "Wirtschaftliche und politische Betrachtungen zur alten und neuen Welt (Italien und die Vereinigten Staaten von Nordamerika)" (Economic and political observations on the old and new world [Italy and the United States of America]), *Kölner Vorträge* 3, no. 2 (Winter 1927–28): 32.

54. Freud, quoted in Gay, *Freud,* 566–67.

55. J. Baudrillard, *Amérique,* 156, 167.

56. U. Eco, *Travels in Hyperreality* (London: Picador, 1987), 43.

57. J. Derrida, *Memoirs for Paul de Man* (New York: Columbia University Press, 1986), 18.

CHAPTER 2: HIGH AND LOW

1. A. Camus, *American Journals* (London: Sphere, 1990), 43.

2. L. Levine, *Highbrow/Lowbrow: The Emergence of Cultural Hierarchy in America* (Cambridge, Mass.: Harvard University Press, 1988).

3. Quoted in P. C. Marzio, *The Democratic Art: Pictures for a 19th-Century America* (Boston: David R. Godine, 1979), 1, 2.

4. ". . . un ciel où clignotent des étoiles et que parcourent des nuées légères. Bien entendu, c'est un faux ciel, avec de fausses étoiles, de faux nuages. Il nous verse une fausse impression de fraîcheur. Car, ici, tout est faux. Fausse, la vie des ombres sur l'écran. Le monde est faux. Je ne suis peut-être plus, moi-même, qu'un simulacre d'homme, une imitation de Duhamel. . . . Je ne peux déjà plus penser ce que je veux. Les images mouvantes se substituent à mes propres pensées. La musique . . . C'est vrai! La musique! Qu'est donc cette musique? On l'entend sans l'écouter. Elle coule comme le vent, elle passe comme un insensible vent. Allons! Un effort de protestation. Que j'écoute cette musique! Je veux! Je veux! Je veux écouter cette musique et non pas seulement l'entendre. Je le pensais bien: c'est de la fausse musique. De la musique de conserve. . . . Cela s'appelle 'les disques.' C'est de la musique en boîtes de conserve" (G. Duhamel, *Scènes de la vie future* [Scenes from future life] [Paris: Mercure de France, 1931], 51, 52, 53).

5. B. Russell, "Is Nationalism Moribund," *The Seven Arts* 2 (Oct. 1917): 673–87.

6. Ibid., 676.

7. Ibid., 684.

8. R. Rolland, "America and the Arts," trans. Waldo Frank, *The Seven Arts* 1 (Nov. 1916): 47–51; quotation on 47.

9. Ibid., 48.

10. Ibid., 49.

11. Ibid, 49–50.

12. Ibid., 51.

13. V. W. Brooks, "Young America," *The Seven Arts* 1 (Dec. 1916), 149.

14. V. W. Brooks, "The Splinter of Ice," *The Seven Arts* 1 (Jan. 1917): 270

15. P. Rosenfeld, "Our Day (Aspects of Johannes V. Jensen)," *The Seven Arts* 1 (Jan. 1917): 281–86; quotation on 284.

16. W. Frank, "Vicarious Fiction," *The Seven Arts* 1 (Jan. 1917): 294–304; quotation on 294.

17. L. Adamic, *Laughing in the Jungle: The Autobiography of an Immigrant in America* (New York: Harper and Row, 1932); cited in T. L. Gross, ed., *A Nation of Nations: Ethnic Literature in America* (New York: Free Press, 1971), 79.

18. "American Independence and the War," *The Seven Arts*, supplement to the April issue (May 16, 1917).

19. P. Strand, "Photography," *The Seven Arts* 2 (Aug. 1917): 524–26; quotation on 524.

20. H. James, *The American Scene*, ed. L. Edel (Bloomington: Indian University Press, 1968), 85.

21. T. Benton, quoted in B. Rose, ed., *Readings in American Art, 1900–1975* (New York: Praeger, 1975), 87, 88.

22. R. Stryker, quoted in P. Daniel, ed., *America in the Depression Years: Photographs from the Farm Security Administration and the Office of War Information Collections, 1935–1943* (Laurel, Md.: Instructional Resources Corporation, 1979), 9.

CHAPTER 3: FILM AS A MECHANICAL ART

1. In J. Kirkpatrick, ed., *Charles E. Ives Memos* (New York: Norton, 1972), 120.

2. "Pourtant ce confort à la portée de tous, qui vaut à chaque ouvrier sa maison, sa baignoire et son auto, se paie d'un prix presque tragique, celui de millions d'hommes réduits à l'automatisme dans le travail. La 'fordisation,' nécessité sans laquelle il n'est pas d'industrie américaine, aboutit à la standardisation de l'individu lui-même. L'artisanat, forme démodée de la production, n'a pas de place dans le nouveau monde, mais avec lui disparaît une certaine conception de l'homme, associée dans notre pensée à l'idée de civilisation même" (André Siegfried, *Les Etats-Unis d'aujourdhui* [The contemporary United States] [Paris: Librarie Armand Colin, 1927], 347).

3. For Huizinga's views on the mechanization of contemporary life, see his *Mensch en menigte in Amerika: vier essays over moderne beschavingsgeschiedenis* (Man and the masses in America: four essays about modern civilization history) (Haarlem: Tjeenk Willink, 1918) and *Amerika levend en denkend: Losse opmerkingen* (America living and thinking: loose observations) (Haarlem: Tjeenk Willink, 1927). Both books have come out in an English translation by Herbert H. Rowen in one volume

entitled *America: A Dutch Historian's Vision, from Afar and Near* (New York: Harper and Row, 1972). The first quotation is from *Mensch en menigte*, 61; the second, from ibid., 129; and the third, from *Amerika levend en denkend*, 14, 15.

4. Huizinga, *Amerika levend en denkend*, 21

5. André Siegfried, "Préface," in A. Philip, *Le Problème ouvrier aux Etats-Unis* (The labor problem in the United States), vii–xix (Paris: Librairie Félix Alcan, 1927), xi.

6. G. Duhamel, *Scènes de la vie future* (Scenes from future life) (Paris: Mercure de France, 1931).

7. A. Halfeld, *Amerika und der Amerikanismus: Kritische Betrachtungen eines Deutschen und Europäers* (America and Americanism: critical observations by a German and European) (Jena: Eugen Diederichs, 1927).

8. Ibid., 37

9. Ibid.

10. R. Müller-Freienfels, "Amerikanismus und Europäische Kultur," *Der Deutsche Gedanke* 4, no. 1 (1927): 30–35; quotations on 34, 35.

11. H. Keyserling, *Amerika: Der Aufgang eines neuen Welt* (America: the rise of a new world) (Stuttgart: Deutsche Verlags Anstalt, 1931), 425.

12. H. G. Wells, *The Future in America: A Search after Realities* (Leipzig: Bernhard Tauchnitz, 1907), 44.

13. Ibid., 47–48.

14. Ibid., 63.

15. Ibid., 57.

16. T. van Doesburg, "Licht en tijdsbeelding (film)" (The plasticism of light and time), *De Stijl* 6 (1923): 5, 62.

17. Huizinga, *Mensch en Menigte*, 28.

18. Ibid.

19. G. de Waal, "De ontwikkeling van de filmkunst in de kapitalistische maatschappij, I" (The development of film in capitalist society), *Communisme* 2 (Apr. 1926): 184–89; "De ontwikkeling van de filmkunst in de kapitalistische maatschappij, II," *Communisme* 2 (June 1926): 266–73.

20. L. J. Jordaan, "De strijd om het witte doek" (The struggle for the silver screen), *NU* 1 (Oct. 1927): 71–75.

21. A. M. de Jong, "Ter inleiding" (Introduction), *NU* 1 (Oct. 1927): 8.

22. Jordaan, "De strijd," 73.

23. L. J. Jordaan, "Het Americanisme en de film" (Americanism and film), *NU* 1 (1928): 418–22.

24. *Jaarboek Media Geschiedenis* (Yearbook media history) (Amsterdam: Stichting Mediageschiedenis, 1989), 75.

25. *Manifest Film Liga Amsterdam* (Amsterdam: Film Liga, 1927).

26. M. ter Braak, *De Propria Curesartikelen, 1923–1925*, ed. Carel Peters (The Hague: Bzztôh, 1978), 216, 217.

27. M. ter Braak, "'Americanisme' in de filmwereld" ("Americanism" in the film world), *Nieuwe Rotterdamsche Courant,* February 15, 1930.

28. Siegfried, "Préface," xi, xv.

29. H. Brugmans, "Nederlandse filmkunst" (Dutch film art), *Socialisme en democratie* 1 (Apr. 7, 1939): 237.

30. A. van Domburg, *Levende schaduwen: Aantekeningen over film* (Living shadows: notes about film) (Utrecht: Uitgeverij Het Spectrum, 1936), 25, 80.

31. Ibid., 93.

32. See J. Heijs, ed., *Filmliga 1927–1931* (Nijmegen: Socialistiese Uitgeverij Nijmegen, 1982).

33. W. Bonger is quoted in T. Beckers, *Planning voor vrijheid: Een historisch-sociologische studie van de overheidsinterventie in rekreatie en vrije tijd* (Planning for freedom: a historical-sociological study of governmental intervention in recreation and leisure) (Wageningen: Vakgroep sociologie, 1983), 130.

34. D. van Staveren, "Een bioscoopwetsontwerp" (A draft cinema law), *De Socialistische Gids* 7 (1922): 947–59.

35. H. G. Cannegieter, "Marlene Dietrich," *De Socialistische Gids* 16 (1931): 888–94.

36. T. Lichthart, "Een ander filmpraatje" (Another film chat), *Tijd en Taak—Religieus-Socialistisch Weekblad* 35, 45, 21 (Aug. 1937): 6–7; quotation on 7.

37. *Het Witte Doek* 1, no. 15 (1937): 228.

38. Ibid., 1, no. 1 (1937): 23.

39. See P. Slot, "'Een vloek en een zegen': De Katholieken en film in Nederland, 1912–1942" ("A curse and a blessing": Catholics and film in the Netherlands), M.A. thesis, University of Amsterdam, 1986.

CHAPTER 4: ADVERTISING

1. R. Marchand, *Advertising the American Dream: Making Way for Modernity, 1920–1940* (Berkeley: University of California Press, 1985).

2. See, for example, J. Fiske, *Reading the Popular* (Boston: Unwin Hyman, 1989).

CHAPTER 5: THE FIFTH FREEDOM AND THE COMMODIFICATION OF CIVIC VIRTUE

1. Roosevelt presidential press conferences, number 658, July 5, 1940.

2. About the New York World's Fair see, for example, L. Zim, M. Lerner, and H. Rollfs, *The World of Tomorrow: The 1939 New York World's Fair* (New York: Harper and Row, 1988); R. Wurts et al., *The New York World's Fair, 1939/1940, in 155 Photographs,* text by S. Appelbaum (New York: Dover, 1977).

3. As regards Roosevelt's own input see L. Crowell, "The Building of the 'Four Freedoms' Speech," *Speech Monographs* 22 (1955): 266–83; S. I. Rosenman, *Working with Roosevelt* (New York: Da Capo, 1972 [1952]), 262–63.

4. See Rosenman, *Working with Roosevelt*, 263.

5. Like so many trends that strike observers as typically American, this one too had its European precursors, in the serialized newspaper publications of nineteenth-century novels, known as "feuilletons." As in other cases, though, the implied modularizing logic was taken to much greater lengths in the United States.

6. D. J. Boorstin, *The Image: Or What Happened to the American Dream* (Harmondsworth: Penguin, 1963 [1962]), 183.

7. A. MacLeish, quoted in W. Safire, *The New Language of Politics: An Anecdotal Dictionary of Catchwords, Slogans, and Political Usage* (New York: Random House, 1968), 14.

8. J. T. Adams, *The Epic of America* (Boston: Little, Brown, 1931), 415, viii.

9. For a reproduction of this poster, see Robert H. Fossum and John K. Roth, *The American Dream* (Durham: British Association for American Studies, 1981), 4.

10. As pointed out in a piece on U.S. pop culture in Europe by Elizabeth Neuffer, *Boston Sunday Globe*, October 9, 1994, 22.

CHAPTER 6: MEDIATED HISTORY

1. J. Baudrillard, *Amérique* (Paris: Bernard Grasset, 1986), 99: "C'est pourquoi la guerre a été gagnée des deux côtés: par les Vietnamiens sur le terrain, par les Américains dans l'espace mental électronique" (That is why the war was won on two sides: by the Vietnamese on the ground, and by the Americans in the electronic mental space).

2. This point is convincingly argued by Michael Mandelbaum; see his "Vietnam: The Television War," *Daedalus* 111, no. 4 (Fall 1982): 157–71.

3. See T. Gitlin, *The Whole World Is Watching: Mass Media in the Making and Unmaking of the New Left* (Berkeley: University of California Press, 1980).

4. See J. E. Mueller, *War, Presidents and Public Opinion* (New York: Wiley, 1973).

CHAPTER 7: BREATHLESS

1. On this latest episode, see Mario Vargas Llosa, "Fields of Dreams," *The Sunday Times* (London), October 31, 1993; see also Rob Kroes, "Amerika is niet van onecht te onderscheiden" (America cannot be distinguished from the real thing) *NRC/Handelsblad,* February 12, 1994.

2. André Siegfried, *Les Etats-Unis d'aujourdhui* (The contemporary United States) (Paris: Librarie Armand Colin, 1927), 347

3. T. Elsaesser, "Two Decades in Another Country: Hollywood and the *Cinéphiles,"* in C. W. E. Bigsby, ed., *Super-Culture: American Popular Culture and Europe,* 199–218 (London: Paul Elek, 1975).

CHAPTER 9: AMERICANIZATION

1. See, for example, U. Hannerz, "American Culture, Creolized, Creolizing," in L. Åsard, ed., *American Culture, Creolized, Creolizing,* 7–30 (Uppsala: Swedish Institute for North American Studies, 1988); Hannerz, "Culture between Center and Periphery: Towards a Macro-anthropology," *Ethnos* 54 (1989): 200–216; Hannerz, *Cultural Complexity* (New York: Columbia University Press, 1992).

2. N. Mitford, ed., *Noblesse Oblige: An Enquiry into the Identifiable Characteristics of the English Aristocracy* (London: Atheneum, 1986).

3. J. Kirkpatrick, ed., *Charles E. Ives Memos* (New York: Norton, 1972), 120, 121.

4. J. Blair, *Modular America: Cross-Cultural Perspectives on the Emergence of an American Way* (Westport, Conn.: Greenwood, 1988).

5. David Nye has further elaborated this point in *The Technological Sublime in America* (Cambridge, Mass.: MIT Press, 1995).

6. See my earlier discussion of this point in chapter 2.

7. R. Banham, "Mediated Environments, Or: You Can't Build That Here," in C. W. E. Bigsby, ed., *Super-Culture: American Popular Culture and Europe,* 69–83 (London: Paul Elek, 1975).

8. Without trying fully to remove the mystery, let me simply say that the word *vertrossing* ("trossization") derives from the acronym T.R.O.S., the name of a Dutch broadcasting licensee. Set up as a pirate station transmitting from the North Sea, it successfully filed for legal status when, in the aftermath of the cultural tremors of the late 1960s, the Dutch airwaves were no longer the sole preserve of the established broadcasting corporations. Their cozy oligarchy had been the outcome of an earlier grand compromise in Dutch pacification politics going back to the interwar years. T.R.O.S. and Veronica—another former pirate—entrenched themselves as the unrepenting purveyors of mass culture, catering to the lowest common denominator of mass tastes. Against the old Catholic, Calvinist, Socialist, and Liberal networks and their self-imposed civilizing mission toward their respective "flocks," the new networks were seen by assorted guardians of culture as a fifth column operating behind the lines of the Dutch defensive perimeter of the national culture, disseminating a pernicious American mass culture. Thus, in the paternalist indictment of these broadcasting upstarts, the word *vertrossing* became the Dutch equivalent of a process of Americanization, although in fact, as I have have argued, through mediation and selective appropriation, the result can more appropriately be understood as Dutchification. Ironically, and unwittingly, the word *vertrossing* seems to illustrate this latter point rather aptly.

Index

Adamic, Louis, 53
Adams, Henry, 20, 39, 69, 74, 75
Adams, James T., 122
advertising: and conformism, 96; and
cultural frontiers, 105; and culture
of consumption, 95–105, 116; and
democracy, 116–29; iconography
of, 104; and modernity, 96, 102;
and production of virtual reality,
100, 101; and representation of
women, 97, 99, 100, 105; as socializing tool, ix, 97, 98
Aerosmith, 160, 161
Alien II, 105
America: as embodiment of capitalism, 27; as Europe's future, 15, 16,
18, 20, 24, 27, 71, 102; as identical
with West, 102, 103, 104, 124;
lacking tragic sense, 21, 22, 182*n;*
as last beach of European culture,
39; in light of modernity, 18, 102,
103; as metaphorical construct, xiii,
xiv, 5, 13 16, 18; and metaphor of
organic cohesion, xiii, 32–36, 41;
and metaphor of space, xiii, 16–28,
31, 43; and metaphor of time, xiii,
17, 28–32; as primitivism, 18, 31;
seen in negative light, 1, 10, 13, 17;
seen in positive light, 1, 8, 9, 10, 11,
13, 18, 36–40
American art: and democratic ethos,
44–47, 61, 165; and mechanical reproduction, 46, 47, 48, 69
American culture: and hierarchy, 44,
47, 56, 63; modularizing logic of,

118, 165, 173; transformation rule
of, 41, 44, 68, 105, 106, 140, 153,
165–71, 173
American Dream, 121–29
Americanism, x, xi, 19, 20, 21, 72, 73,
80, 82, 83, 85, 91, 95, 172
Americanization, x, xi, xii, 172, 176;
and advertising, 127–29; and American Dream, 124
American System of Manufactures, 32
anomie, 16
anti-Americanism: cultural, 10, 20,
21, 27, 72, 81, 143
Antin, Mary, 54
Armstrong, Louis, 143

Banham, Reyner, 175, 176
Barber, Samuel, 138
Barlow, Joel, 12
Bates, Katherine L., 122
Baudrillard, Jean, 27, 31, 32, 37–40
passim, 171; on Vietnam War, 134,
136, 137
Bazin, André, 146–49 passim, 153
Beauvoir, Simone de, 26
behaviorism, 73
Belmondo, Jean-Paul, 150
Benton, Thomas Hart, 61, 62
Berkeley, George, 8, 9
Bernstein, Leonard, 110
Bertina, Bob J., 90
Bisset, Jacqueline, 149
Blair, John G., 165
Bogart, Humphrey, 151, 152
Bonger, W. A., 88

9424

ROB KROES, a professor in and chairman of the American Studies department at the University of Amsterdam, was president of the European Association for American Studies (EAAS) for four years (1992–96). He is the author of several books, including *Students and Soldiers: Studies in Left- and Right-Wing Radicalism* (London, 1975) and *The Persistence of Ethnicity: Dutch Calvinist Pioneers in Amsterdam, Montana* (University of Illinois Press, 1992). He is the general editor of European Contributions to American Studies, a series of multiauthor volumes published in Amsterdam.

940 Kro

Kroes, Rob.

If you've seen one, you've
seen the mall